HIGH ROLLERS

ANDREW COSBY
ROSS RICHIE
founders

MARK WAID
editor-in-chief

ADAM FORTIER
vice president,
new business

CHIP MOSHER
marketing &
sales director

MATT GAGNON
managing editor

ED DUKESHIRE
designer

First Edition: December 2008

10 9 8 7 6 5 4 3 2 1
PRINTED IN KOREA

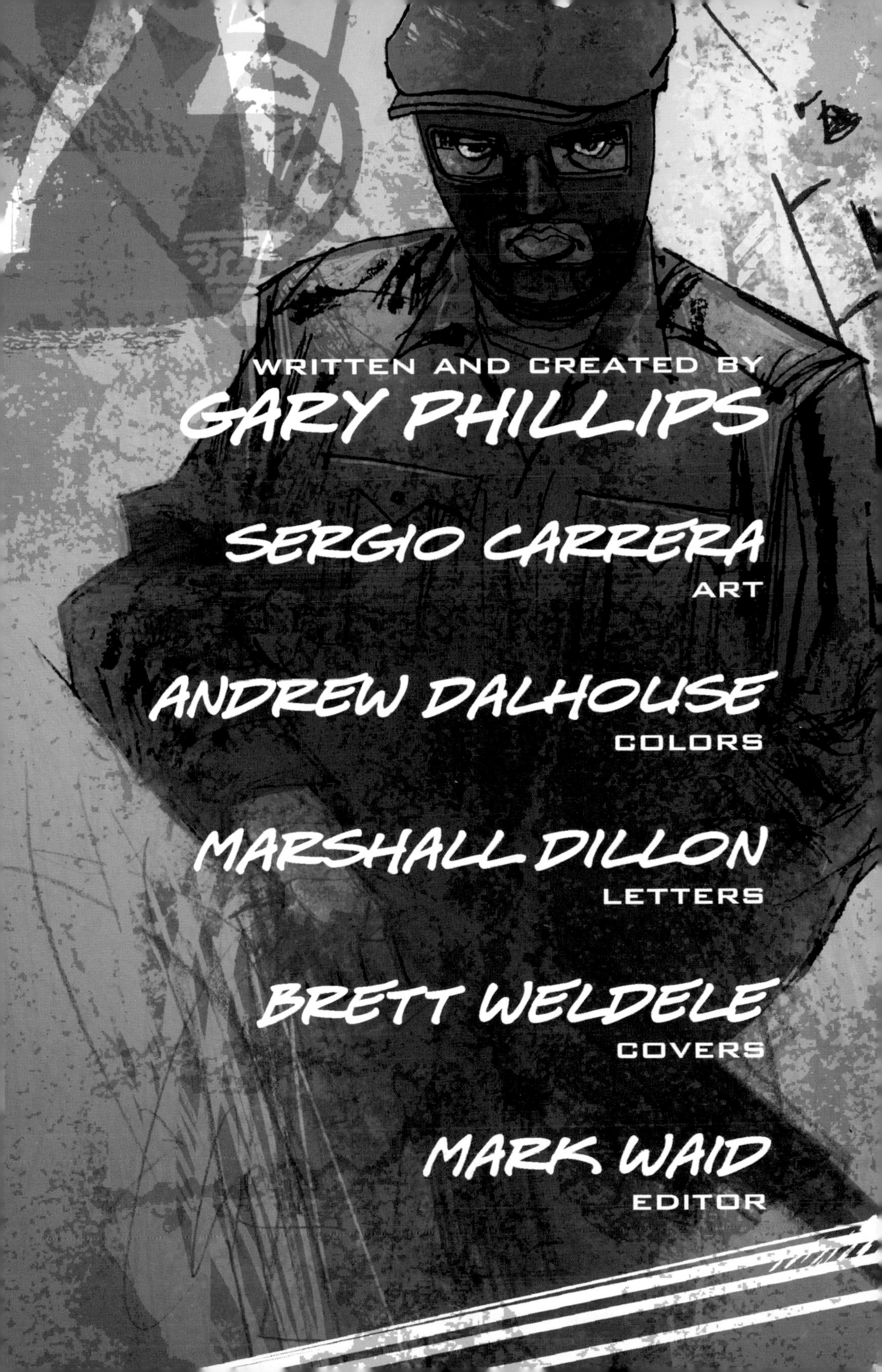

WRITTEN AND CREATED BY
GARY PHILLIPS

SERGIO CARRERA
ART

ANDREW DALHOUSE
COLORS

MARSHALL DILLON
LETTERS

BRETT WELDELE
COVERS

MARK WAID
EDITOR

DEDICATION

To Freddie Hubbard and
Donald "Richard Stark" Westlake,
two who knew the score
only too well.

Foreword by Walter Mosley

The world we live in is a delicate and infinitely complex structure comprised of the interconnections of many different physical schemas and logical systems. Each of us (us being all the living and non-sentient beings on this planet – and beyond) experiences a very limited range of these logical systems. The fly makes a circuit from flower to dung heap, from a young woman's moist brow to a stallion's sweaty ass. That winged insect might create an entire philosophy based upon these experiences, concluding that it has mapped out the major truths of the physical and spiritual world. The sperm whale has her ocean. The sun flings its satellites in what seems like an eternity.

A young child is raised in a peaceful suburb with gentle loving parents. She goes to school and learns her ABCs. Her world is generally pleasant, deftly defined, and absolute. Teachers and relatives and school-friends, for the most part, support this vision and system of belief. There is no reason for the child, and later the young woman, to question the superiority of her religion, race, language, and perceived system of right and wrong.

Her world is the only world.

And then Gary Phillips comes along.

Mr. Phillips, with the help of his friend CQ, breaks down the logic of one human system replacing it with a close relative. In this world men and women don't have the same support-systems, they cannot rely on friends and family in the same ways.

In HIGH ROLLERS we are presented with a system based on the concept of raw power tempered by a strength of will that is almost impossible to imagine in a world where the belief in external laws guides (and often misguides) the masses. The characters in this novel move from the realm of Law into a more primal system of Chaos. In this, truly existential, world history rises and suddenly disappears based upon the strength of character of a solitary individual.

This novel is noir, existential, and ultimately the counterpoint to the world of that young woman, a world that is even now sputtering and failing to keep its image in place.

— Walter Mosley, 2008.

Walter Mosley has written twenty-nine critically acclaimed and widely read novels. Mosley's series of Easy Rawlins mysteries have been mainstays on the New York Times Bestsellers list. He currently resides in New York City.

PROLOGUE

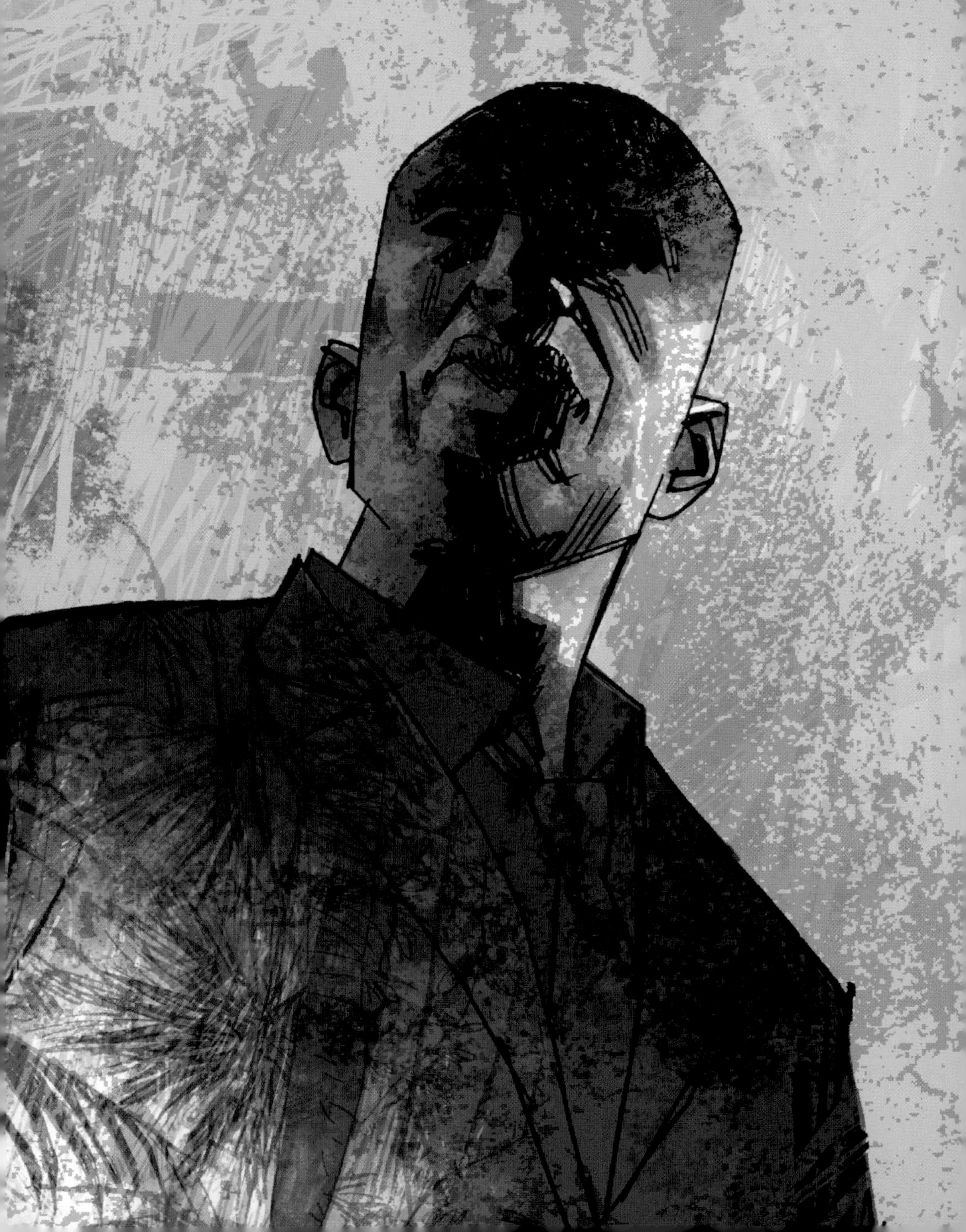

THE SET-UP

LENA HOLT let her mouth fall away from the stem of the crack pipe, clamping her lips tight so as to hold in the narcotic fumes invading her bloodstream. She envisioned cartoonish globules of crack essence floating into her corpuscles, which breathed in and out, opening giant pores. She sat back, the music from the smooth jazz station wrapping itself around her like silken scarves intermittently festooned with small razors that prickled her skin. Holt opened her red eyes, staring at the gray concrete wall of the parking structure. She sighed heavily and regarded the time on her watch. In less than half an hour she had to be in court, defending a client accused of an injury hit-and-run. She shook her head, morose and bemused.

Her client was a middle-aged housekeeper who drove a fifteen-year-old beater of a Toyota. She'd been running late that morning and had to get from her apartment in working-class Inglewood to the house she cleaned for a gay fashion designer couple in Beverly Hills. The woman, Heidy Solano was her name, had come around a corner and grazed a young man, a teen, jaywalking across La Brea with his friends. The kid was over six feet, tatted and built like a baller, wearing a wife-beater, oversized shorts, and sporting cornrows. Heidy had the piss scared out of her as the young man was helped to his feet by his dawgs and he started calling her all sorts of names, variations of "blind-ass ho" and "no-driving bitch." As she zoomed off, fearful of what he and his homies would do to her, mindful too she hadn't been able to renew her car insurance, one of the youngsters had taken a picture of her back plate with the camera built into his cell phone.

Holt clicked the ignition power off and put eyedrops in her eyes to temper her bloodshot whites. She also chewed two breath mints while dropping her cell phone into her briefcase, having impotently tried for the second time since parking to reach Trey Loc Simmons. Bastard, she reflected. Holt pulled down the visor and gazed lovingly at the photo of her daughter, Amelia. She then got out of her parked Volkswagen Beetle and worked the wrinkles out of her skirt. She checked herself in the outside mirror, praying her mask of respectability was still in place. Holt's high heels sounded along the concrete of the criminal courts parking structure as she strode off toward the courtroom, reminding herself of Law School Edict 101—project confidence and assurance. Never let 'em see you sweat. For, in reality, Lena Holt, well-dressed crackhead and criminal defense attorney, knew somewhere inside of her she was trying to scale Everest in a pair of Pradas, and it was only a matter of time before she tumbled.

CAMERON QUINN eased his athletic frame out of the tumbled black satin sheets on his bed. Next to him, the video vixen—would-be singer Reva, real name Nancy—snored lightly, sleeping on her stomach. He grinned wolfishly, gazing at that magnificent ass of hers bathed in a light, cooling sheen of sweat, while he tied his kimono closed. He padded barefoot into his living room, passing by the smiling picture of his sister, Rita, who he hadn't seen in person for years—though he always let her know how to contact him. CQ TiVo'd the Lakers game but wasn't in the mood for Kobe and company just now. He poured a neat draft of McClellan's and settled in his comfortable chair with the book he'd started, *Gang Leader for a Day* by this East Asian cat, Sudhir Venkatesh. The dude was a professor now but, back when he was a grad student, he began hanging with this Chicago set, the Black Kings, getting to know all about the way they functioned, hierarchy, what it took to run the show, all that. CQ wasn't reading it for crime tips but was cataloguing what Venkatesh had to say about gang culture and the psychology of shot callers.

Taking another sip of his scotch, his cell phone chimed and he didn't have to see the number to know it must be his boss, Trey Loc, calling him at this time of night.

"Yo," he answered.

"Told you I wasn't trippin'."A loud snort underscored Harold "Trey Loc" Simmons' words as he imbibed his product on the other end of the line. "Knew he was chumpin' me."

"Beanbag," CQ said laconically.

Trey Loc made more nasal sounds. "That's right. Petey caught him with his hand all up in my cookie jar."

CQ laughed briefly, derisively. "You goin' on his say-so? Petey couldn't find pale-ass Paris Hilton naked in a room of Zulus."

"Look here, Cam'ron, the boy done confirmed what I been suspicion'ing. Petey got people out there in Montclair. After Bean made his monthly collection from our... associates, Petey back-tracked on him with his connects. They said they turned in one amount, and Bean turned in another, in his favor. Understand?"

"That don't mean Petey got it right." He didn't say he didn't trust Petey since he knew his boss was partial to that knothead who'd taken a bullet for Trey once. "Beanbag's always been down with me."

"Sheee," Trey Loc said, "Don't you go underestimating Petey, he got more goin' on that you give him credit for. And like I said, me comin' up short from Beanbag's count, I might be willing to jus' go for a friendly warning, broke leg, somethin' like that, but this ain't the first time Bean done tried to punk me." He paused, snorting again. "But you damn sure better make sure it's the last."

A feeling CQ was hard pressed to name ebbed through the enforcer but he resigned himself to his role. "I got it."

"That's right, you got it," Trey Loc hissed, clicking off.

CQ stared at the disposable cell phone for a beat, then put it aside. He finished his drink, had another, and finished another chapter in the book.

"Hey, you," Reva called dreamily and invitingly from the bedroom. "Come back to bed."

"In a minute, baby girl." He crossed one leg over another and made a call. "Cee Cee," he said after the line connected. He then laid out what he wanted her to do. She was looking to move up the chain and wanted her own franchise. She was also lusted after by Beanbag. Badly.

CQ clicked off after working out the plan with Cee Cee and rose to re-enter the bedroom. Passing by a darkened window, he momentarily spied a reflection of himself. He looked old for his age.

ROGER MARSTON sobered quickly, watching his king-high flush turn to dust before the well-hidden full house the old lady wearing the sun visor and orthopedic tennis shoes threw down. Murmurs and curses went around the table as she raked in the chips. He nodded to her curtly. Marston didn't have to look over his shoulder to know that the two linebackers who'd drifted into the Gardena Gardens Casino some forty minutes ago, past two in the morning, were no longer lingering in the background. No, they'd be waiting for him by his car in the open-air parking lot. Or, God forbid, at his home. Please not that, he silently pleaded. He could not visit his failings on his wife, Rita. She was so good to him, so understanding.

Pausing at the door, he considered jumping in a cab and running off to Mexico. But cabs didn't prowl so much in the greater Southern California area and, well, hell, what would he do in Mexico? Now Paris, he could flee to Paris. If he had the money. And if he had the money, he would have paid the vig and then some to what he owed that goniff moneychanger Machete Ortiz. Yeah, if. He took a deep breath and, on shaky legs, headed for his leased Beemer, a month behind on those payments, too.

The first one, ponytail and chest the size of a front-loader, emerged from the gloom, a wide grin on his pleasant face. "Machete says we can do you up proper, but not hurt your hands. Says you need them hands to make him his money."

"Tell Ma—" but the other one hit him in his gut and he didn't get to finish his sentence. Blissfully, in the process of the silent beating—save for his grunts and wails, particularly when one of them heel-kicked him on the side of his knee— Marston hit his head on the bumper of that sweet piece of German engineering. Blacking out, he had a brief inner image of himself tumbling into nothingness.

The two emissaries calmly and casually took Roger Marston and dumped him in front of the emergency room, then peeled off into the early morning.

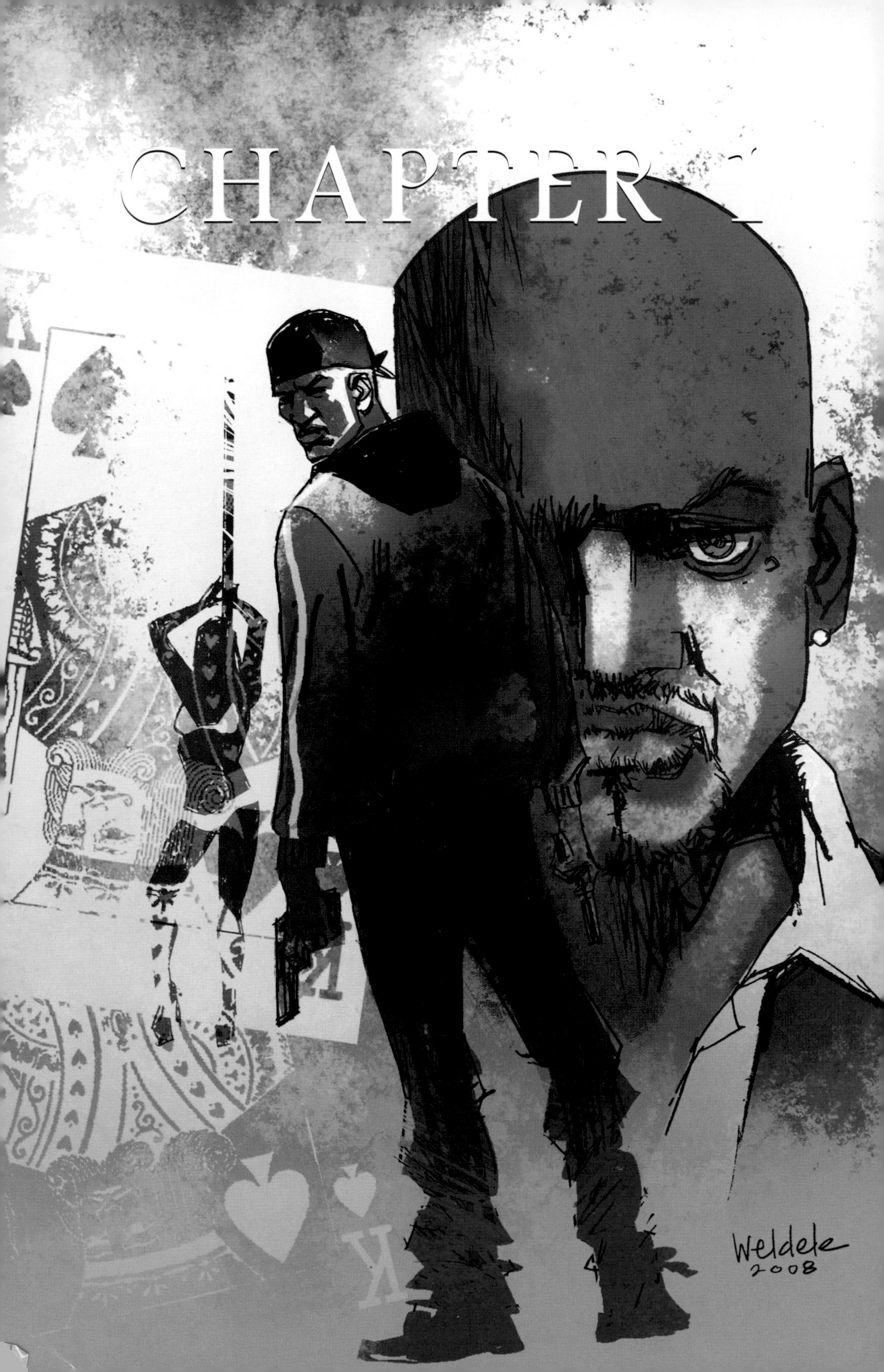
CHAPTER 1
Weldele
2008

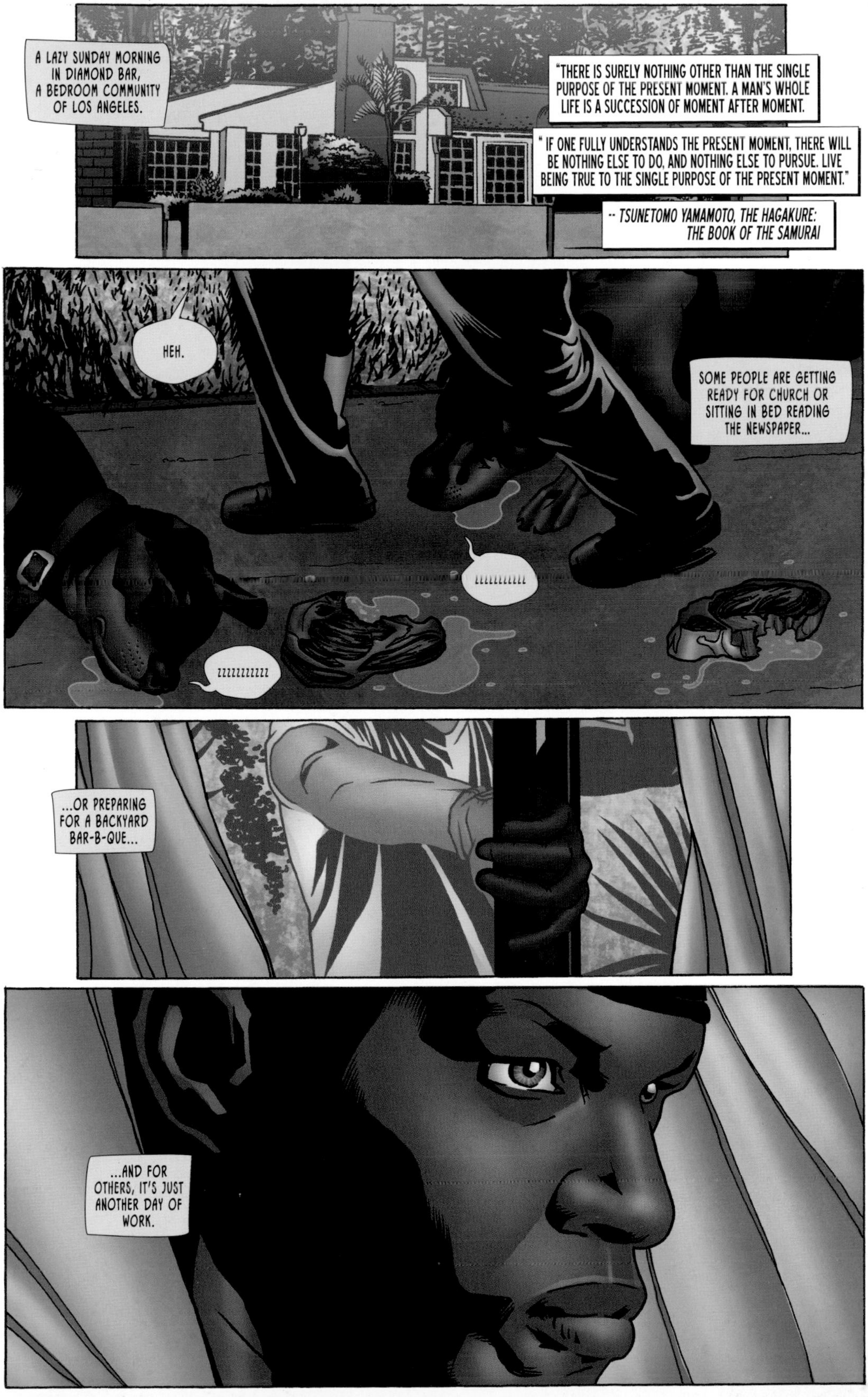
A LAZY SUNDAY MORNING IN DIAMOND BAR, A BEDROOM COMMUNITY OF LOS ANGELES.
"THERE IS SURELY NOTHING OTHER THAN THE SINGLE PURPOSE OF THE PRESENT MOMENT. A MAN'S WHOLE LIFE IS A SUCCESSION OF MOMENT AFTER MOMENT.
" IF ONE FULLY UNDERSTANDS THE PRESENT MOMENT, THERE WILL BE NOTHING ELSE TO DO, AND NOTHING ELSE TO PURSUE. LIVE BEING TRUE TO THE SINGLE PURPOSE OF THE PRESENT MOMENT."
-- TSUNETOMO YAMAMOTO, THE HAGAKURE: THE BOOK OF THE SAMURAI
HEH.
SOME PEOPLE ARE GETTING READY FOR CHURCH OR SITTING IN BED READING THE NEWSPAPER...
ZZZZZZZZZZZ
ZZZZZZZZZZ
...OR PREPARING FOR A BACKYARD BAR-B-QUE...
...AND FOR OTHERS, IT'S JUST ANOTHER DAY OF WORK.

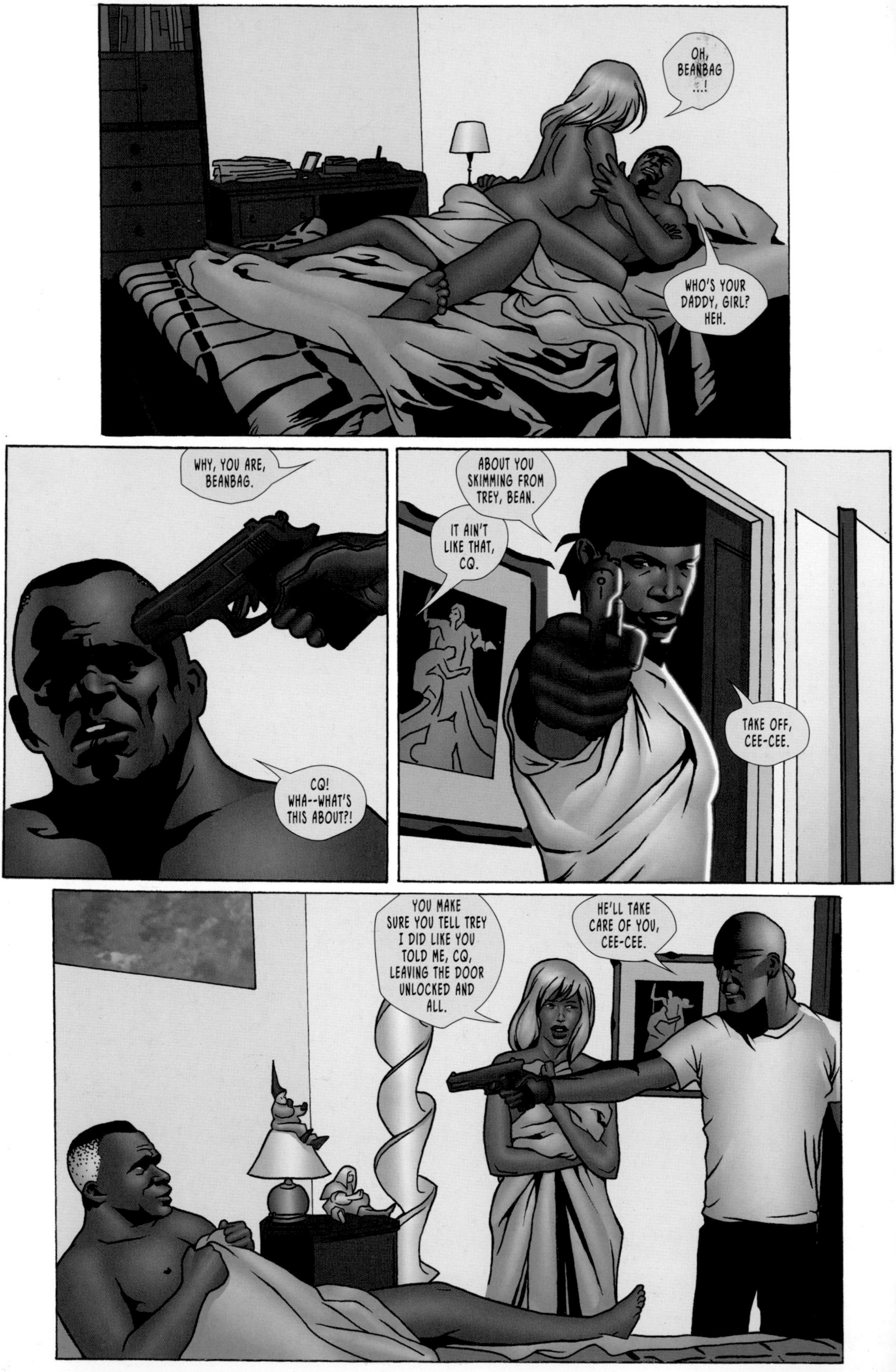
OH, BEANBAG ...!
WHO'S YOUR DADDY, GIRL? HEH.
WHY, YOU ARE, BEANBAG.
CQ! WHA--WHAT'S THIS ABOUT?!
ABOUT YOU SKIMMING FROM TREY, BEAN.
IT AIN'T LIKE THAT, CQ.
TAKE OFF, CEE-CEE.
YOU MAKE SURE YOU TELL TREY I DID LIKE YOU TOLD ME, CQ, LEAVING THE DOOR UNLOCKED AND ALL.
HE'LL TAKE CARE OF YOU, CEE-CEE.

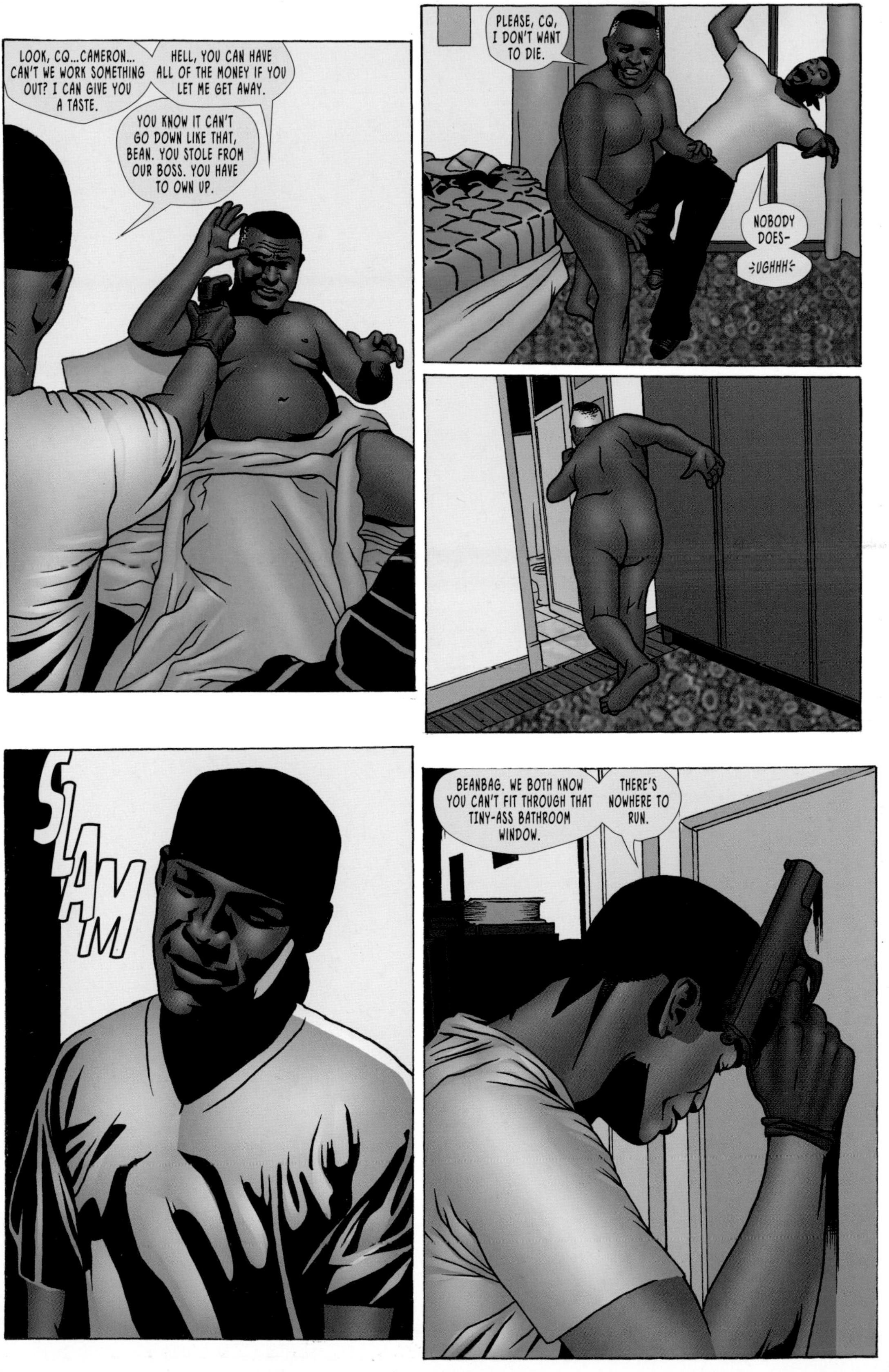
LOOK, CQ...CAMERON... CAN'T WE WORK SOMETHING OUT? I CAN GIVE YOU A TASTE.
HELL, YOU CAN HAVE ALL OF THE MONEY IF YOU LET ME GET AWAY.
YOU KNOW IT CAN'T GO DOWN LIKE THAT, BEAN. YOU STOLE FROM OUR BOSS. YOU HAVE TO OWN UP.
PLEASE, CQ, I DON'T WANT TO DIE.
NOBODY DOES-
UGHHH
SLAM
BEANBAG. WE BOTH KNOW YOU CAN'T FIT THROUGH THAT TINY-ASS BATHROOM WINDOW.
THERE'S NOWHERE TO RUN.

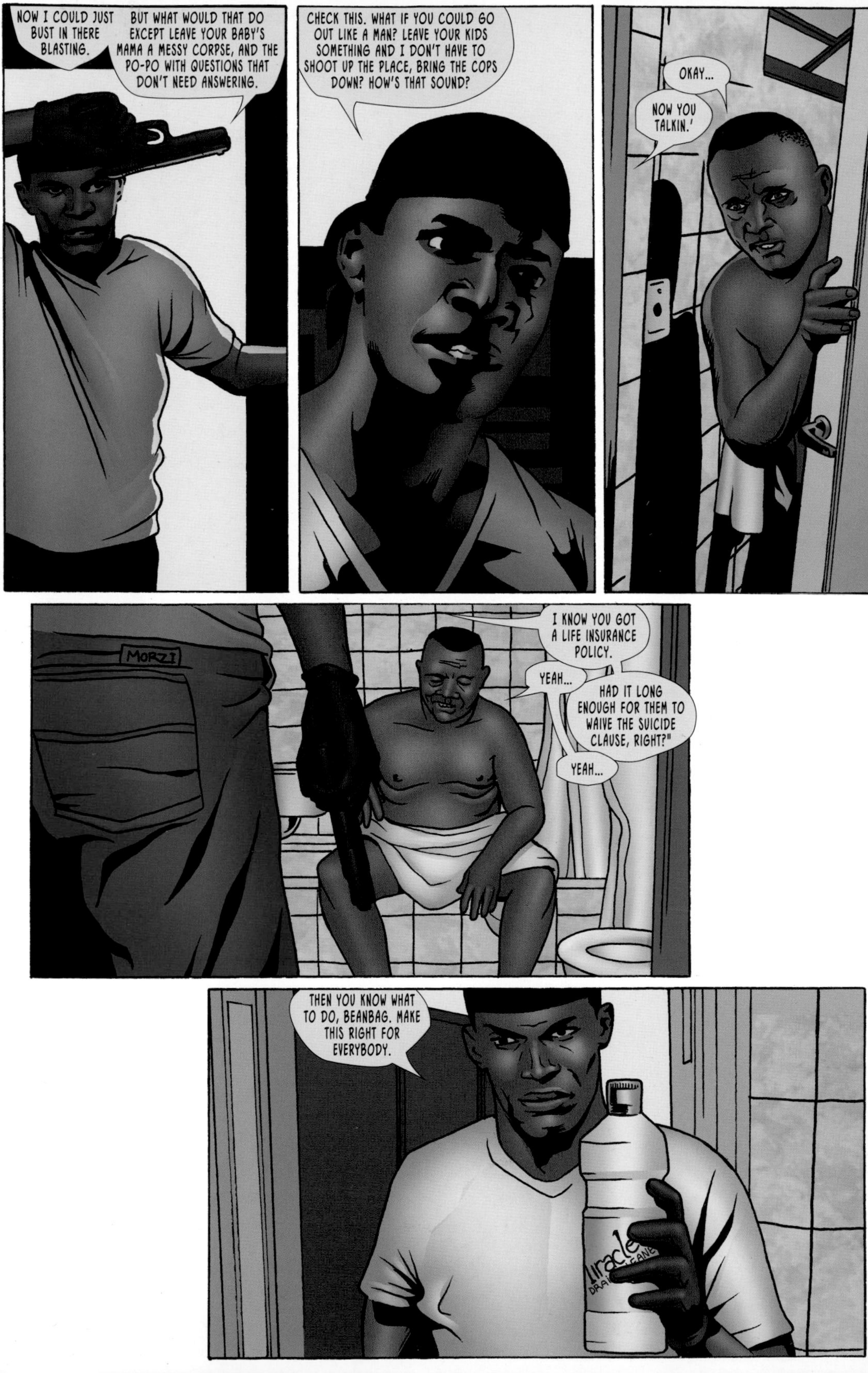
NOW I COULD JUST BUST IN THERE BLASTING.
BUT WHAT WOULD THAT DO EXCEPT LEAVE YOUR BABY'S MAMA A MESSY CORPSE, AND THE PO-PO WITH QUESTIONS THAT DON'T NEED ANSWERING.
CHECK THIS. WHAT IF YOU COULD GO OUT LIKE A MAN? LEAVE YOUR KIDS SOMETHING AND I DON'T HAVE TO SHOOT UP THE PLACE, BRING THE COPS DOWN? HOW'S THAT SOUND?
OKAY...
NOW YOU TALKIN.'
MORZI
I KNOW YOU GOT A LIFE INSURANCE POLICY.
YEAH...
HAD IT LONG ENOUGH FOR THEM TO WAIVE THE SUICIDE CLAUSE, RIGHT?"
YEAH...
THEN YOU KNOW WHAT TO DO, BEANBAG. MAKE THIS RIGHT FOR EVERYBODY.

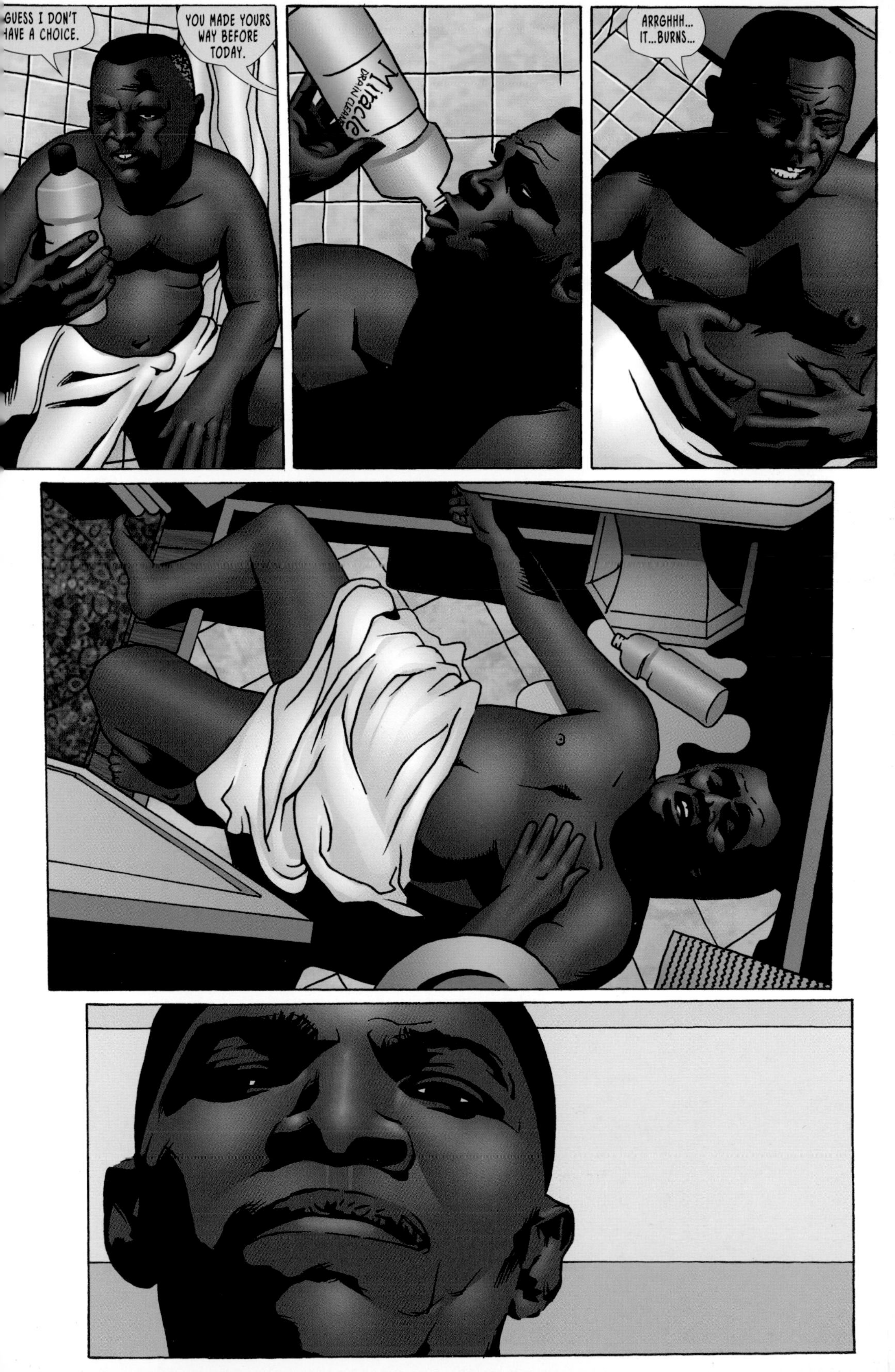
GUESS I DON'T HAVE A CHOICE.
YOU MADE YOURS WAY BEFORE TODAY.
Miracle
ARRGHHH... IT...BURNS...

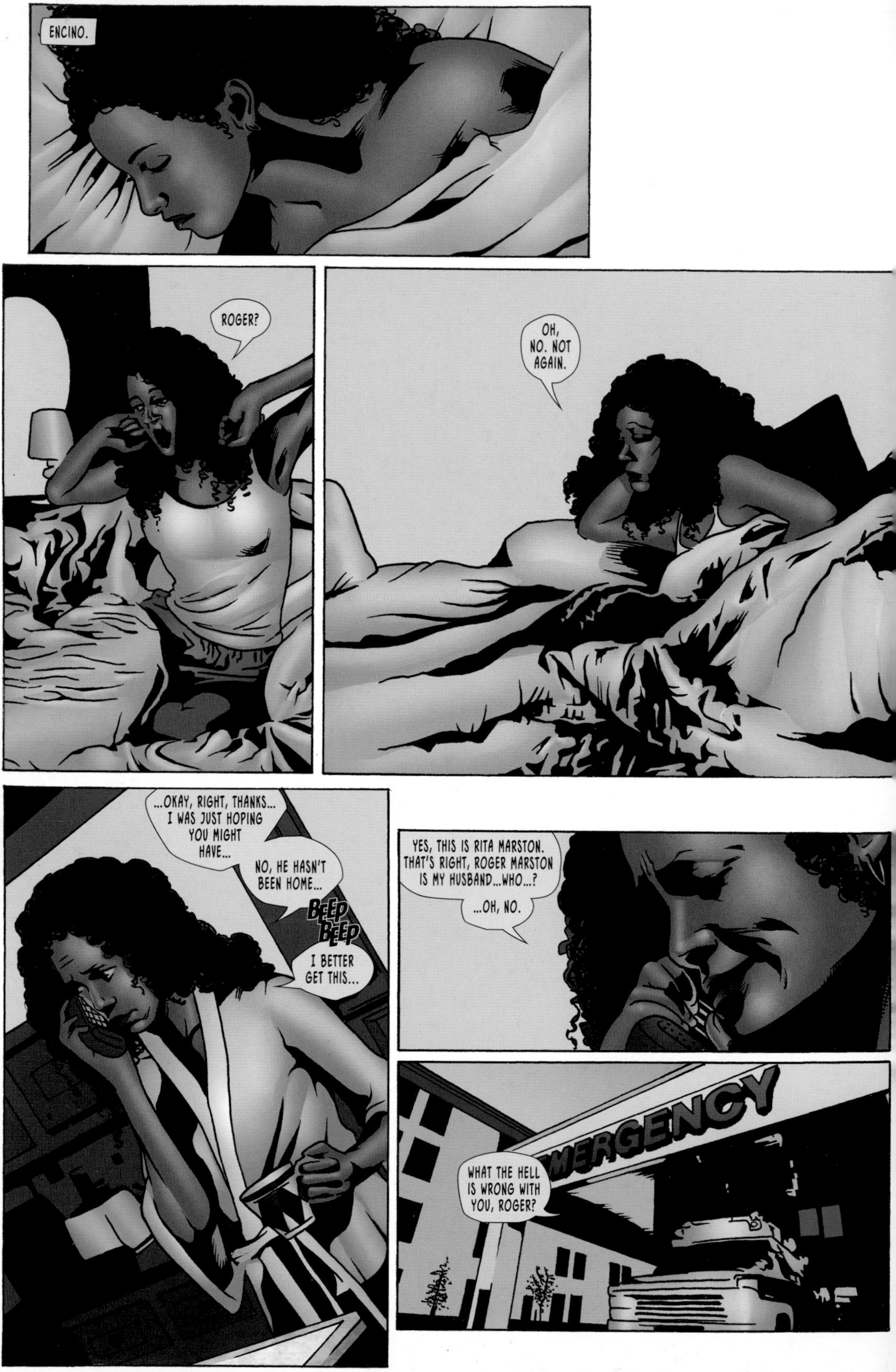
ENCINO.
ROGER?
OH, NO. NOT AGAIN.
...OKAY, RIGHT, THANKS... I WAS JUST HOPING YOU MIGHT HAVE...
NO, HE HASN'T BEEN HOME...
BEEP BEEP
I BETTER GET THIS...
YES, THIS IS RITA MARSTON. THAT'S RIGHT, ROGER MARSTON IS MY HUSBAND...WHO...?
...OH, NO.
EMERGENCY
WHAT THE HELL IS WRONG WITH YOU, ROGER?

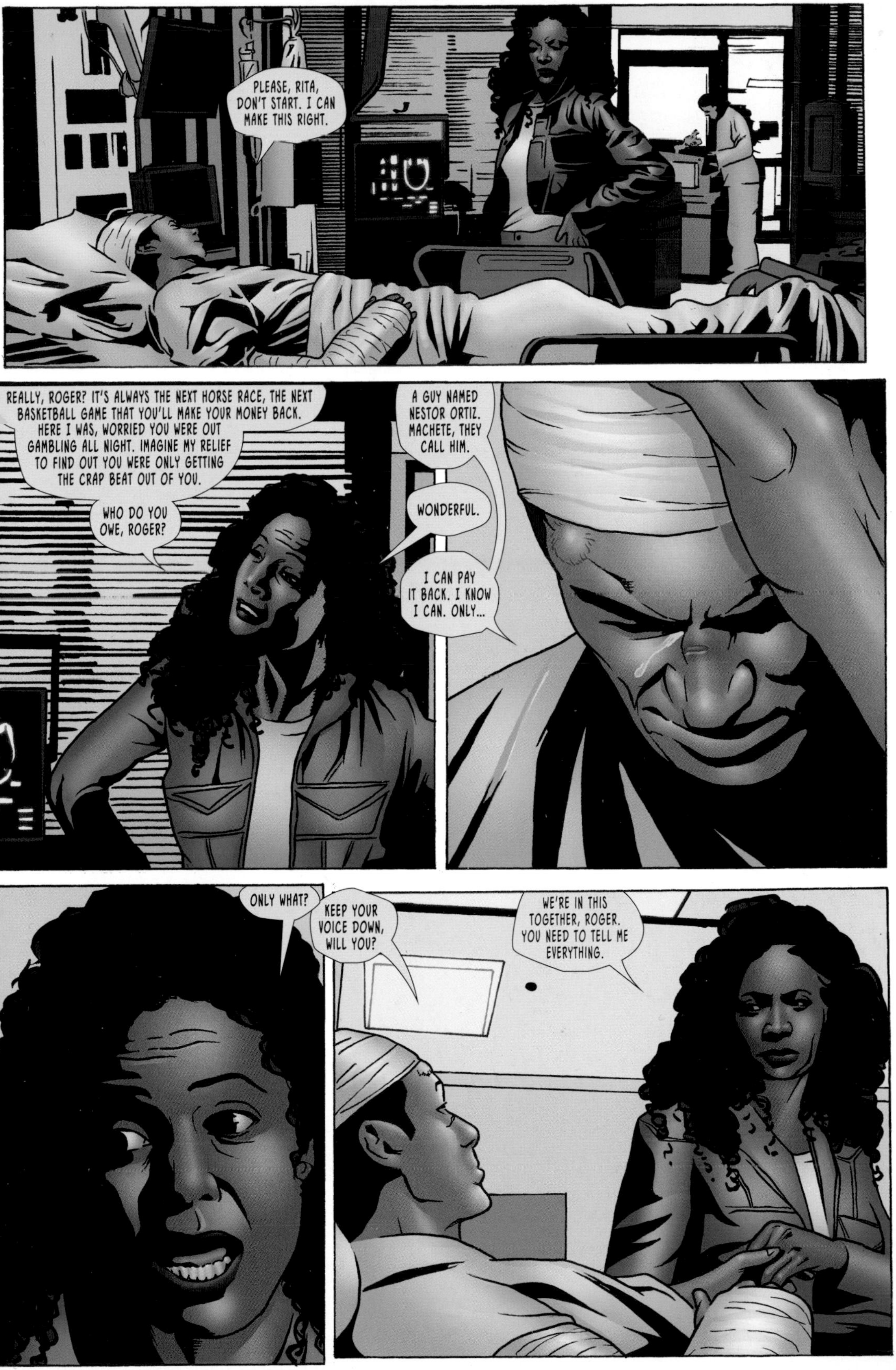
PLEASE, RITA, DON'T START. I CAN MAKE THIS RIGHT.
REALLY, ROGER? IT'S ALWAYS THE NEXT HORSE RACE, THE NEXT BASKETBALL GAME THAT YOU'LL MAKE YOUR MONEY BACK. HERE I WAS, WORRIED YOU WERE OUT GAMBLING ALL NIGHT. IMAGINE MY RELIEF TO FIND OUT YOU WERE ONLY GETTING THE CRAP BEAT OUT OF YOU.
WHO DO YOU OWE, ROGER?
A GUY NAMED NESTOR ORTIZ. MACHETE, THEY CALL HIM.
WONDERFUL.
I CAN PAY IT BACK. I KNOW I CAN. ONLY...
ONLY WHAT?
KEEP YOUR VOICE DOWN, WILL YOU?
WE'RE IN THIS TOGETHER, ROGER. YOU NEED TO TELL ME EVERYTHING.

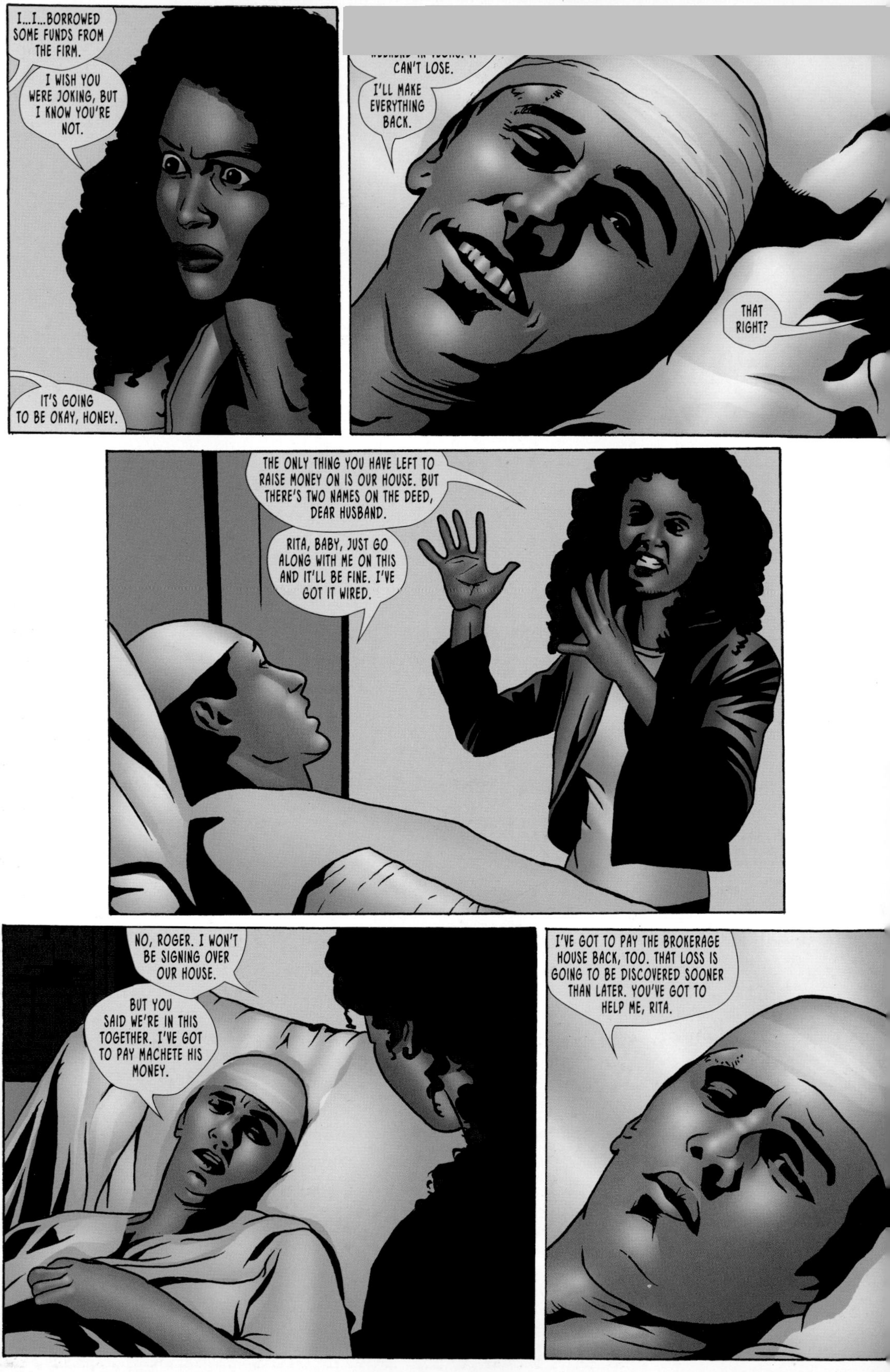

I...I...BORROWED SOME FUNDS FROM THE FIRM.
I WISH YOU WERE JOKING, BUT I KNOW YOU'RE NOT.
IT'S GOING TO BE OKAY, HONEY.
CAN'T LOSE.
I'LL MAKE EVERYTHING BACK.
THAT RIGHT?
THE ONLY THING YOU HAVE LEFT TO RAISE MONEY ON IS OUR HOUSE. BUT THERE'S TWO NAMES ON THE DEED, DEAR HUSBAND.
RITA, BABY, JUST GO ALONG WITH ME ON THIS AND IT'LL BE FINE. I'VE GOT IT WIRED.
NO, ROGER. I WON'T BE SIGNING OVER OUR HOUSE.
BUT YOU SAID WE'RE IN THIS TOGETHER. I'VE GOT TO PAY MACHETE HIS MONEY.
I'VE GOT TO PAY THE BROKERAGE HOUSE BACK, TOO. THAT LOSS IS GOING TO BE DISCOVERED SOONER THAN LATER. YOU'VE GOT TO HELP ME, RITA.

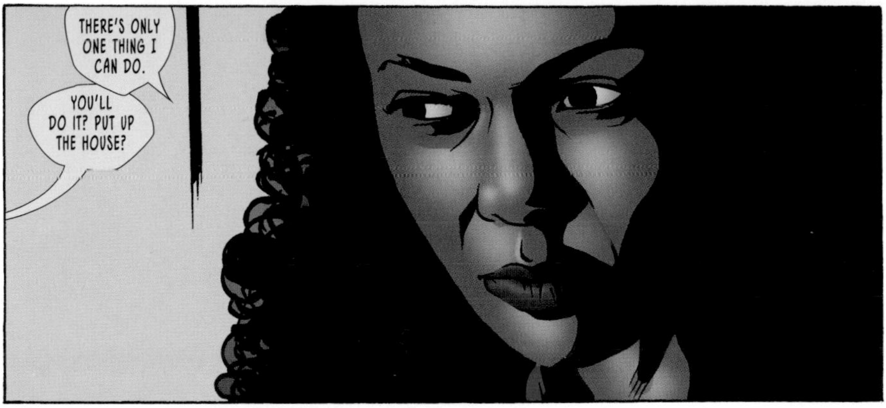
THERE'S ONLY ONE THING I CAN DO.
YOU'LL DO IT? PUT UP THE HOUSE?

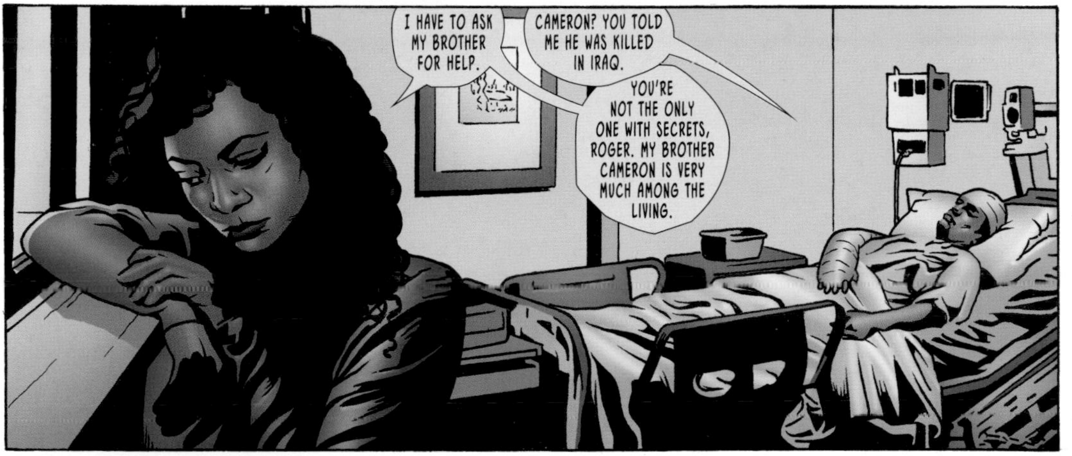
I HAVE TO ASK MY BROTHER FOR HELP.
CAMERON? YOU TOLD ME HE WAS KILLED IN IRAQ.
YOU'RE NOT THE ONLY ONE WITH SECRETS, ROGER. MY BROTHER CAMERON IS VERY MUCH AMONG THE LIVING.

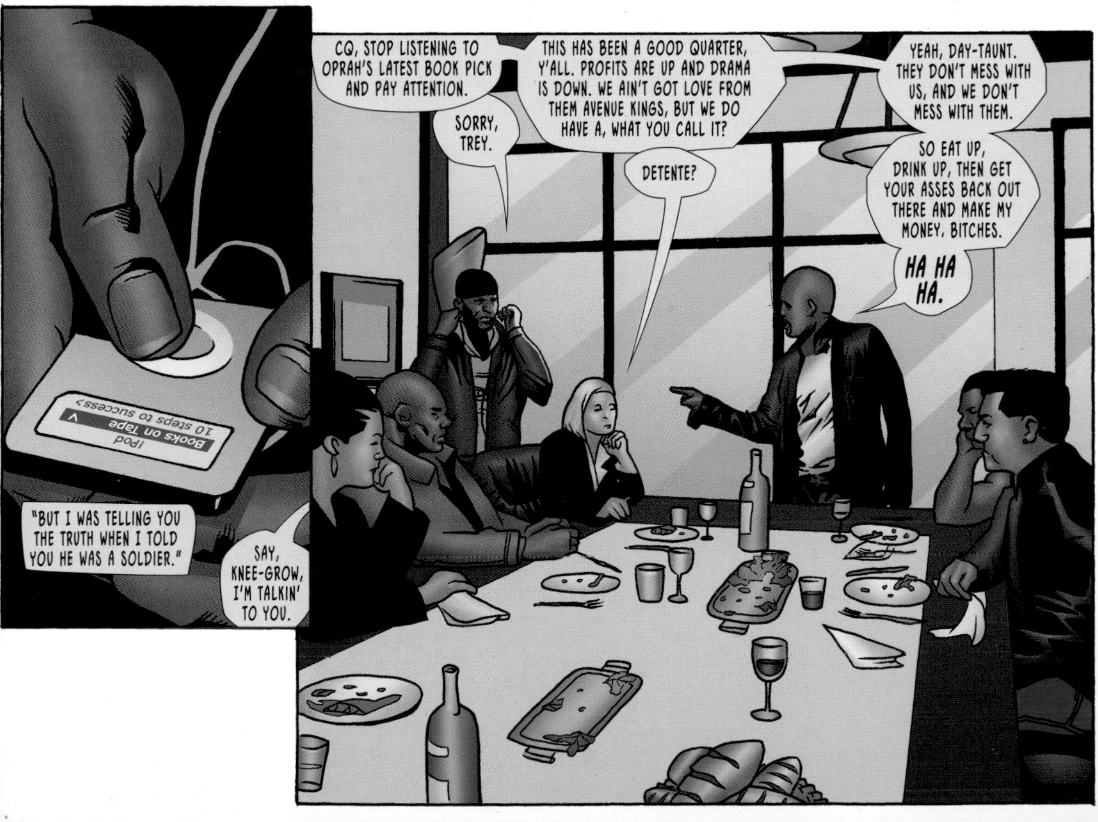
iPod
Books on Tape
10 steps to success
"BUT I WAS TELLING YOU THE TRUTH WHEN I TOLD YOU HE WAS A SOLDIER."
SAY, KNEE-GROW, I'M TALKIN' TO YOU.
CQ, STOP LISTENING TO OPRAH'S LATEST BOOK PICK AND PAY ATTENTION.
SORRY, TREY.
THIS HAS BEEN A GOOD QUARTER, Y'ALL. PROFITS ARE UP AND DRAMA IS DOWN. WE AIN'T GOT LOVE FROM THEM AVENUE KINGS, BUT WE DO HAVE A, WHAT YOU CALL IT?
DETENTE?
YEAH, DAY-TAUNT. THEY DON'T MESS WITH US, AND WE DON'T MESS WITH THEM.
SO EAT UP, DRINK UP, THEN GET YOUR ASSES BACK OUT THERE AND MAKE MY MONEY, BITCHES.
HA HA HA.

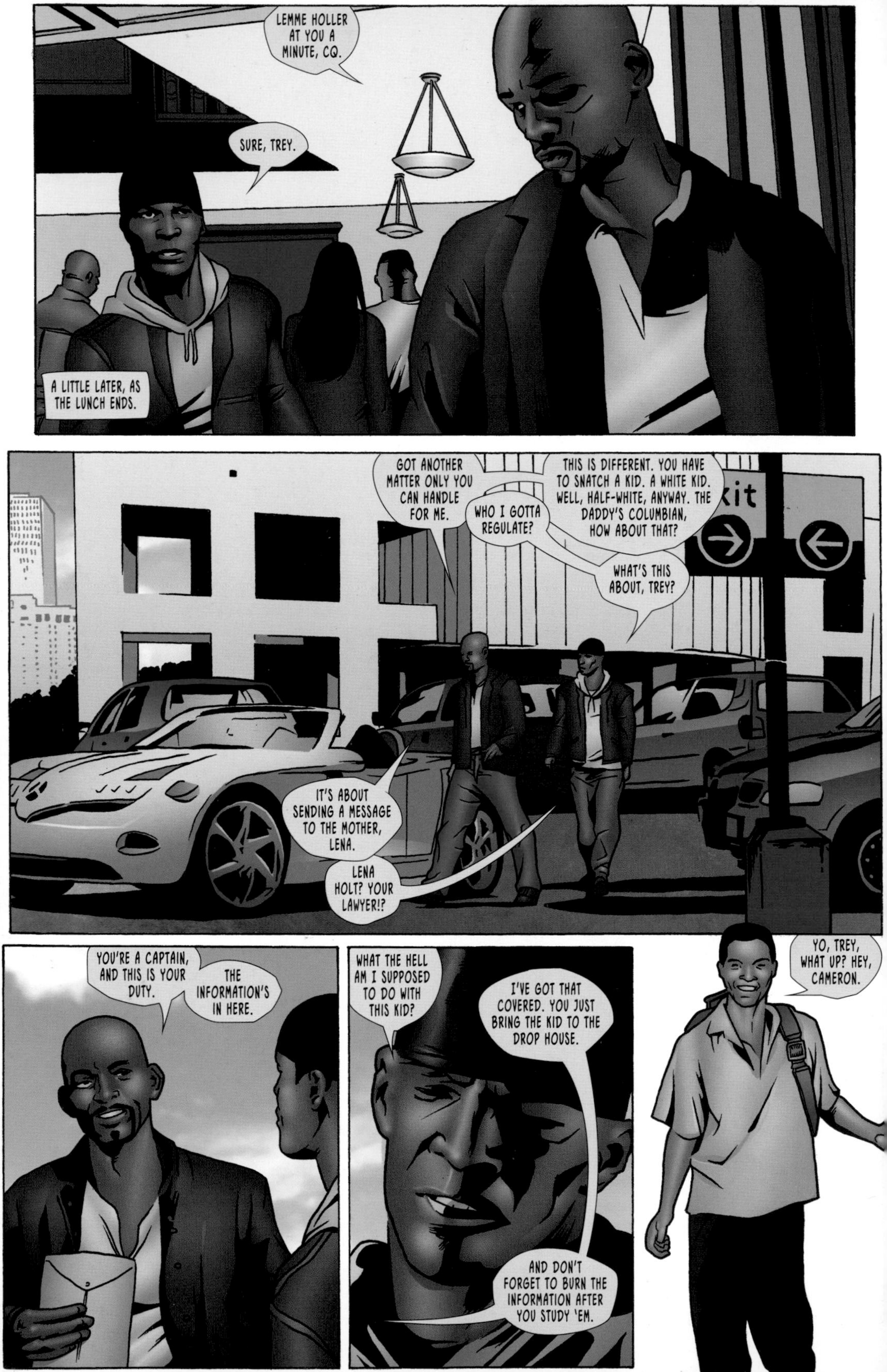
A LITTLE LATER, AS THE LUNCH ENDS.
LEMME HOLLER AT YOU A MINUTE, CQ.
SURE, TREY.
GOT ANOTHER MATTER ONLY YOU CAN HANDLE FOR ME.
WHO I GOTTA REGULATE?
THIS IS DIFFERENT. YOU HAVE TO SNATCH A KID. A WHITE KID. WELL, HALF-WHITE, ANYWAY. THE DADDY'S COLUMBIAN, HOW ABOUT THAT?
WHAT'S THIS ABOUT, TREY?
IT'S ABOUT SENDING A MESSAGE TO THE MOTHER, LENA.
LENA HOLT? YOUR LAWYER!?
YOU'RE A CAPTAIN, AND THIS IS YOUR DUTY.
THE INFORMATION'S IN HERE.
WHAT THE HELL AM I SUPPOSED TO DO WITH THIS KID?
I'VE GOT THAT COVERED. YOU JUST BRING THE KID TO THE DROP HOUSE.
AND DON'T FORGET TO BURN THE INFORMATION AFTER YOU STUDY 'EM.
YO, TREY, WHAT UP? HEY, CAMERON.

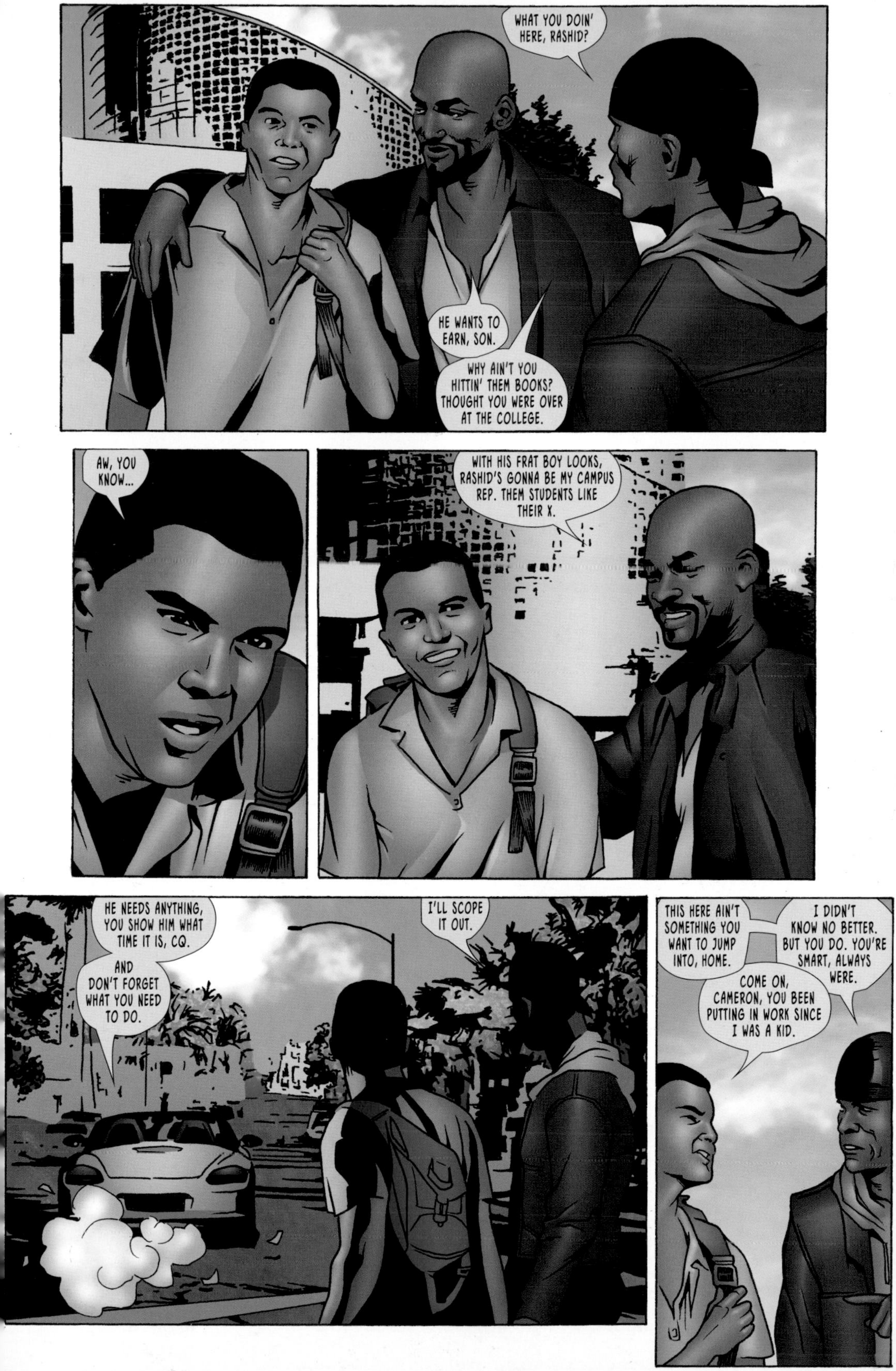
WHAT YOU DOIN' HERE, RASHID?
HE WANTS TO EARN, SON.
WHY AIN'T YOU HITTIN' THEM BOOKS? THOUGHT YOU WERE OVER AT THE COLLEGE.
AW, YOU KNOW...
WITH HIS FRAT BOY LOOKS, RASHID'S GONNA BE MY CAMPUS REP. THEM STUDENTS LIKE THEIR X.
HE NEEDS ANYTHING, YOU SHOW HIM WHAT TIME IT IS, CQ.
AND DON'T FORGET WHAT YOU NEED TO DO.
I'LL SCOPE IT OUT.
THIS HERE AIN'T SOMETHING YOU WANT TO JUMP INTO, HOME.
I DIDN'T KNOW NO BETTER. BUT YOU DO. YOU'RE SMART, ALWAYS WERE.
COME ON, CAMERON, YOU BEEN PUTTING IN WORK SINCE I WAS A KID.

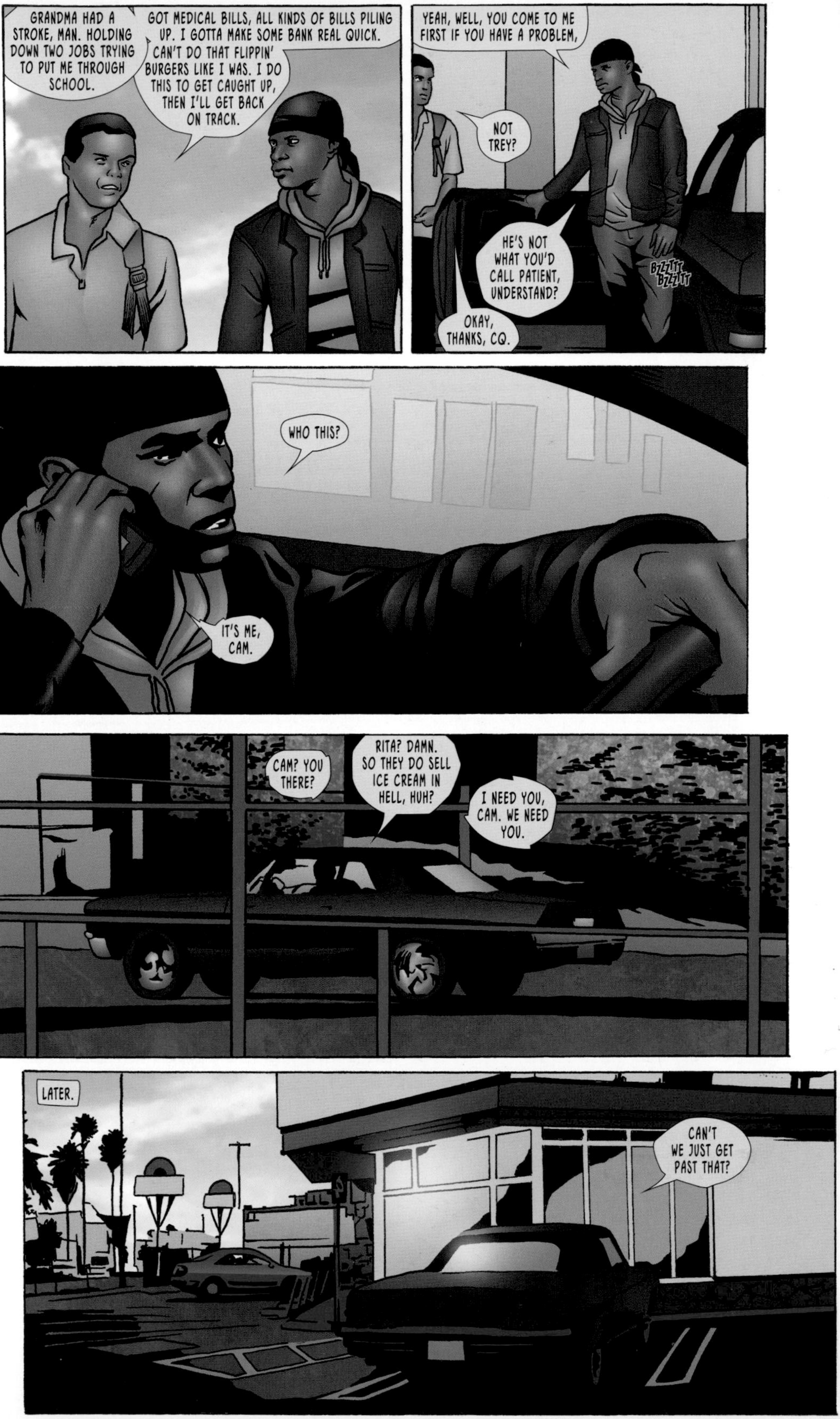
GRANDMA HAD A STROKE, MAN. HOLDING DOWN TWO JOBS TRYING TO PUT ME THROUGH SCHOOL.
GOT MEDICAL BILLS, ALL KINDS OF BILLS PILING UP. I GOTTA MAKE SOME BANK REAL QUICK.
CAN'T DO THAT FLIPPIN' BURGERS LIKE I WAS. I DO THIS TO GET CAUGHT UP, THEN I'LL GET BACK ON TRACK.
YEAH, WELL, YOU COME TO ME FIRST IF YOU HAVE A PROBLEM,
NOT TREY?
HE'S NOT WHAT YOU'D CALL PATIENT, UNDERSTAND?
BZZZTT BZZZTT
OKAY, THANKS, CQ.
WHO THIS?
IT'S ME, CAM.
CAM? YOU THERE?
RITA? DAMN. SO THEY DO SELL ICE CREAM IN HELL, HUH?
I NEED YOU, CAM. WE NEED YOU.
LATER.
CAN'T WE JUST GET PAST THAT?

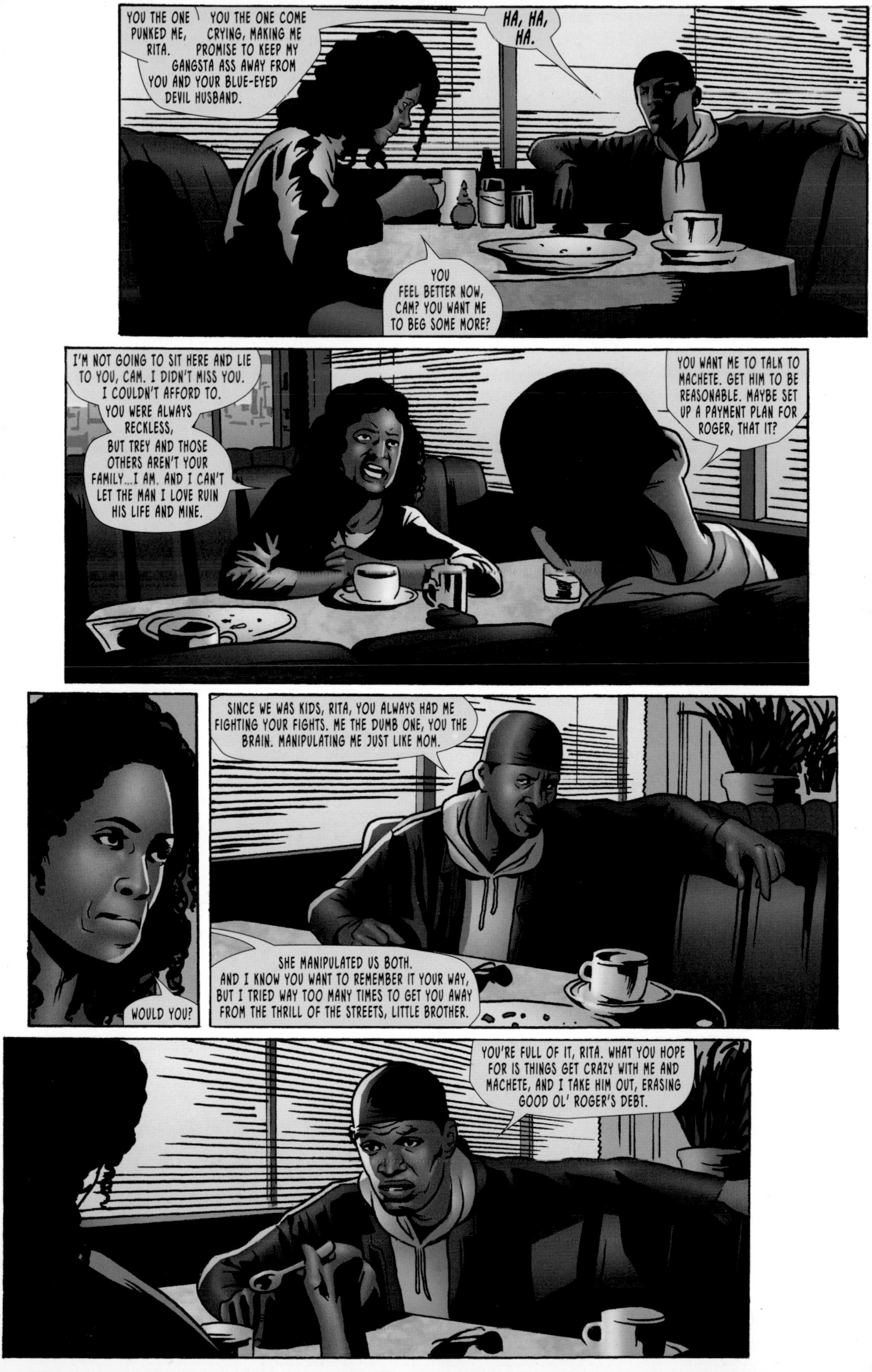
YOU THE ONE PUNKED ME, RITA.
YOU THE ONE COME CRYING, MAKING ME PROMISE TO KEEP MY GANGSTA ASS AWAY FROM YOU AND YOUR BLUE-EYED DEVIL HUSBAND.
HA, HA, HA.
YOU FEEL BETTER NOW, CAM? YOU WANT ME TO BEG SOME MORE?
I'M NOT GOING TO SIT HERE AND LIE TO YOU, CAM. I DIDN'T MISS YOU. I COULDN'T AFFORD TO. YOU WERE ALWAYS RECKLESS,
BUT TREY AND THOSE OTHERS AREN'T YOUR FAMILY...I AM. AND I CAN'T LET THE MAN I LOVE RUIN HIS LIFE AND MINE.
YOU WANT ME TO TALK TO MACHETE. GET HIM TO BE REASONABLE. MAYBE SET UP A PAYMENT PLAN FOR ROGER, THAT IT?
SINCE WE WAS KIDS, RITA, YOU ALWAYS HAD ME FIGHTING YOUR FIGHTS. ME THE DUMB ONE, YOU THE BRAIN. MANIPULATING ME JUST LIKE MOM.
SHE MANIPULATED US BOTH. AND I KNOW YOU WANT TO REMEMBER IT YOUR WAY, BUT I TRIED WAY TOO MANY TIMES TO GET YOU AWAY FROM THE THRILL OF THE STREETS, LITTLE BROTHER.
WOULD YOU?
YOU'RE FULL OF IT, RITA. WHAT YOU HOPE FOR IS THINGS GET CRAZY WITH ME AND MACHETE, AND I TAKE HIM OUT, ERASING GOOD OL' ROGER'S DEBT.

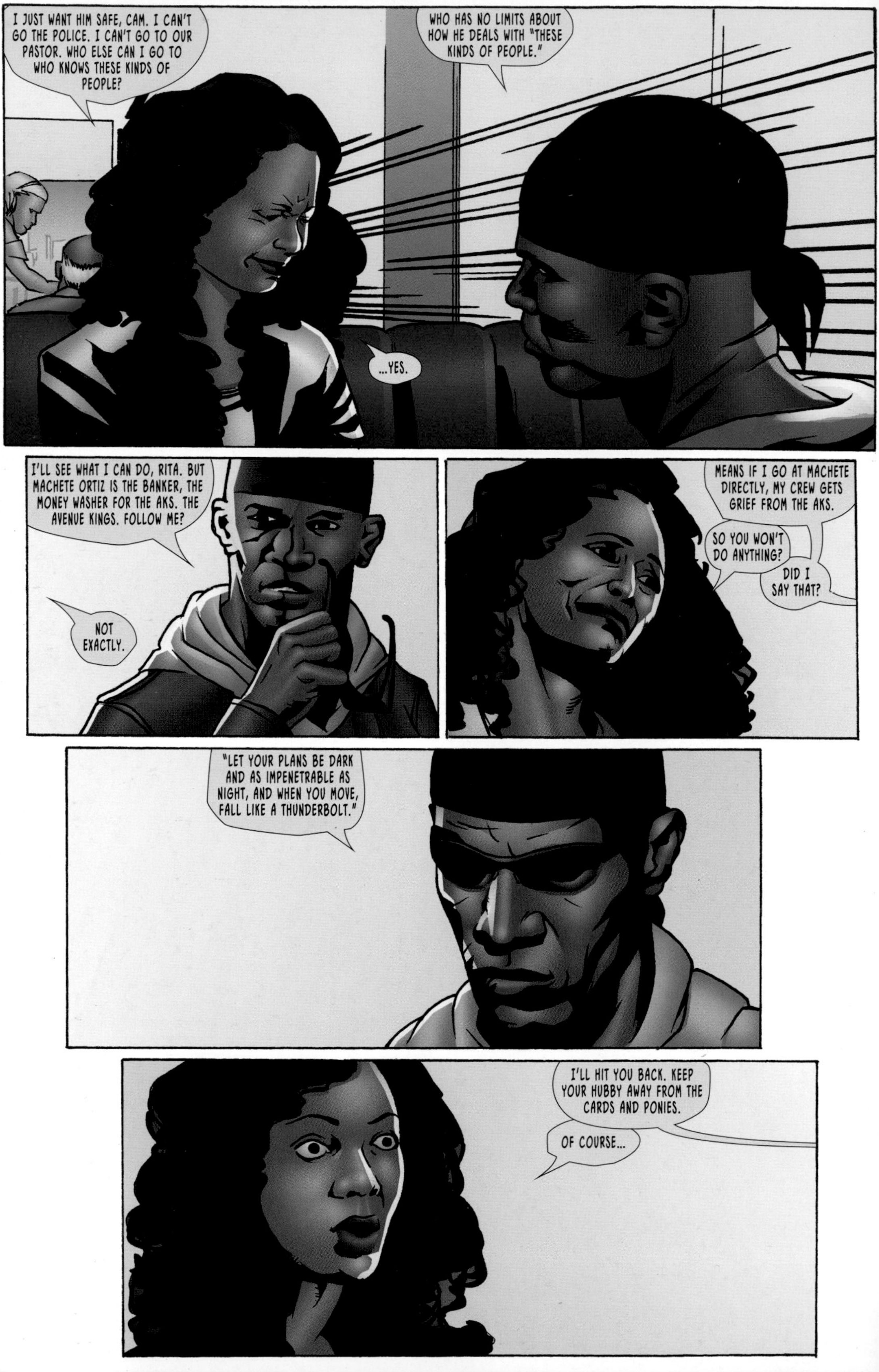
I JUST WANT HIM SAFE, CAM. I CAN'T GO THE POLICE. I CAN'T GO TO OUR PASTOR. WHO ELSE CAN I GO TO WHO KNOWS THESE KINDS OF PEOPLE?
WHO HAS NO LIMITS ABOUT HOW HE DEALS WITH "THESE KINDS OF PEOPLE."
...YES.
I'LL SEE WHAT I CAN DO, RITA. BUT MACHETE ORTIZ IS THE BANKER, THE MONEY WASHER FOR THE AKS. THE AVENUE KINGS. FOLLOW ME?
NOT EXACTLY.
MEANS IF I GO AT MACHETE DIRECTLY, MY CREW GETS GRIEF FROM THE AKS.
SO YOU WON'T DO ANYTHING?
DID I SAY THAT?
"LET YOUR PLANS BE DARK AND AS IMPENETRABLE AS NIGHT, AND WHEN YOU MOVE, FALL LIKE A THUNDERBOLT."
I'LL HIT YOU BACK. KEEP YOUR HUBBY AWAY FROM THE CARDS AND PONIES.
OF COURSE...

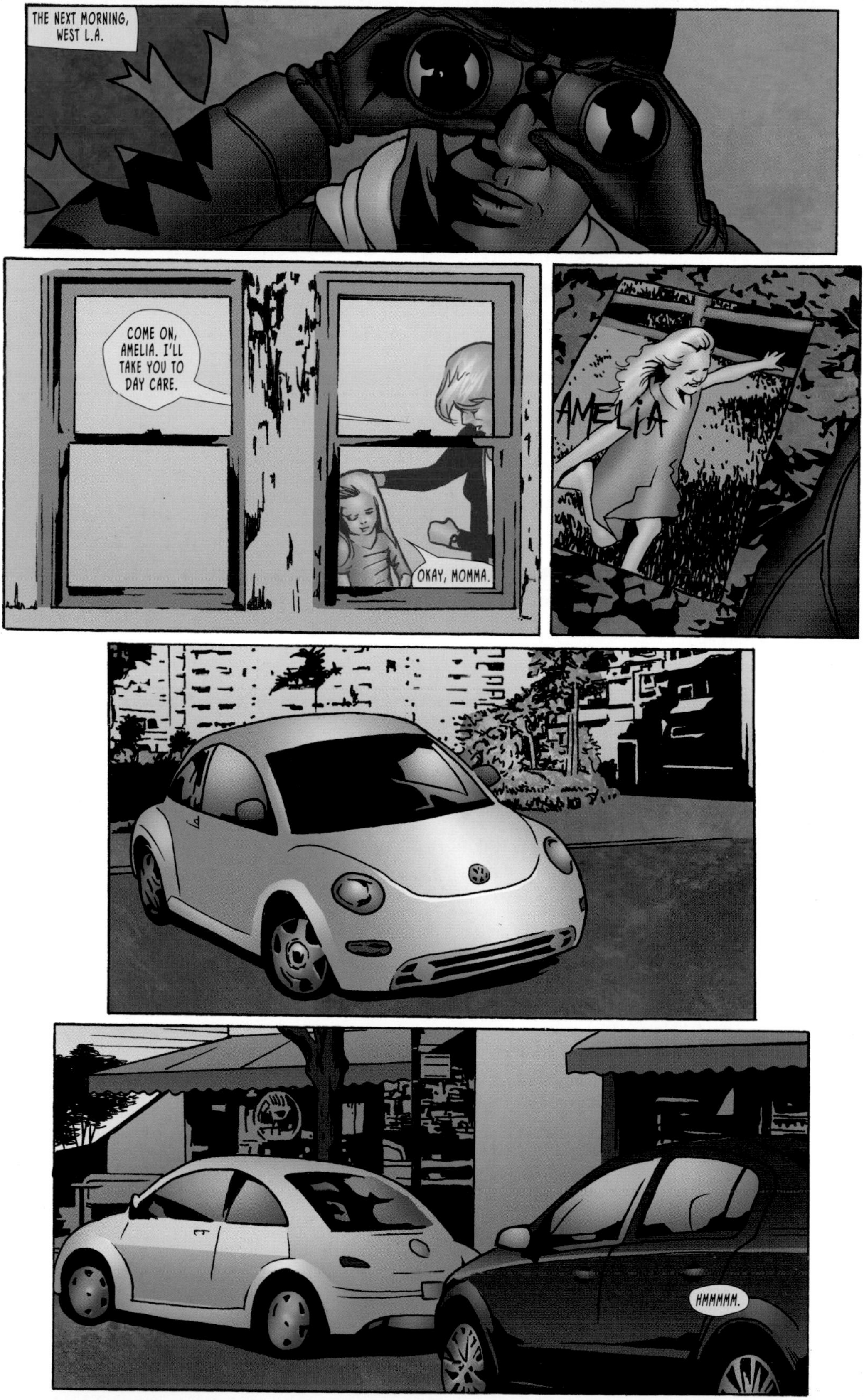
THE NEXT MORNING, WEST L.A.
COME ON, AMELIA. I'LL TAKE YOU TO DAY CARE.
OKAY, MOMMA.
AMELIA
HMMMMM.

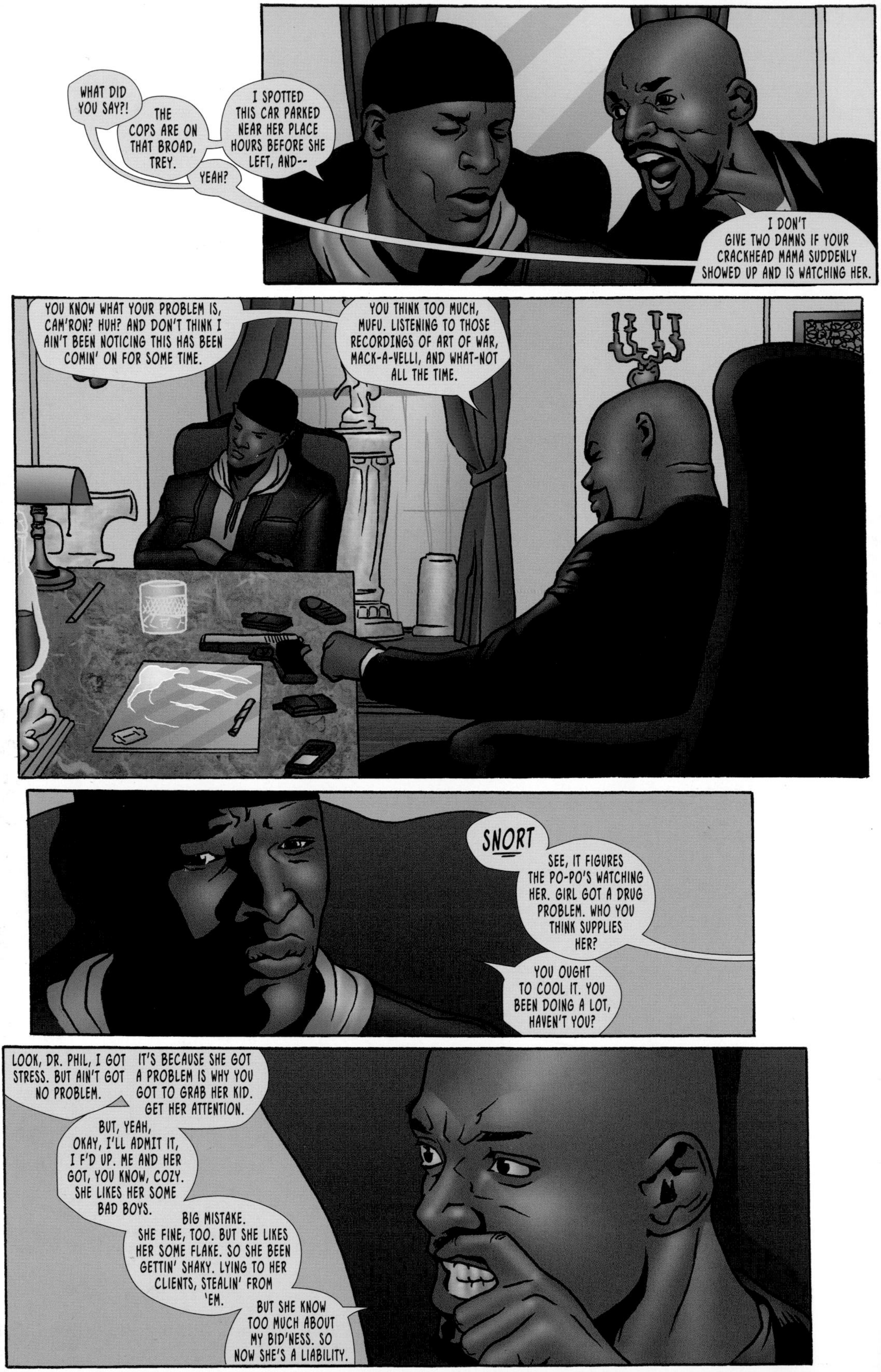
WHAT DID YOU SAY?!
THE COPS ARE ON THAT BROAD, TREY.
I SPOTTED THIS CAR PARKED NEAR HER PLACE HOURS BEFORE SHE LEFT, AND--
YEAH?
I DON'T GIVE TWO DAMNS IF YOUR CRACKHEAD MAMA SUDDENLY SHOWED UP AND IS WATCHING HER.
YOU KNOW WHAT YOUR PROBLEM IS, CAM'RON? HUH? AND DON'T THINK I AIN'T BEEN NOTICING THIS HAS BEEN COMIN' ON FOR SOME TIME.
YOU THINK TOO MUCH, MUFU. LISTENING TO THOSE RECORDINGS OF ART OF WAR, MACK-A-VELLI, AND WHAT-NOT ALL THE TIME.
SNORT
SEE, IT FIGURES THE PO-PO'S WATCHING HER. GIRL GOT A DRUG PROBLEM. WHO YOU THINK SUPPLIES HER?
YOU OUGHT TO COOL IT. YOU BEEN DOING A LOT, HAVEN'T YOU?
LOOK, DR. PHIL, I GOT STRESS. BUT AIN'T GOT NO PROBLEM.
IT'S BECAUSE SHE GOT A PROBLEM IS WHY YOU GOT TO GRAB HER KID. GET HER ATTENTION.
BUT, YEAH, OKAY, I'LL ADMIT IT, I F'D UP. ME AND HER GOT, YOU KNOW, COZY. SHE LIKES HER SOME BAD BOYS.
BIG MISTAKE. SHE FINE, TOO. BUT SHE LIKES HER SOME FLAKE. SO SHE BEEN GETTIN' SHAKY. LYING TO HER CLIENTS, STEALIN' FROM 'EM.
BUT SHE KNOW TOO MUCH ABOUT MY BID'NESS. SO NOW SHE'S A LIABILITY.

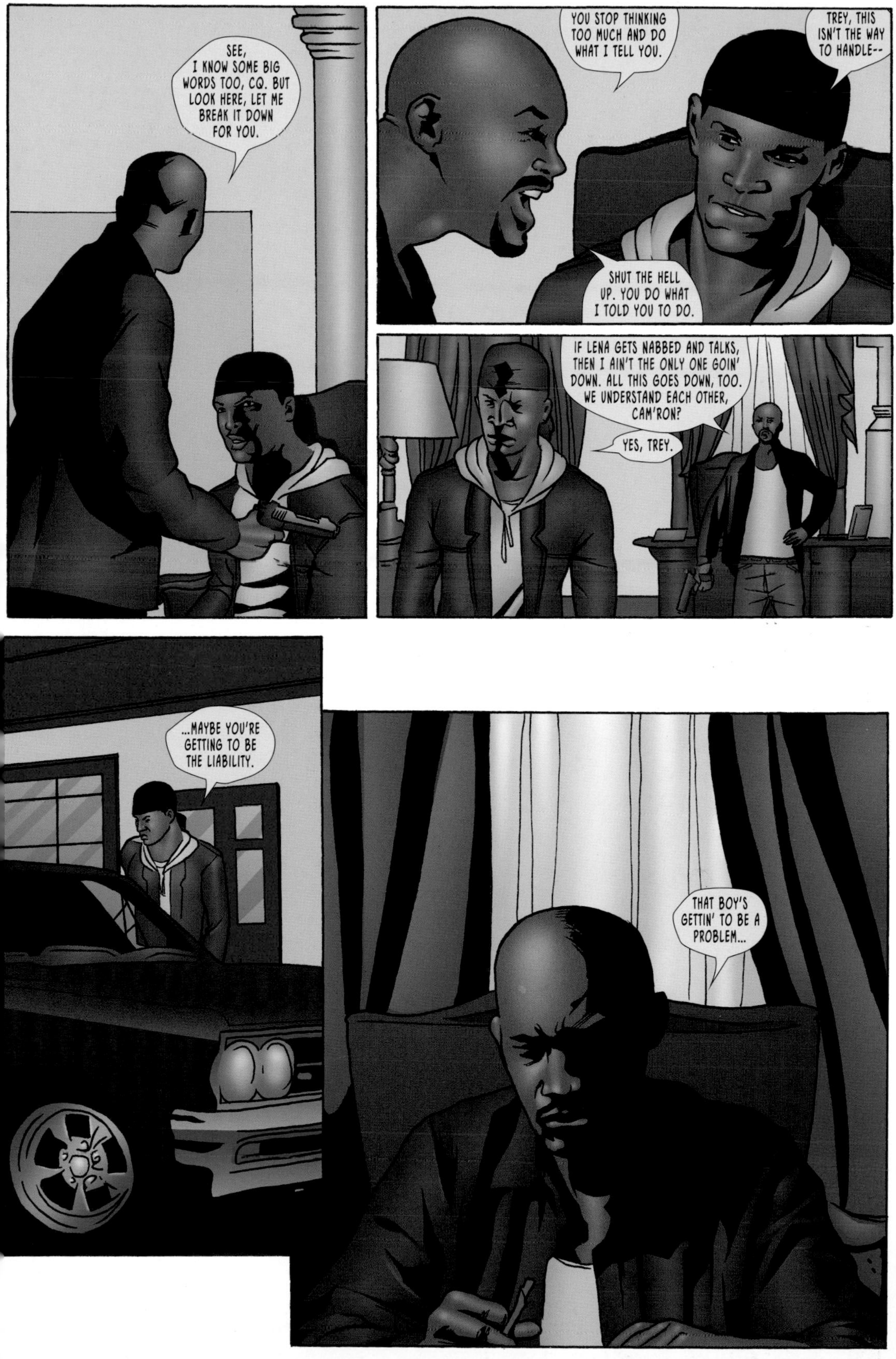
SEE, I KNOW SOME BIG WORDS TOO, CQ. BUT LOOK HERE, LET ME BREAK IT DOWN FOR YOU.
YOU STOP THINKING TOO MUCH AND DO WHAT I TELL YOU.
TREY, THIS ISN'T THE WAY TO HANDLE--
SHUT THE HELL UP. YOU DO WHAT I TOLD YOU TO DO.
IF LENA GETS NABBED AND TALKS, THEN I AIN'T THE ONLY ONE GOIN' DOWN. ALL THIS GOES DOWN, TOO. WE UNDERSTAND EACH OTHER, CAM'RON?
YES, TREY.
...MAYBE YOU'RE GETTING TO BE THE LIABILITY.
THAT BOY'S GETTIN' TO BE A PROBLEM...

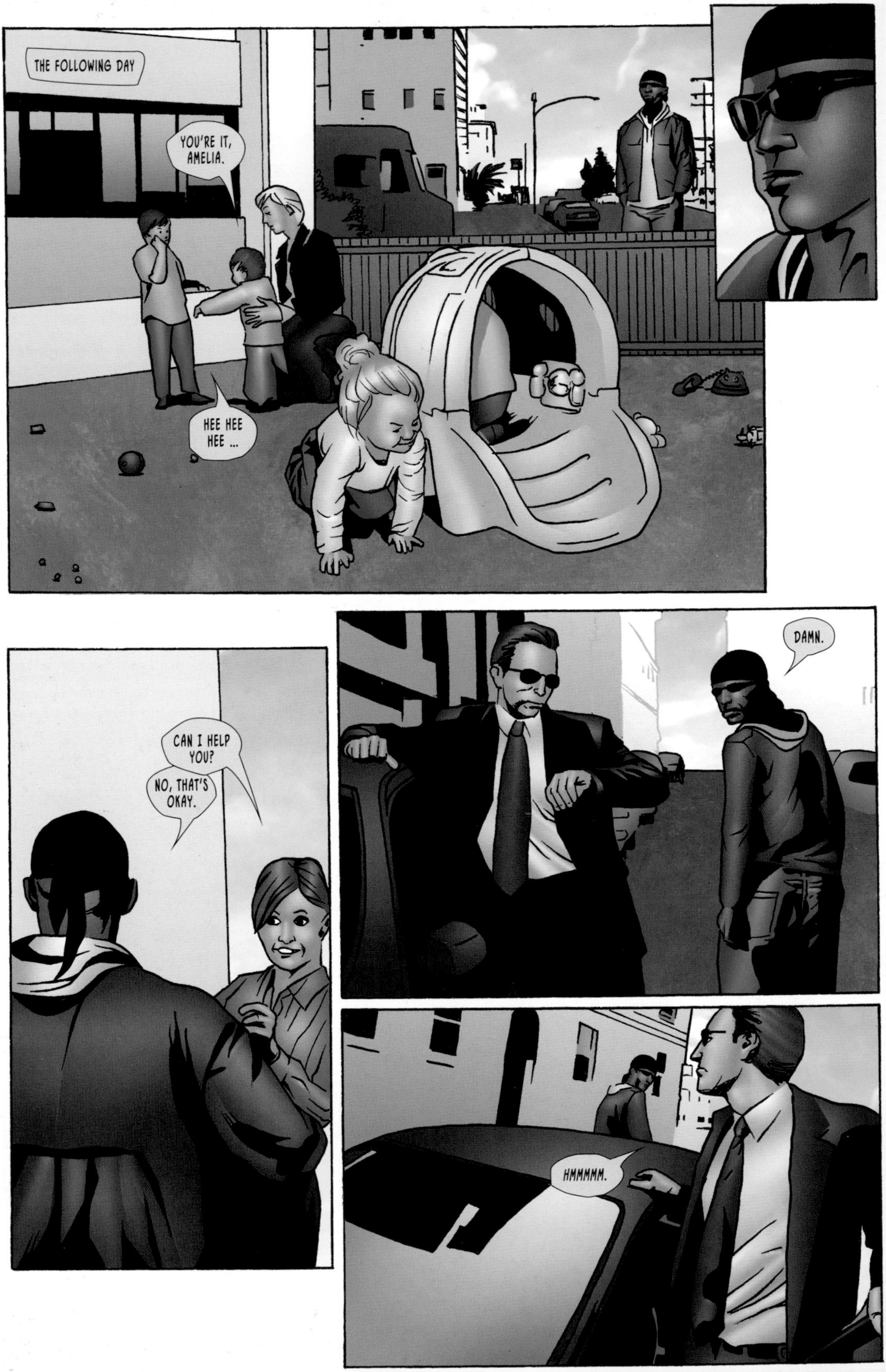
THE FOLLOWING DAY
YOU'RE IT, AMELIA.
HEE HEE HEE ...
CAN I HELP YOU?
NO, THAT'S OKAY.
DAMN.
HMMMMM.

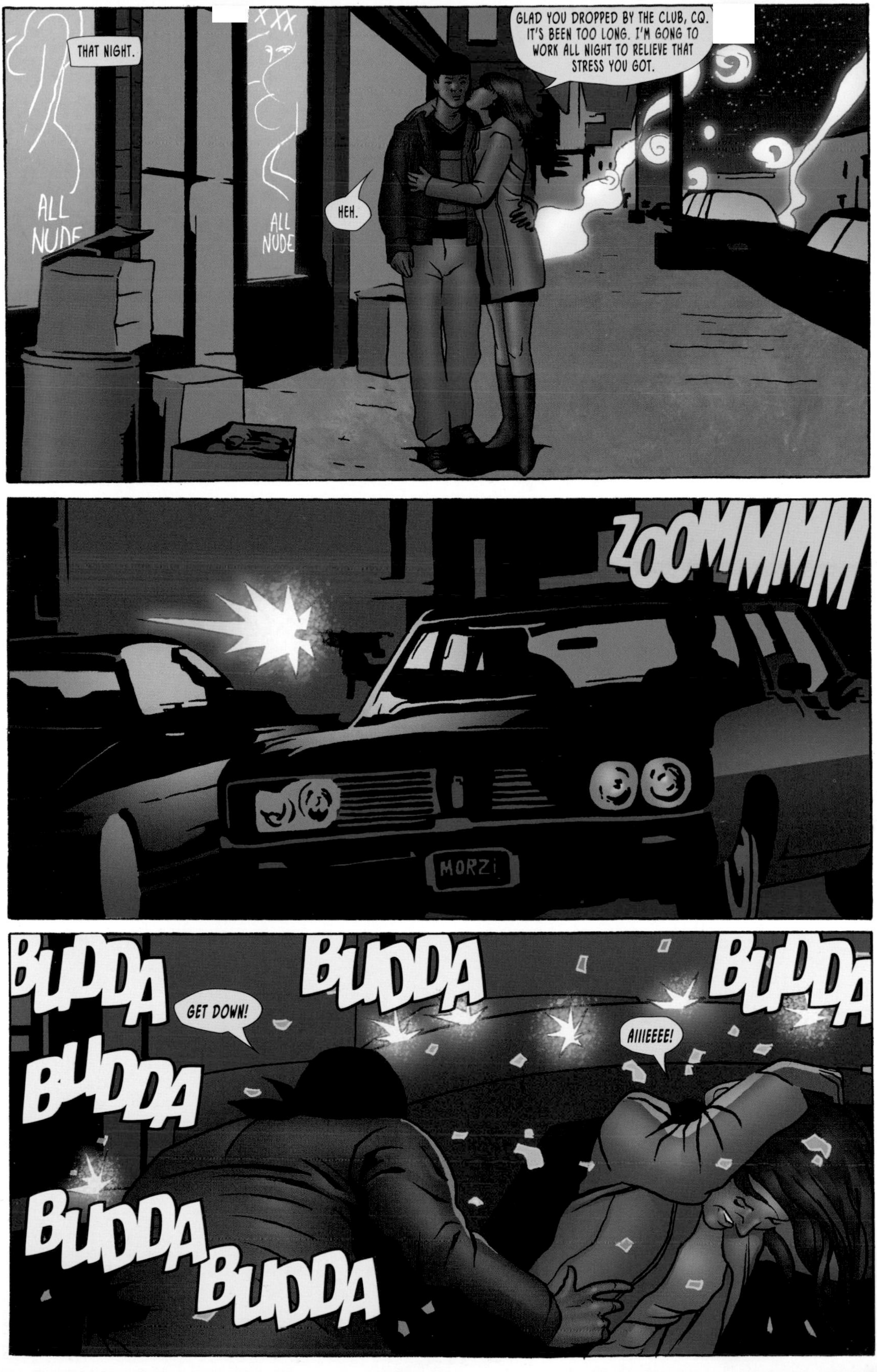
XXX
THAT NIGHT.
GLAD YOU DROPPED BY THE CLUB, CQ. IT'S BEEN TOO LONG. I'M GONG TO WORK ALL NIGHT TO RELIEVE THAT STRESS YOU GOT.
HEH.
ALL NUDE
ALL NUDE
ZOOMMMM
MORZi
BUDDA
BUDDA
BUDDA
GET DOWN!
AIIIEEEE!
BUDDA
BUDDA
BUDDA

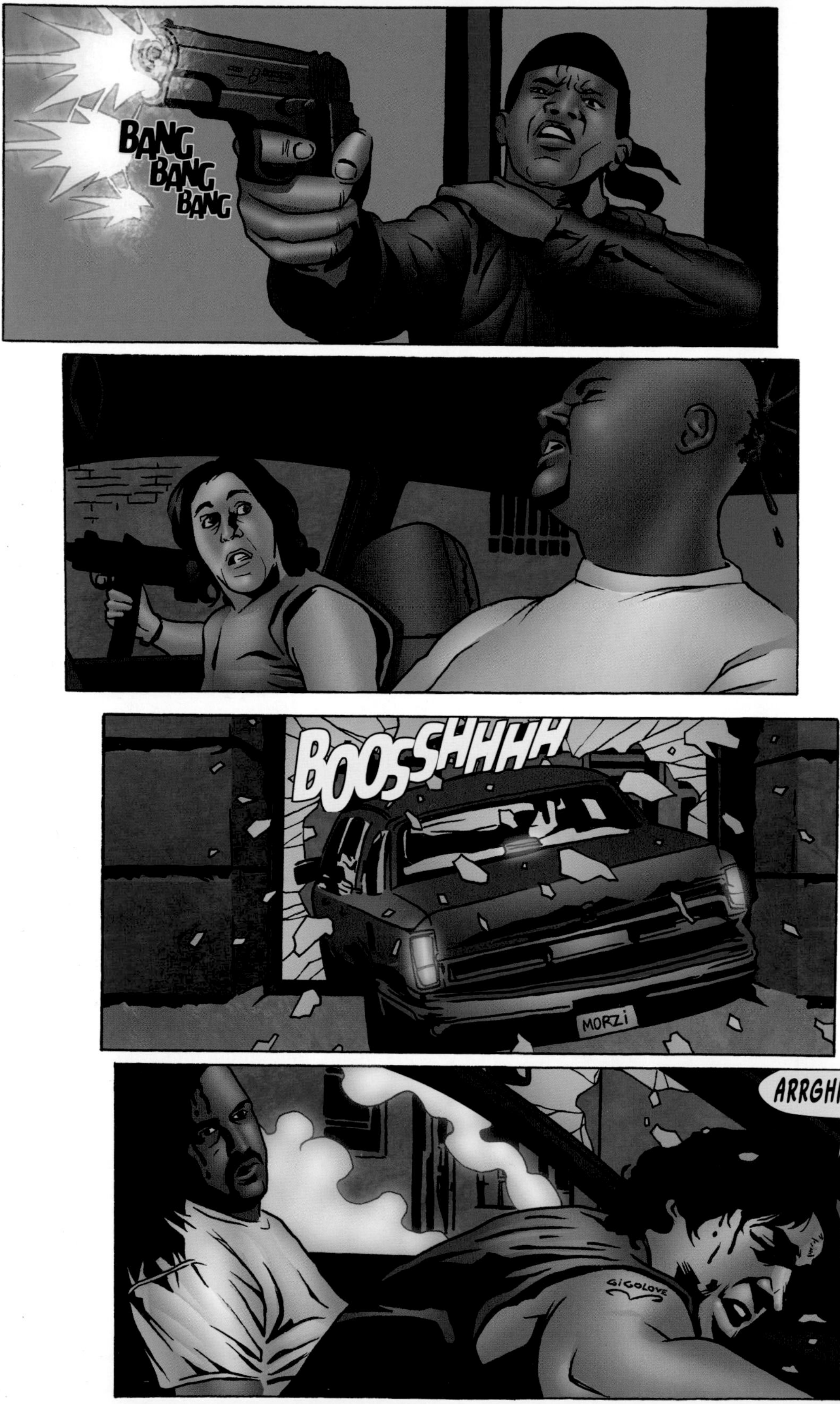
BANG
BANG
BANG
BOOSSHHHH
MORZI
ARRGHHHH!
GIGOLOVE

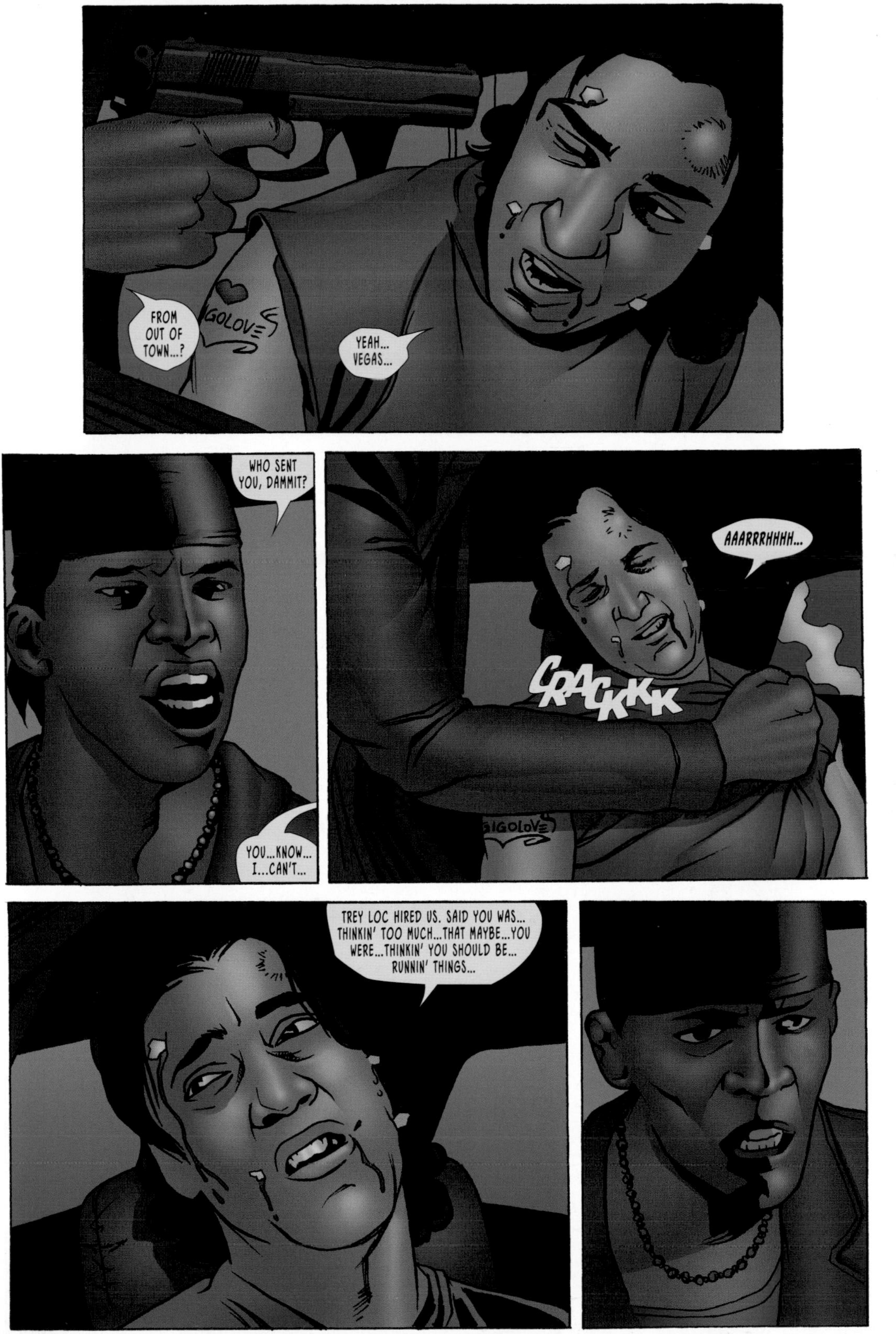
GIGOLOVE
FROM OUT OF TOWN...?
YEAH... VEGAS...
WHO SENT YOU, DAMMIT?
YOU...KNOW... I...CAN'T...
AAARRRHHHH...
CRACKKK
GIGOLOVE
TREY LOC HIRED US. SAID YOU WAS... THINKIN' TOO MUCH...THAT MAYBE...YOU WERE...THINKIN' YOU SHOULD BE... RUNNIN' THINGS...

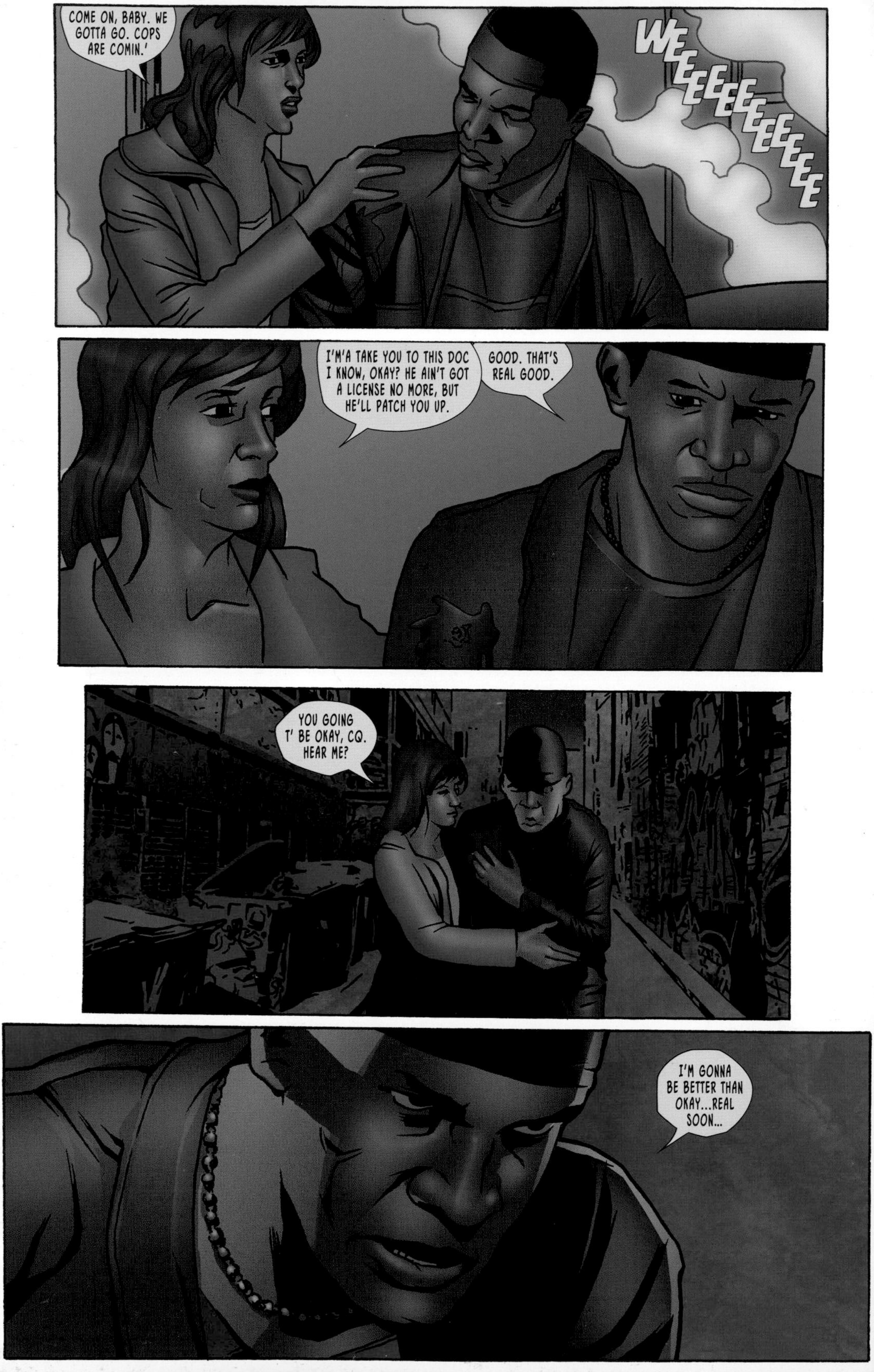
COME ON, BABY. WE GOTTA GO. COPS ARE COMIN.'
WEEEEEEEEEEEE
I'M'A TAKE YOU TO THIS DOC I KNOW, OKAY? HE AIN'T GOT A LICENSE NO MORE, BUT HE'LL PATCH YOU UP.
GOOD. THAT'S REAL GOOD.
YOU GOING T' BE OKAY, CQ. HEAR ME?
I'M GONNA BE BETTER THAN OKAY...REAL SOON...

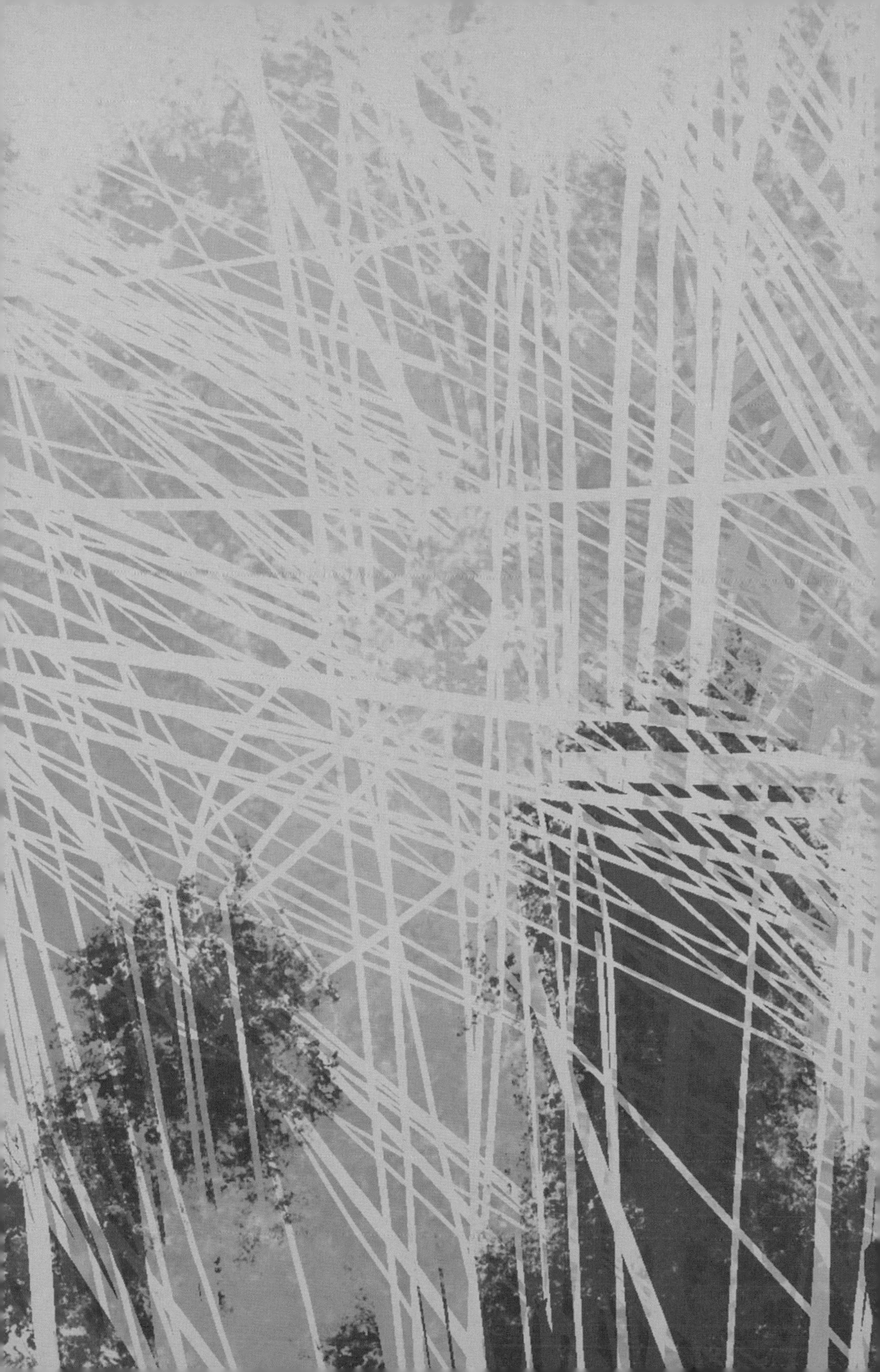

CHAPTER 2

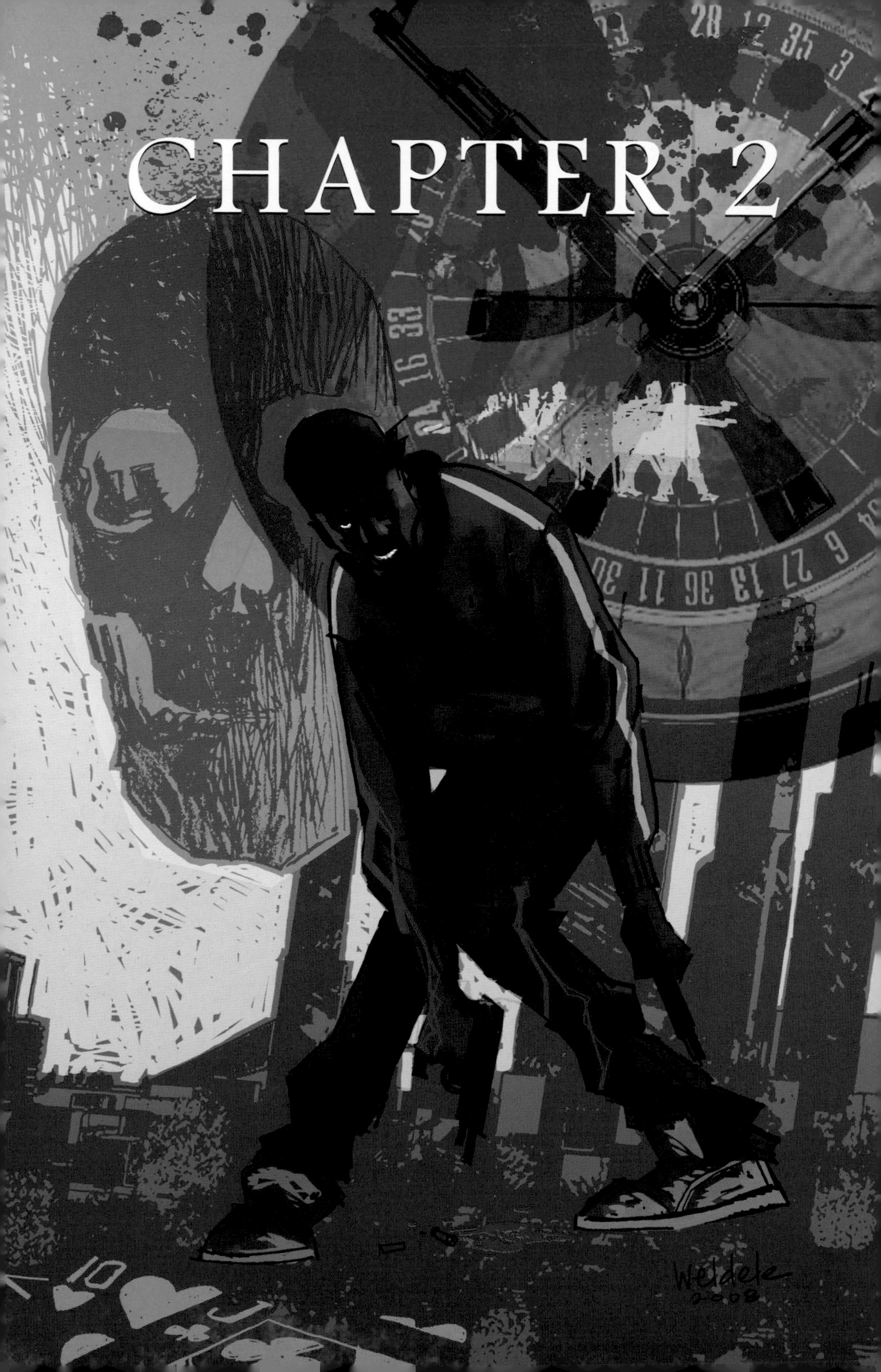
Weldele
2008

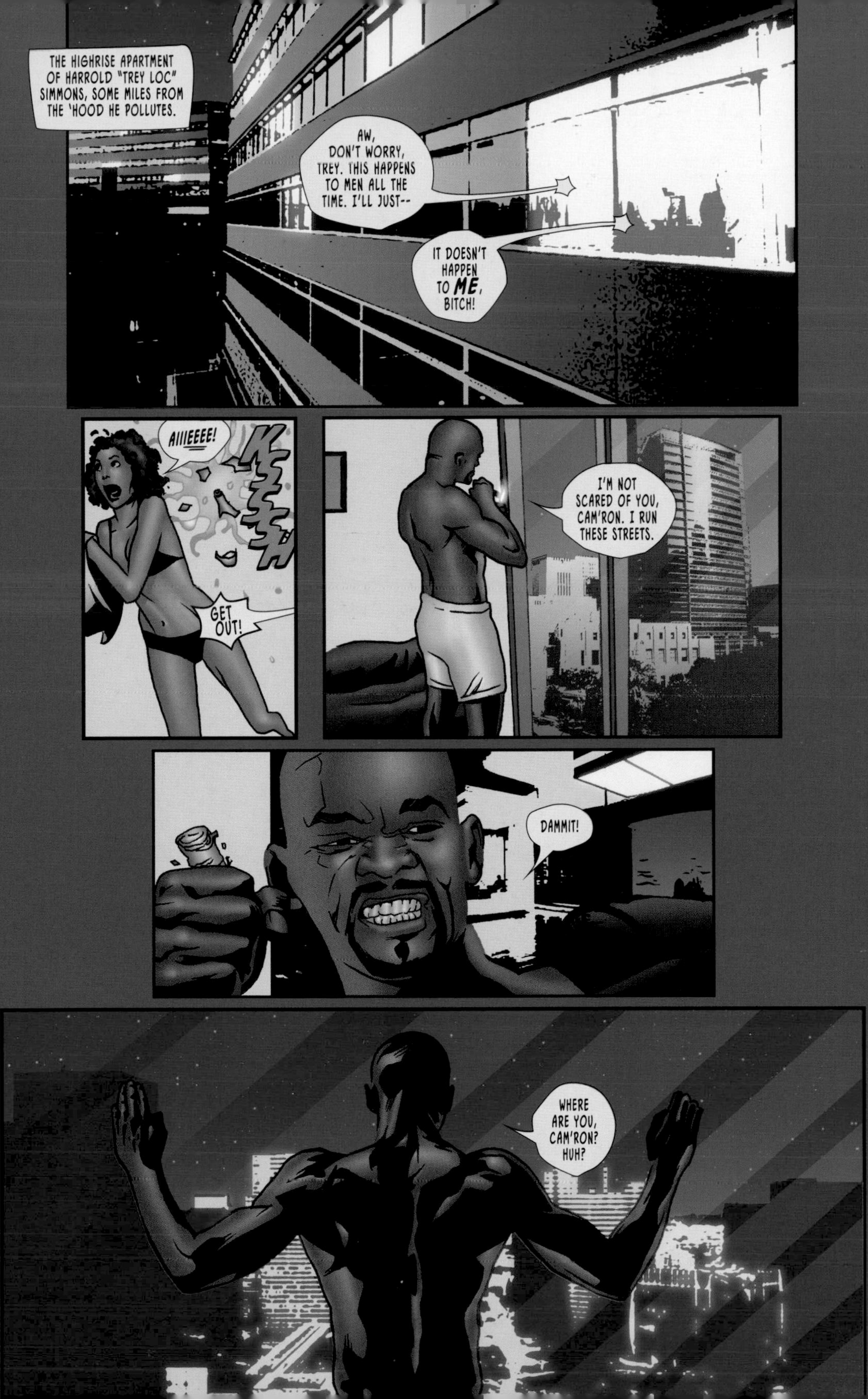
THE HIGHRISE APARTMENT OF HARROLD "TREY LOC" SIMMONS, SOME MILES FROM THE 'HOOD HE POLLUTES.
AW, DON'T WORRY, TREY. THIS HAPPENS TO MEN ALL THE TIME. I'LL JUST--
IT DOESN'T HAPPEN TO ME, BITCH!
AIIIEEEE!
KSSSH
GET OUT!
I'M NOT SCARED OF YOU, CAM'RON. I RUN THESE STREETS.
DAMMIT!
WHERE ARE YOU, CAM'RON? HUH?

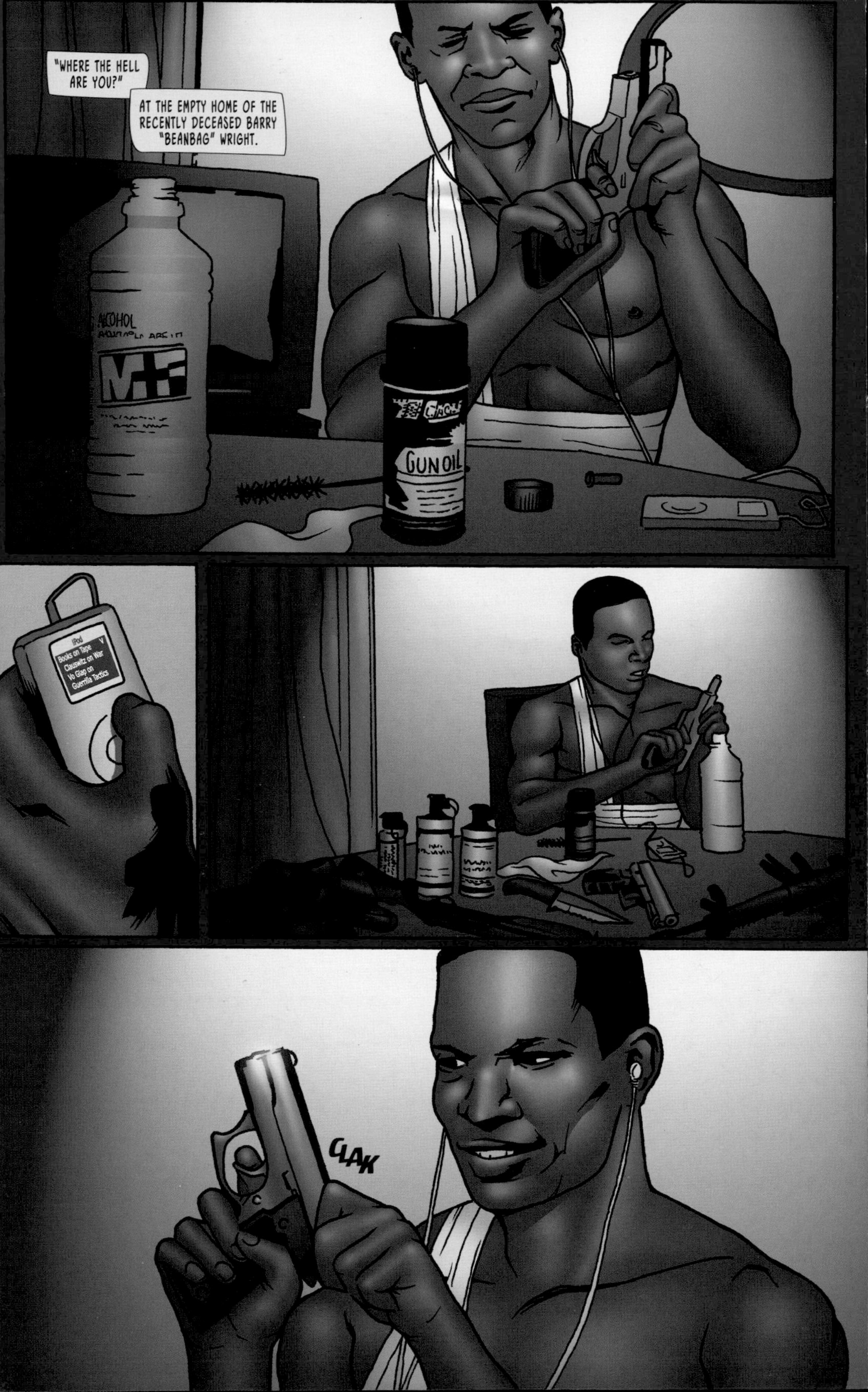
"WHERE THE HELL ARE YOU?"
AT THE EMPTY HOME OF THE RECENTLY DECEASED BARRY "BEANBAG" WRIGHT.
ALCOHOL
GUN OIL
iPod
Books on Tape
Clauswitz on War
Vo Giap on Guerrilla Tactics
CLAK

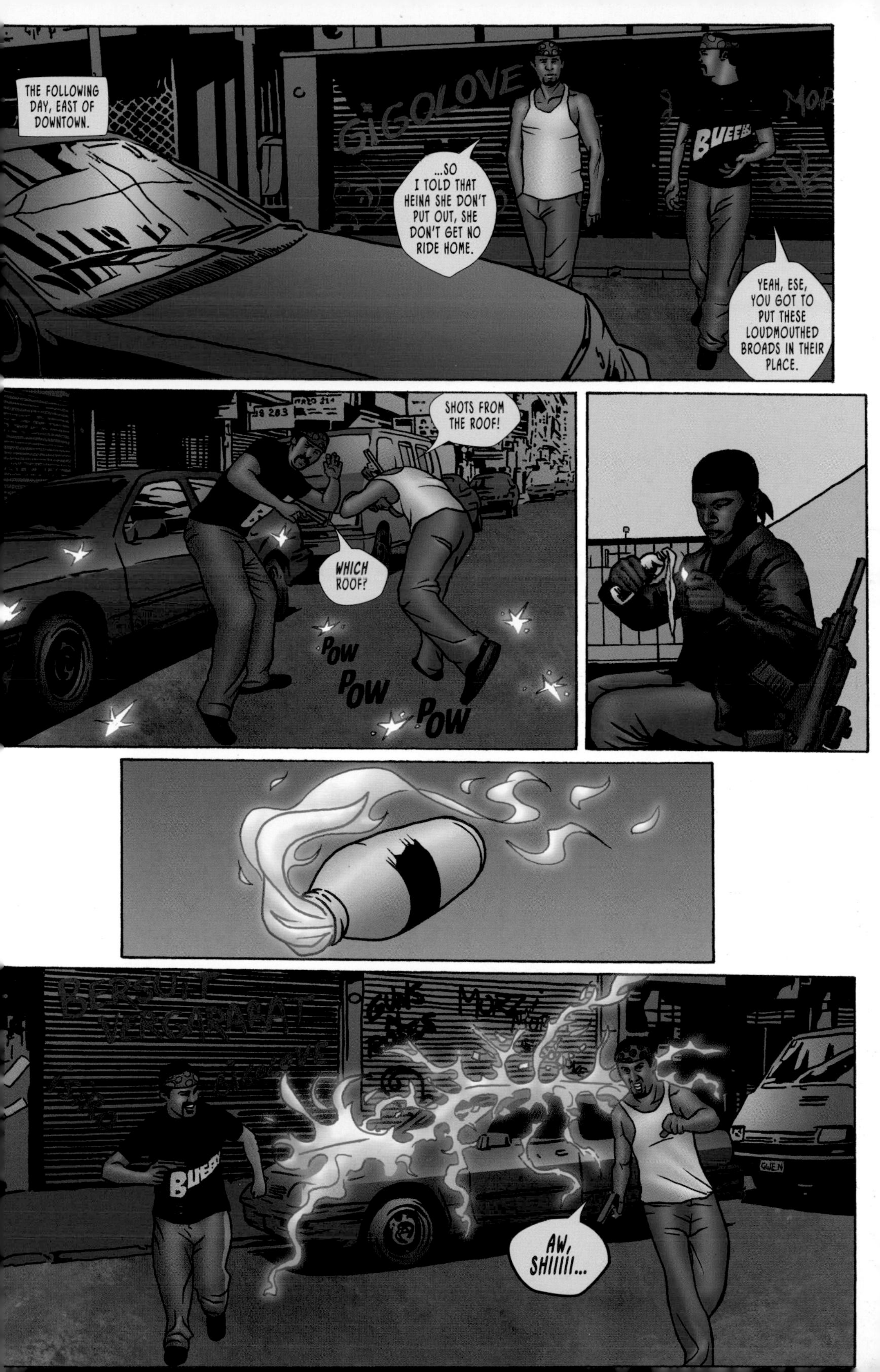
THE FOLLOWING DAY, EAST OF DOWNTOWN.
...SO I TOLD THAT HEINA SHE DON'T PUT OUT, SHE DON'T GET NO RIDE HOME.
YEAH, ESE, YOU GOT TO PUT THESE LOUDMOUTHED BROADS IN THEIR PLACE.
SHOTS FROM THE ROOF!
WHICH ROOF?
POW
POW
POW
AW, SHIIIII...

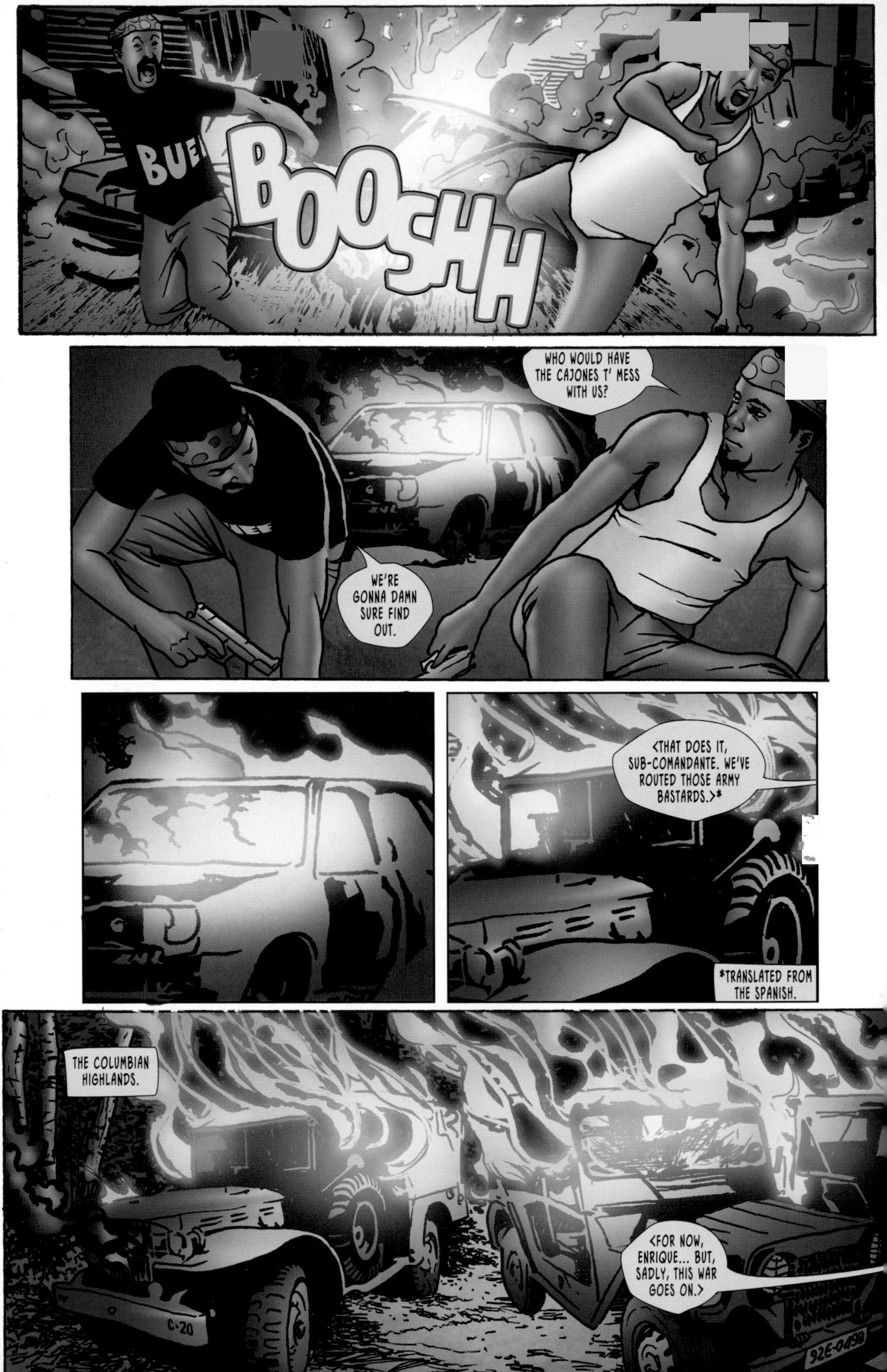
BOOSHH
BUE
WHO WOULD HAVE THE CAJONES T' MESS WITH US?
WE'RE GONNA DAMN SURE FIND OUT.
<THAT DOES IT, SUB-COMANDANTE. WE'VE ROUTED THOSE ARMY BASTARDS.>*
*TRANSLATED FROM THE SPANISH.
THE COLUMBIAN HIGHLANDS.
<FOR NOW, ENRIQUE... BUT, SADLY, THIS WAR GOES ON.>
C-20
32E-0498

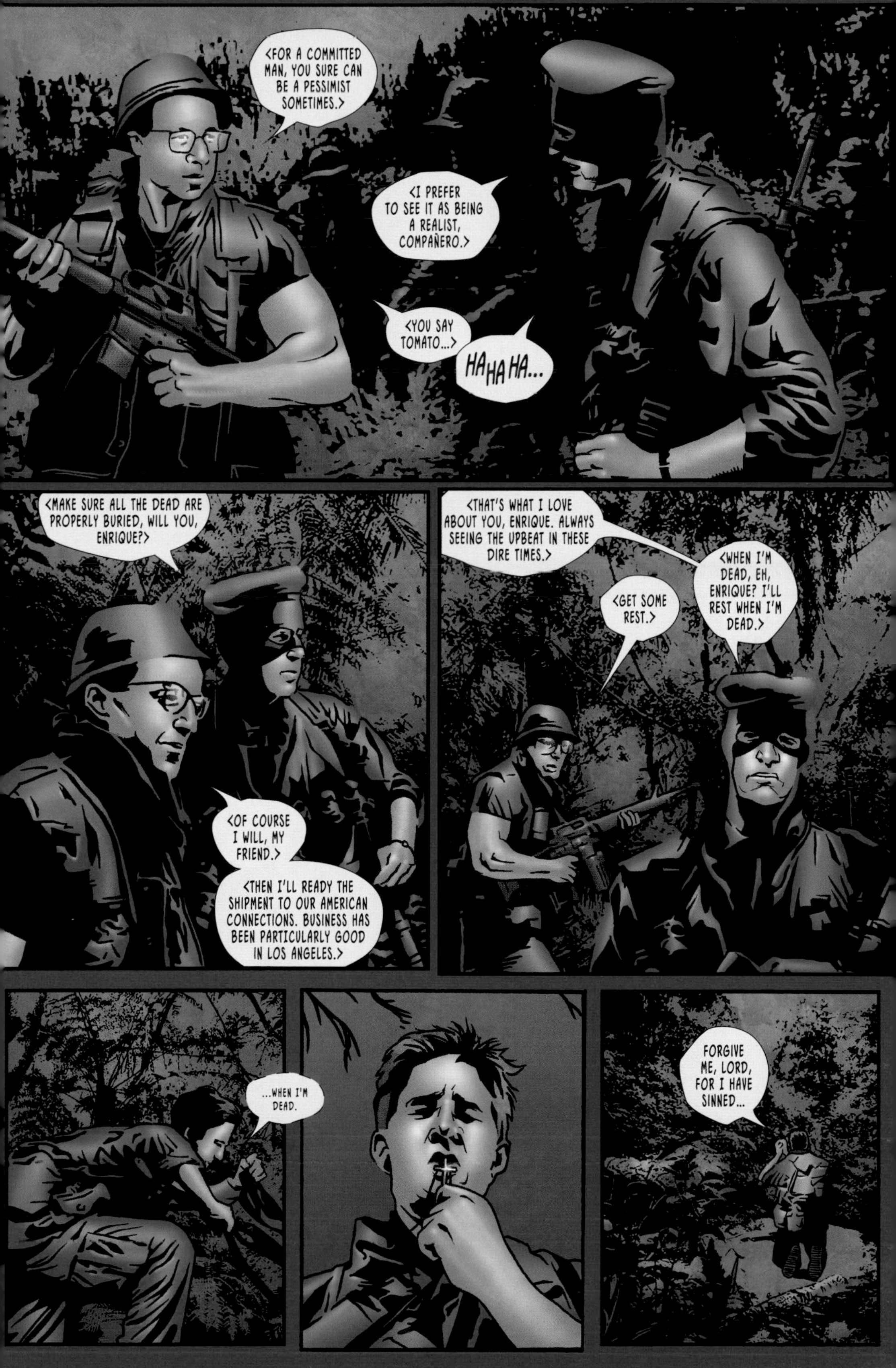
<FOR A COMMITTED MAN, YOU SURE CAN BE A PESSIMIST SOMETIMES.>
<I PREFER TO SEE IT AS BEING A REALIST, COMPAÑERO.>
<YOU SAY TOMATO...>
HAHAHA...
<MAKE SURE ALL THE DEAD ARE PROPERLY BURIED, WILL YOU, ENRIQUE?>
<OF COURSE I WILL, MY FRIEND.>
<THEN I'LL READY THE SHIPMENT TO OUR AMERICAN CONNECTIONS. BUSINESS HAS BEEN PARTICULARLY GOOD IN LOS ANGELES.>
<THAT'S WHAT I LOVE ABOUT YOU, ENRIQUE. ALWAYS SEEING THE UPBEAT IN THESE DIRE TIMES.>
<GET SOME REST.>
<WHEN I'M DEAD, EH, ENRIQUE? I'LL REST WHEN I'M DEAD.>
...WHEN I'M DEAD.
FORGIVE ME, LORD, FOR I HAVE SINNED...

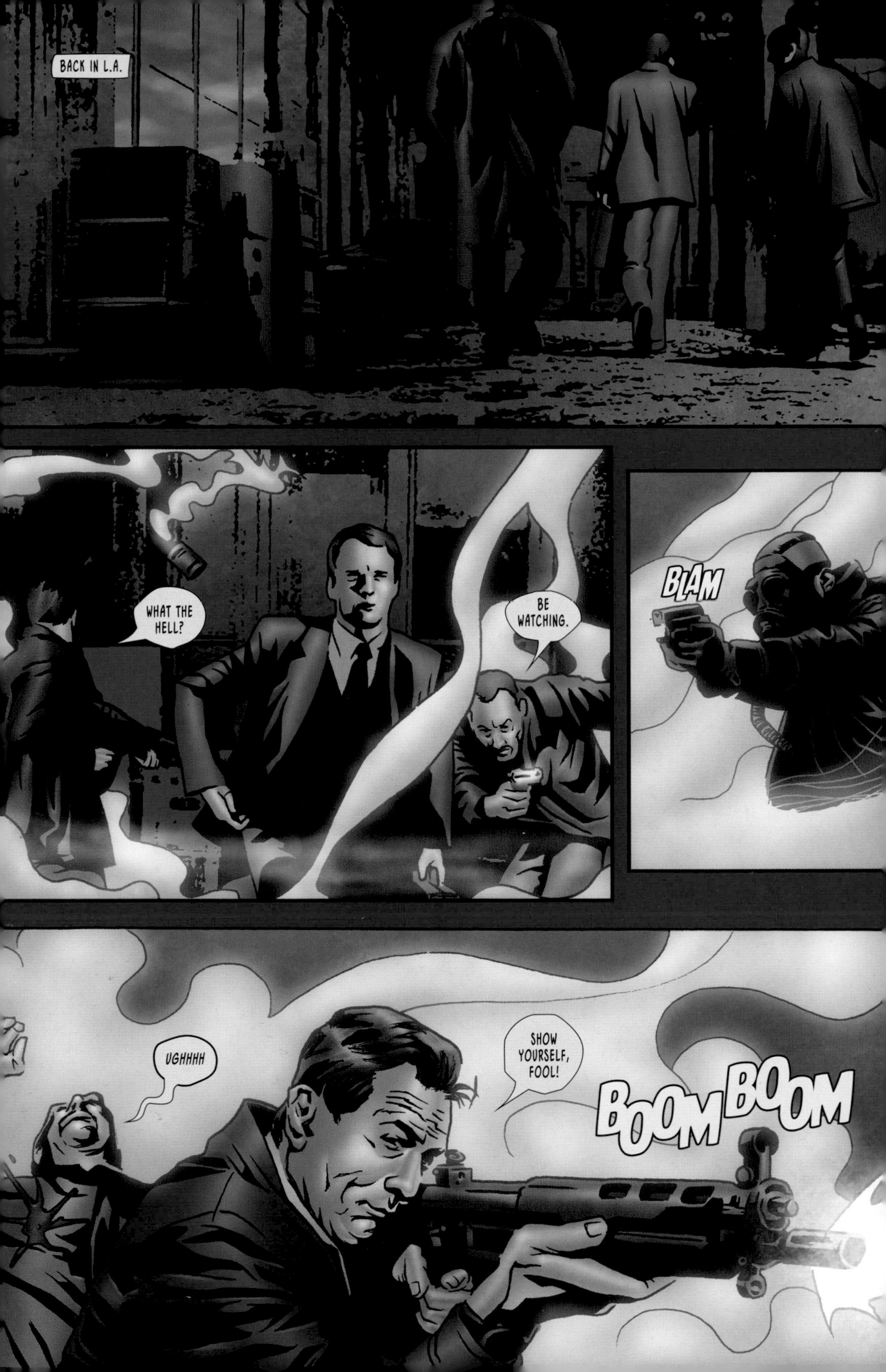
BACK IN L.A.
WHAT THE HELL?
BE WATCHING.
BLAM
UGHHHH
SHOW YOURSELF, FOOL!
BOOM BOOM

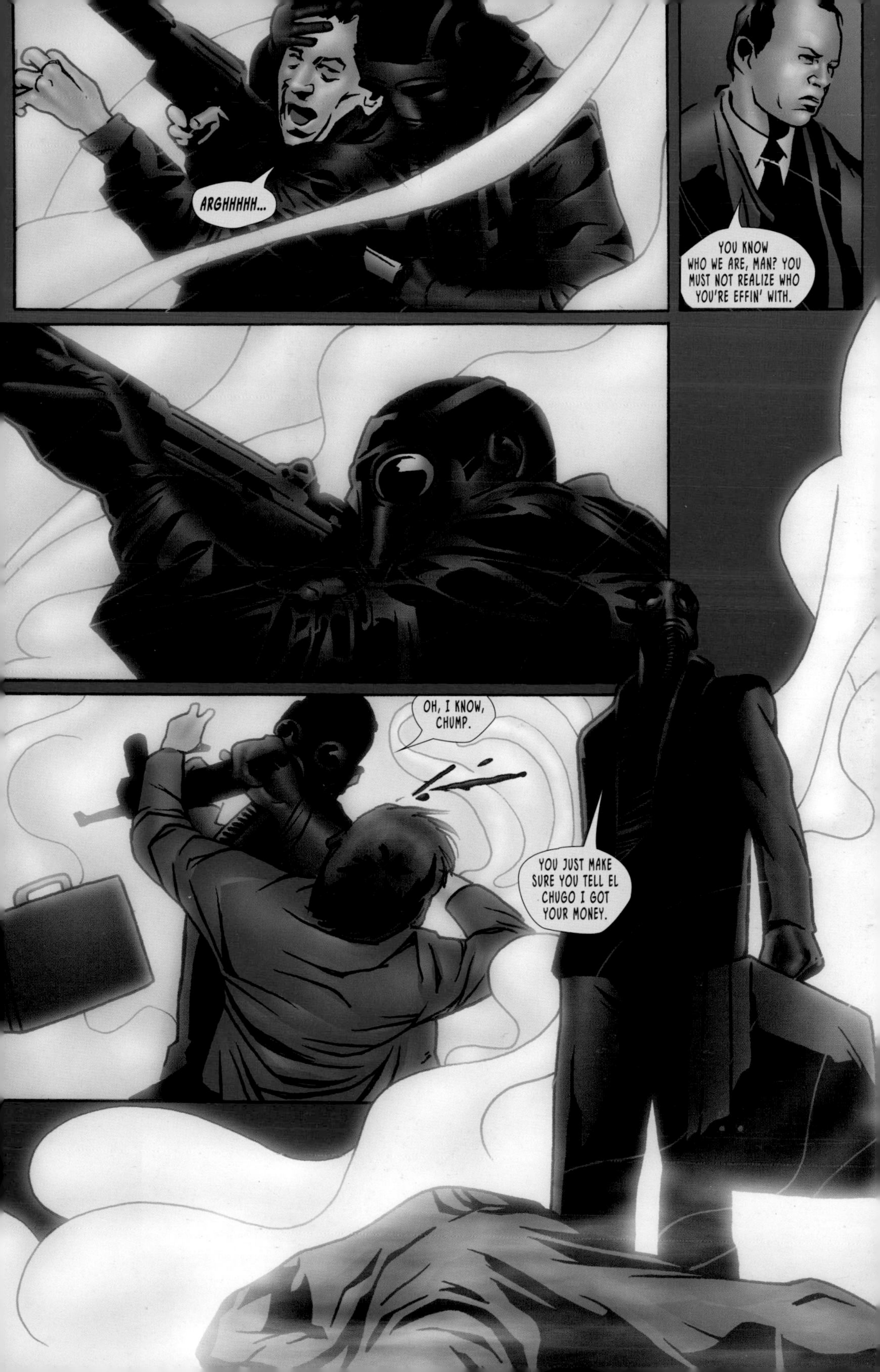
ARGHHHHH...
YOU KNOW WHO WE ARE, MAN? YOU MUST NOT REALIZE WHO YOU'RE EFFIN' WITH.
OH, I KNOW, CHUMP.
YOU JUST MAKE SURE YOU TELL EL CHUGO I GOT YOUR MONEY.

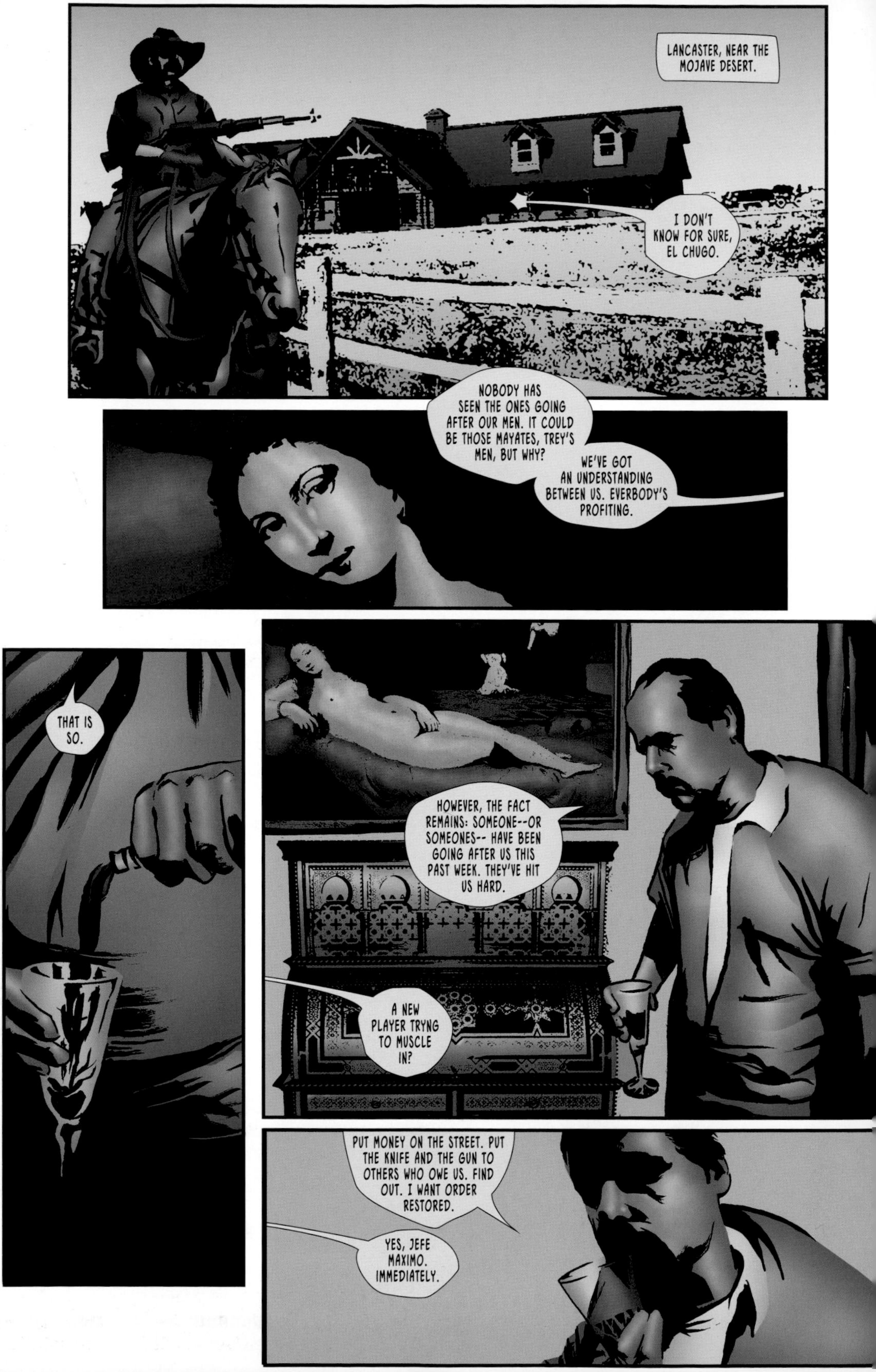
LANCASTER, NEAR THE MOJAVE DESERT.
I DON'T KNOW FOR SURE, EL CHUGO.
NOBODY HAS SEEN THE ONES GOING AFTER OUR MEN. IT COULD BE THOSE MAYATES, TREY'S MEN, BUT WHY?
WE'VE GOT AN UNDERSTANDING BETWEEN US. EVERBODY'S PROFITING.
THAT IS SO.
HOWEVER, THE FACT REMAINS: SOMEONE--OR SOMEONES-- HAVE BEEN GOING AFTER US THIS PAST WEEK. THEY'VE HIT US HARD.
A NEW PLAYER TRYNG TO MUSCLE IN?
PUT MONEY ON THE STREET. PUT THE KNIFE AND THE GUN TO OTHERS WHO OWE US. FIND OUT. I WANT ORDER RESTORED.
YES, JEFE MAXIMO. IMMEDIATELY.

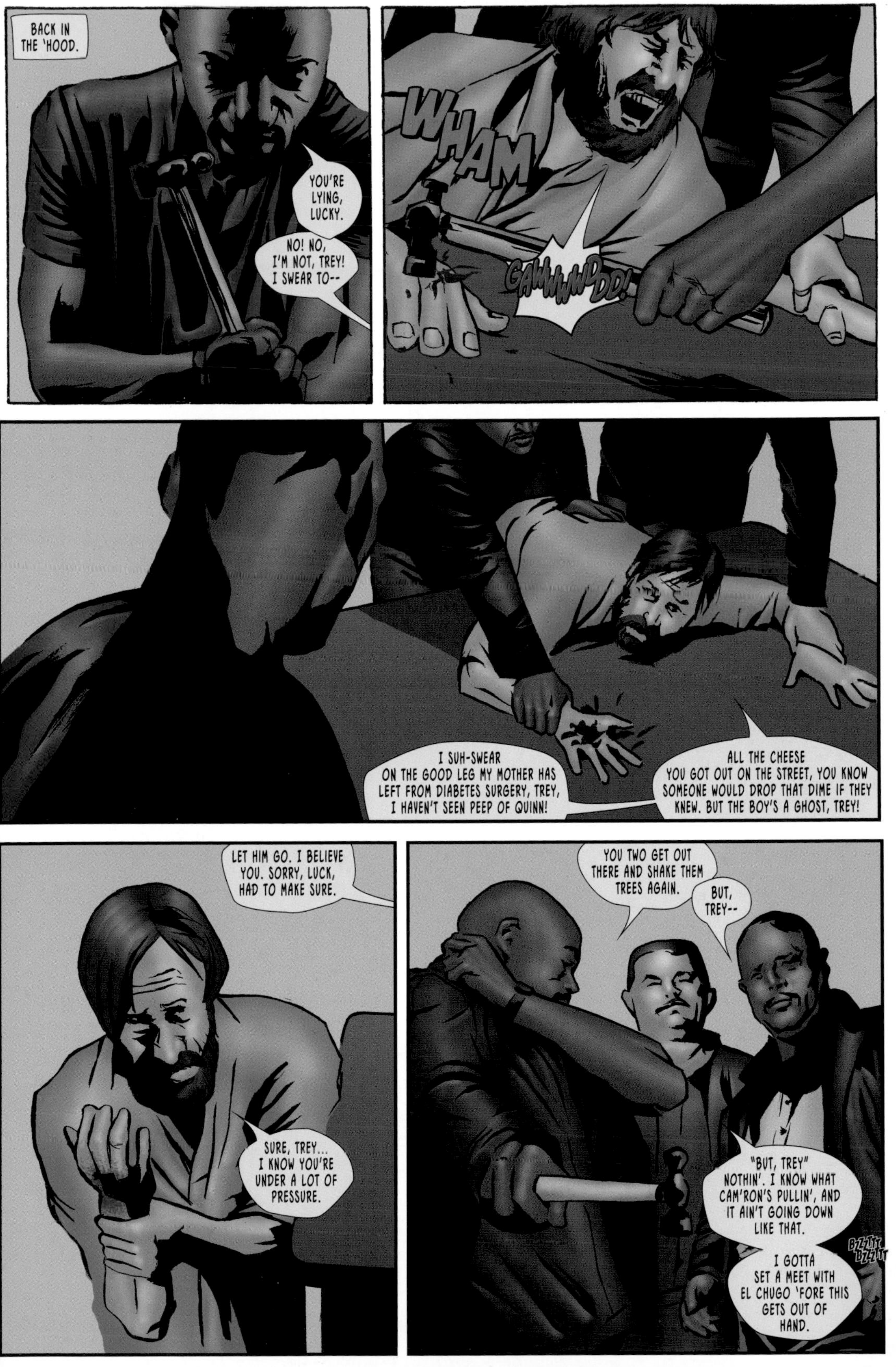
BACK IN THE 'HOOD.
YOU'RE LYING, LUCKY.
NO! NO, I'M NOT, TREY! I SWEAR TO--
WHAM
GAWWWWDDD!
I SUH-SWEAR ON THE GOOD LEG MY MOTHER HAS LEFT FROM DIABETES SURGERY, TREY, I HAVEN'T SEEN PEEP OF QUINN!
ALL THE CHEESE YOU GOT OUT ON THE STREET, YOU KNOW SOMEONE WOULD DROP THAT DIME IF THEY KNEW. BUT THE BOY'S A GHOST, TREY!
LET HIM GO. I BELIEVE YOU. SORRY, LUCK, HAD TO MAKE SURE.
SURE, TREY... I KNOW YOU'RE UNDER A LOT OF PRESSURE.
YOU TWO GET OUT THERE AND SHAKE THEM TREES AGAIN.
BUT, TREY--
"BUT, TREY" NOTHIN'. I KNOW WHAT CAM'RON'S PULLIN', AND IT AIN'T GOING DOWN LIKE THAT.
BZZTTT BZZTTT
I GOTTA SET A MEET WITH EL CHUGO 'FORE THIS GETS OUT OF HAND.

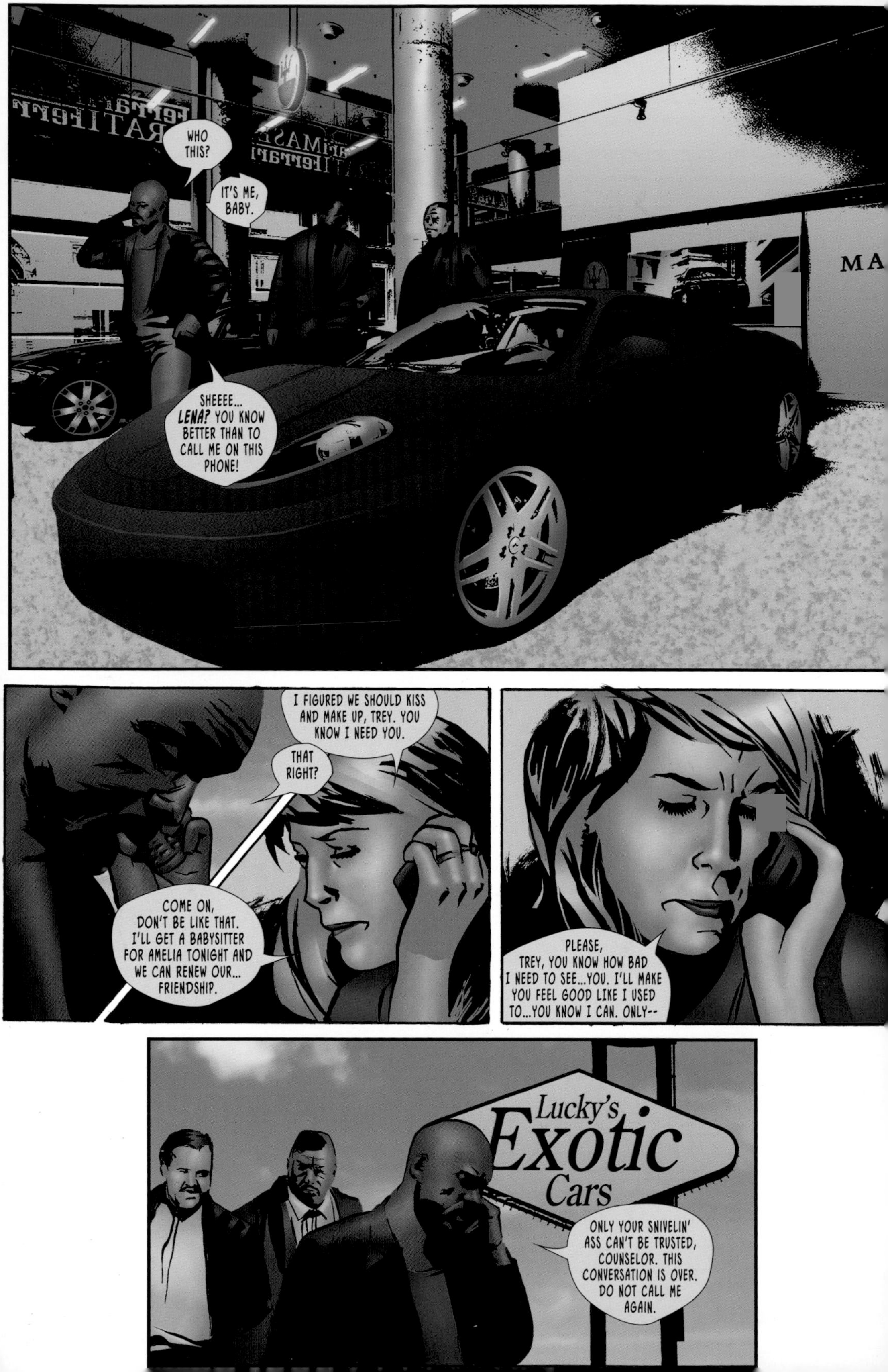

WHO THIS?
IT'S ME, BABY.
SHEEEE... LENA? YOU KNOW BETTER THAN TO CALL ME ON THIS PHONE!
MA
I FIGURED WE SHOULD KISS AND MAKE UP, TREY. YOU KNOW I NEED YOU.
THAT RIGHT?
COME ON, DON'T BE LIKE THAT. I'LL GET A BABYSITTER FOR AMELIA TONIGHT AND WE CAN RENEW OUR... FRIENDSHIP.
PLEASE, TREY, YOU KNOW HOW BAD I NEED TO SEE...YOU. I'LL MAKE YOU FEEL GOOD LIKE I USED TO...YOU KNOW I CAN. ONLY--
Lucky's Exotic Cars
ONLY YOUR SNIVELIN' ASS CAN'T BE TRUSTED, COUNSELOR. THIS CONVERSATION IS OVER. DO NOT CALL ME AGAIN.

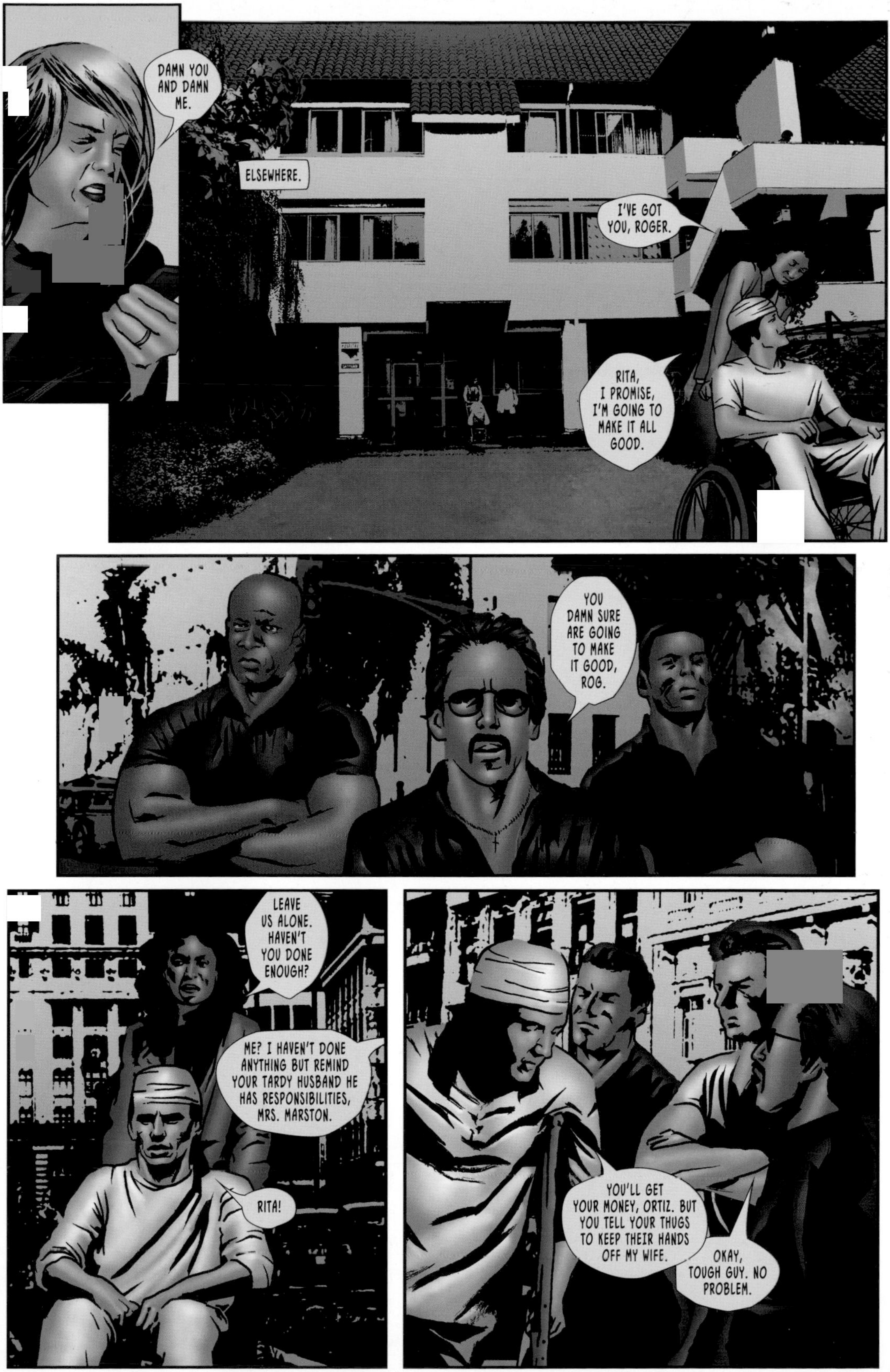
DAMN YOU AND DAMN ME.
ELSEWHERE.
I'VE GOT YOU, ROGER.
RITA, I PROMISE, I'M GOING TO MAKE IT ALL GOOD.
YOU DAMN SURE ARE GOING TO MAKE IT GOOD, ROG.
LEAVE US ALONE. HAVEN'T YOU DONE ENOUGH?
ME? I HAVEN'T DONE ANYTHING BUT REMIND YOUR TARDY HUSBAND HE HAS RESPONSIBILITIES, MRS. MARSTON.
RITA!
YOU'LL GET YOUR MONEY, ORTIZ. BUT YOU TELL YOUR THUGS TO KEEP THEIR HANDS OFF MY WIFE.
OKAY, TOUGH GUY. NO PROBLEM.

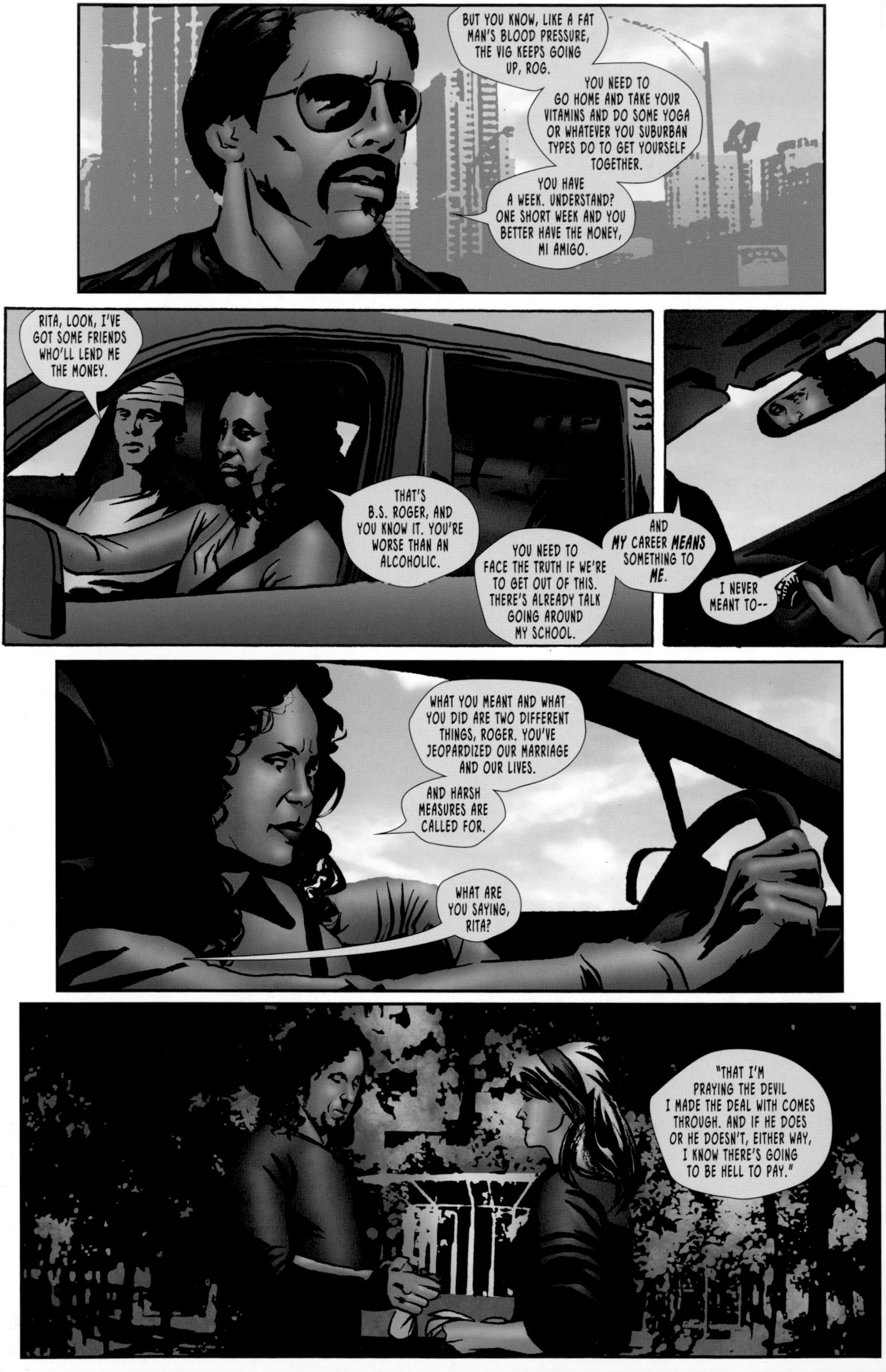
BUT YOU KNOW, LIKE A FAT MAN'S BLOOD PRESSURE, THE VIG KEEPS GOING UP, ROG.
YOU NEED TO GO HOME AND TAKE YOUR VITAMINS AND DO SOME YOGA OR WHATEVER YOU SUBURBAN TYPES DO TO GET YOURSELF TOGETHER.
YOU HAVE A WEEK. UNDERSTAND? ONE SHORT WEEK AND YOU BETTER HAVE THE MONEY, MI AMIGO.
RITA, LOOK, I'VE GOT SOME FRIENDS WHO'LL LEND ME THE MONEY.
THAT'S B.S. ROGER, AND YOU KNOW IT. YOU'RE WORSE THAN AN ALCOHOLIC.
YOU NEED TO FACE THE TRUTH IF WE'RE TO GET OUT OF THIS. THERE'S ALREADY TALK GOING AROUND MY SCHOOL.
AND **MY** CAREER **MEANS** SOMETHING TO **ME**.
I NEVER MEANT TO--
WHAT YOU MEANT AND WHAT YOU DID ARE TWO DIFFERENT THINGS, ROGER. YOU'VE JEOPARDIZED OUR MARRIAGE AND OUR LIVES.
AND HARSH MEASURES ARE CALLED FOR.
WHAT ARE YOU SAYING, RITA?
"THAT I'M PRAYING THE DEVIL I MADE THE DEAL WITH COMES THROUGH. AND IF HE DOES OR HE DOESN'T, EITHER WAY, I KNOW THERE'S GOING TO BE HELL TO PAY."

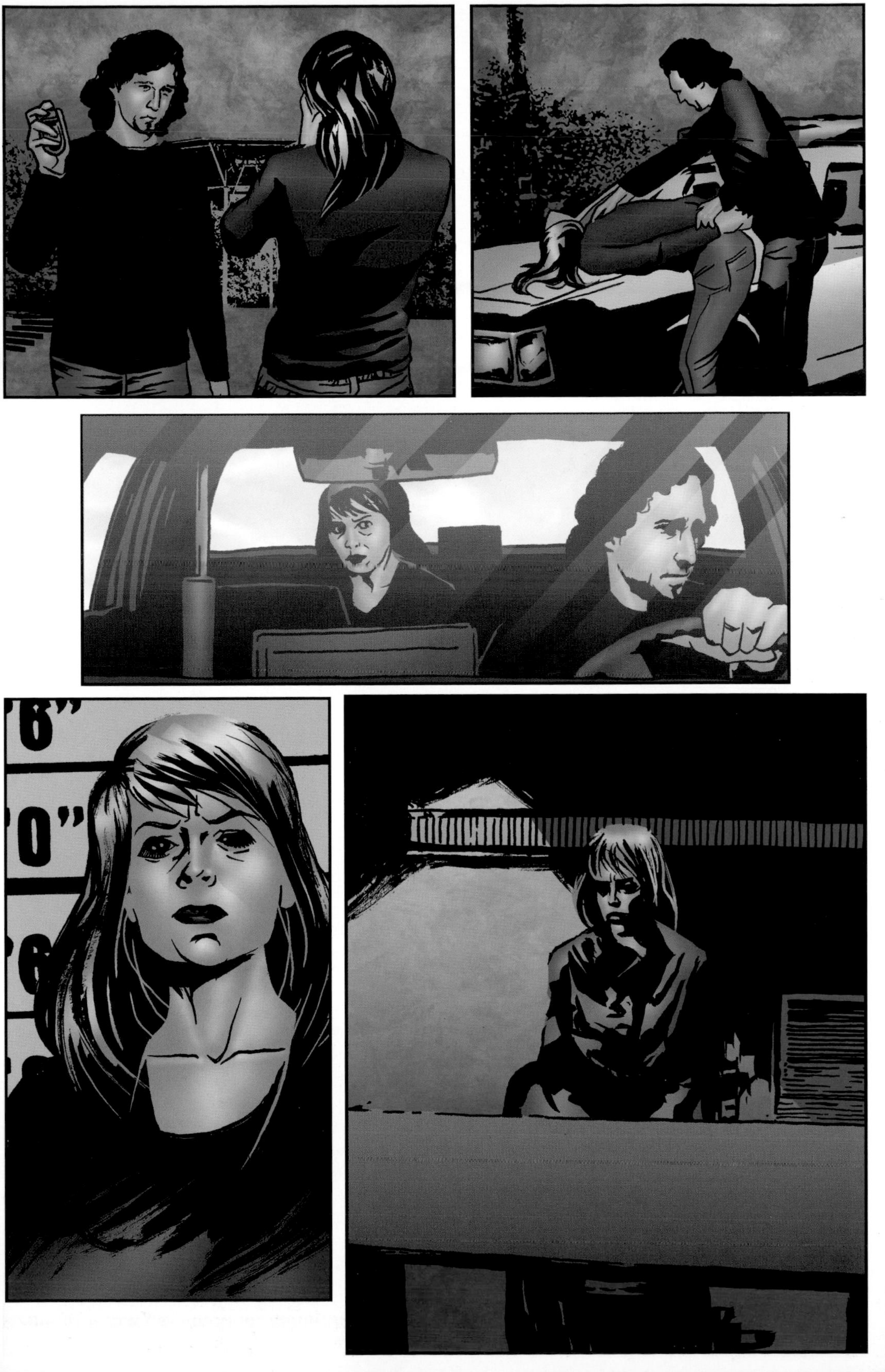

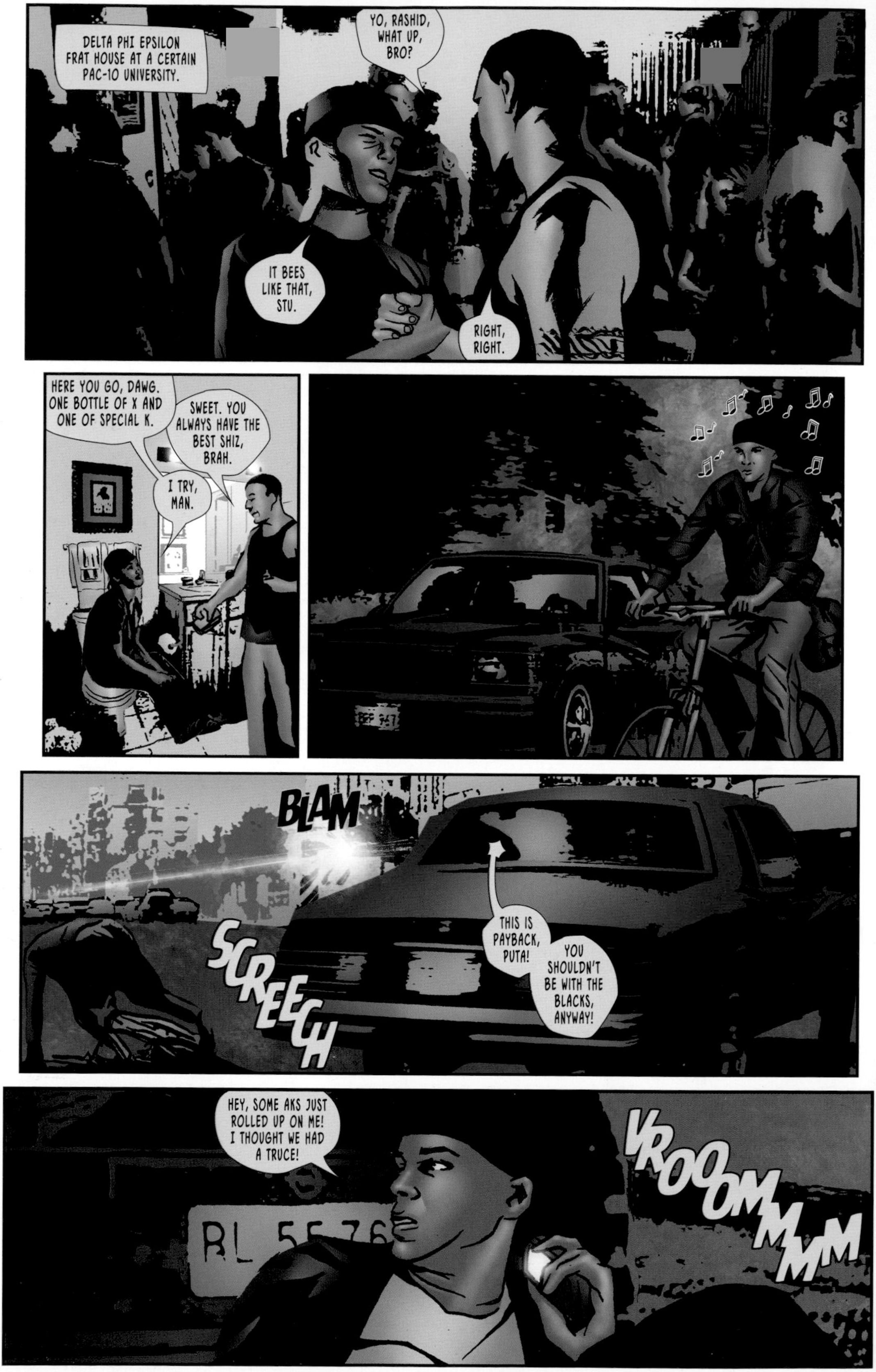
DELTA PHI EPSILON FRAT HOUSE AT A CERTAIN PAC-10 UNIVERSITY.
YO, RASHID, WHAT UP, BRO?
IT BEES LIKE THAT, STU.
RIGHT, RIGHT.
HERE YOU GO, DAWG. ONE BOTTLE OF X AND ONE OF SPECIAL K.
SWEET. YOU ALWAYS HAVE THE BEST SHIZ, BRAH.
I TRY, MAN.
BLAM
SCREECH
THIS IS PAYBACK, PUTA!
YOU SHOULDN'T BE WITH THE BLACKS, ANYWAY!
HEY, SOME AKS JUST ROLLED UP ON ME! I THOUGHT WE HAD A TRUCE!
VROOOMMMMM

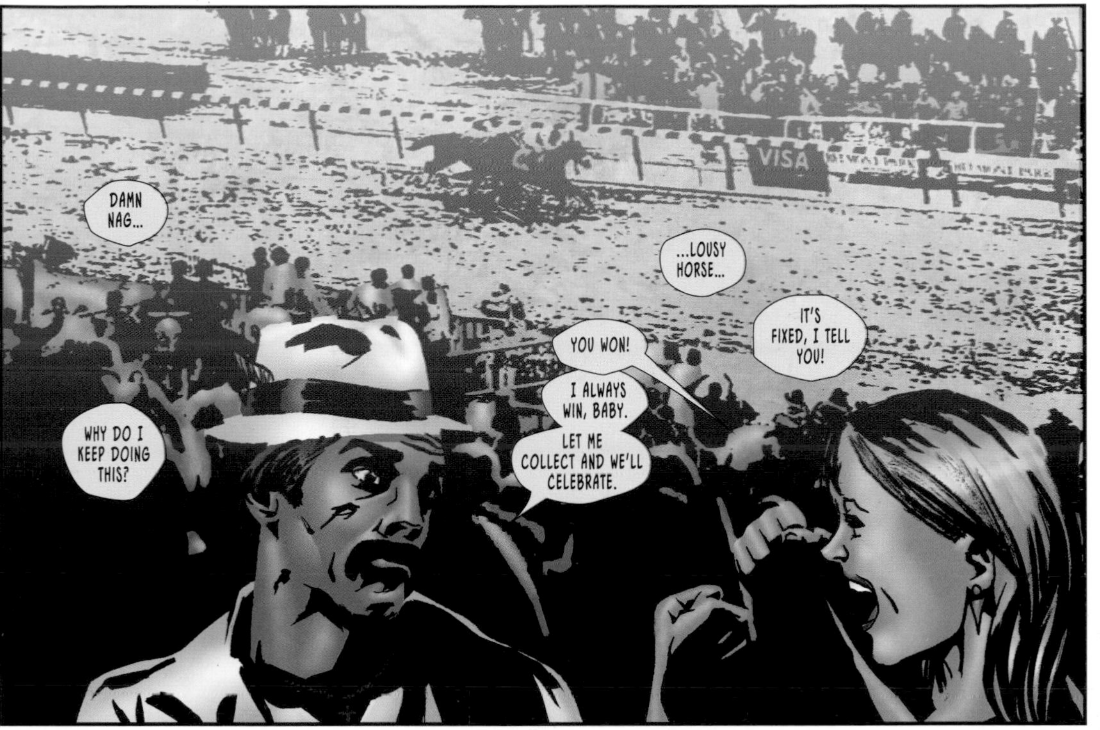
DAMN NAG...
...LOUSY HORSE...
IT'S FIXED, I TELL YOU!
YOU WON!
I ALWAYS WIN, BABY.
LET ME COLLECT AND WE'LL CELEBRATE.
WHY DO I KEEP DOING THIS?
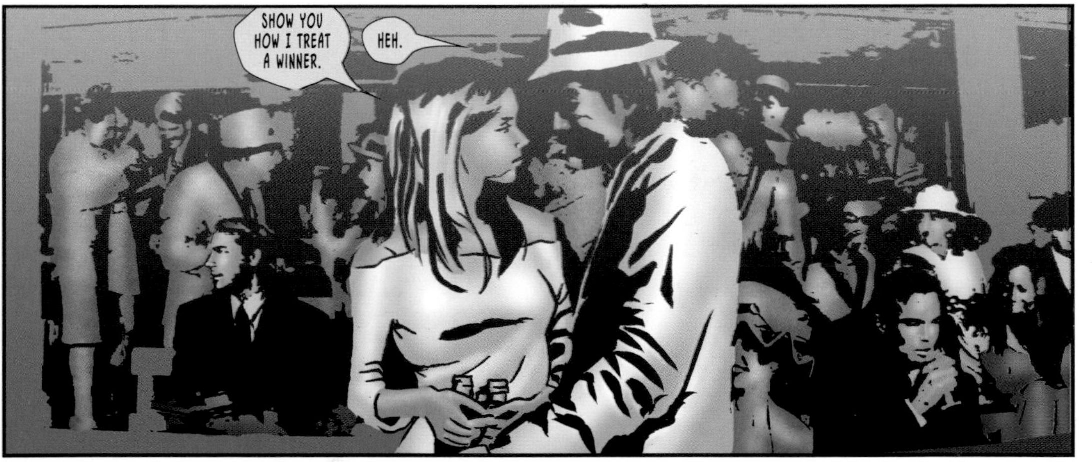
SHOW YOU HOW I TREAT A WINNER.
HEH.
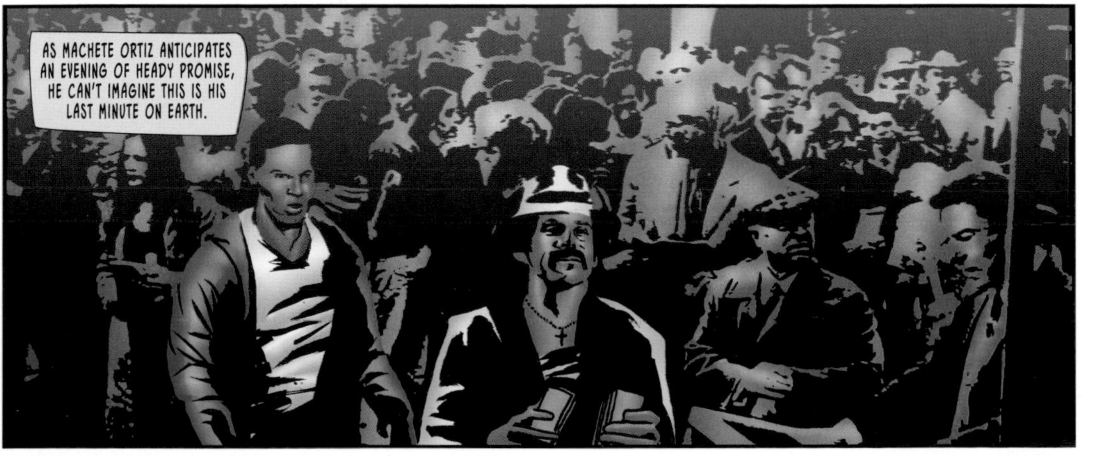
AS MACHETE ORTIZ ANTICIPATES AN EVENING OF HEADY PROMISE, HE CAN'T IMAGINE THIS IS HIS LAST MINUTE ON EARTH.

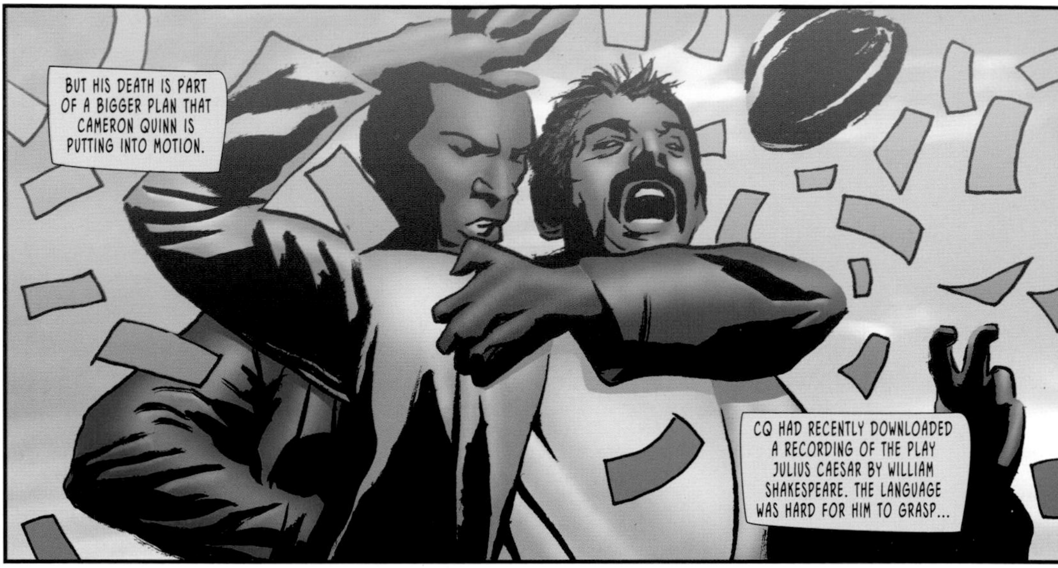
BUT HIS DEATH IS PART OF A BIGGER PLAN THAT CAMERON QUINN IS PUTTING INTO MOTION.
CQ HAD RECENTLY DOWNLOADED A RECORDING OF THE PLAY JULIUS CAESAR BY WILLIAM SHAKESPEARE. THE LANGUAGE WAS HARD FOR HIM TO GRASP...

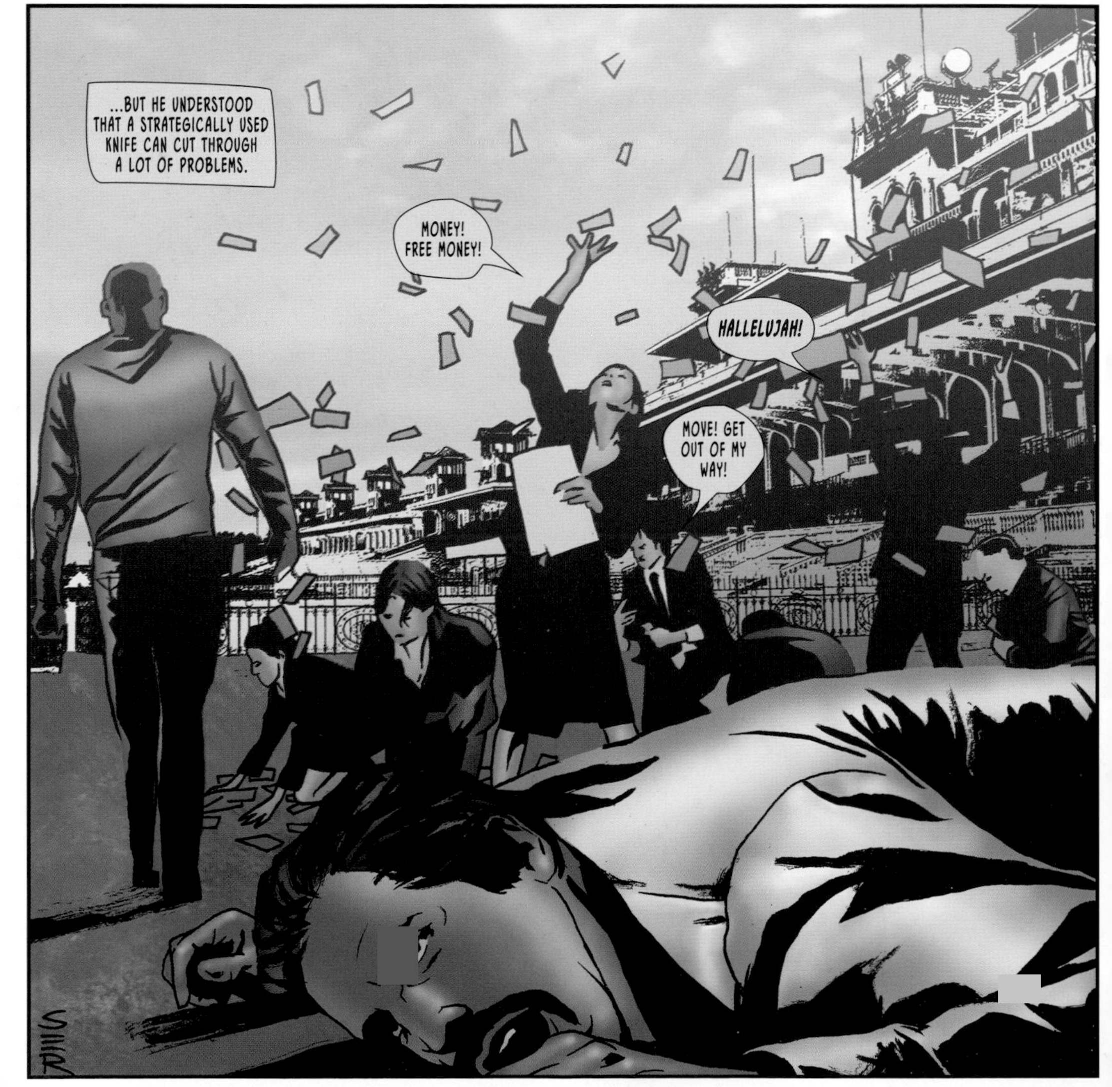
...BUT HE UNDERSTOOD THAT A STRATEGICALLY USED KNIFE CAN CUT THROUGH A LOT OF PROBLEMS.
MONEY! FREE MONEY!
HALLELUJAH!
MOVE! GET OUT OF MY WAY!

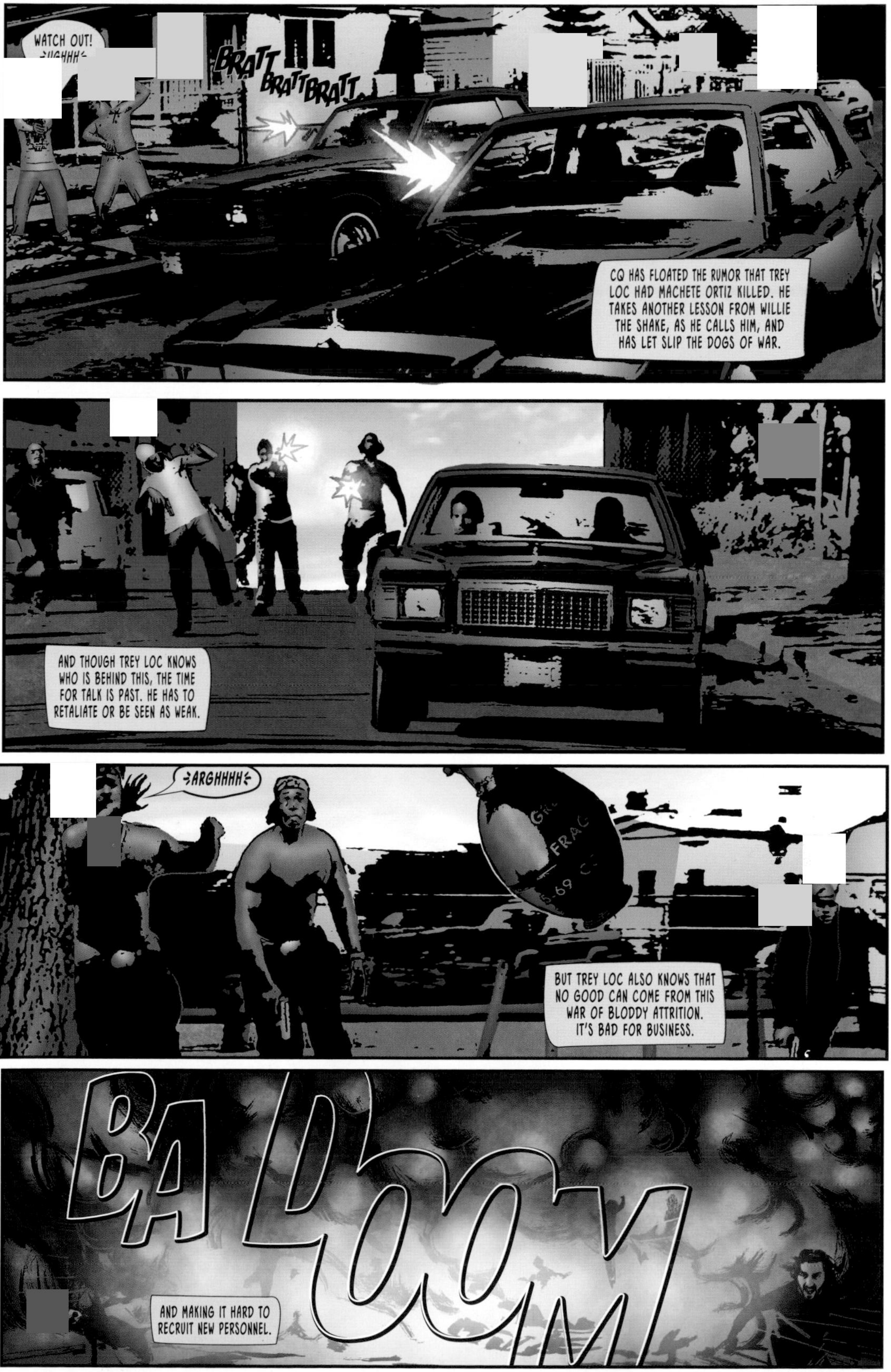
WATCH OUT!
UGHHH
BRATT BRATT BRATT
CQ HAS FLOATED THE RUMOR THAT TREY LOC HAD MACHETE ORTIZ KILLED. HE TAKES ANOTHER LESSON FROM WILLIE THE SHAKE, AS HE CALLS HIM, AND HAS LET SLIP THE DOGS OF WAR.
AND THOUGH TREY LOC KNOWS WHO IS BEHIND THIS, THE TIME FOR TALK IS PAST. HE HAS TO RETALIATE OR BE SEEN AS WEAK.
ARGHHHH
FRAG
BUT TREY LOC ALSO KNOWS THAT NO GOOD CAN COME FROM THIS WAR OF BLOODY ATTRITION. IT'S BAD FOR BUSINESS.
BALOOOM
AND MAKING IT HARD TO RECRUIT NEW PERSONNEL.

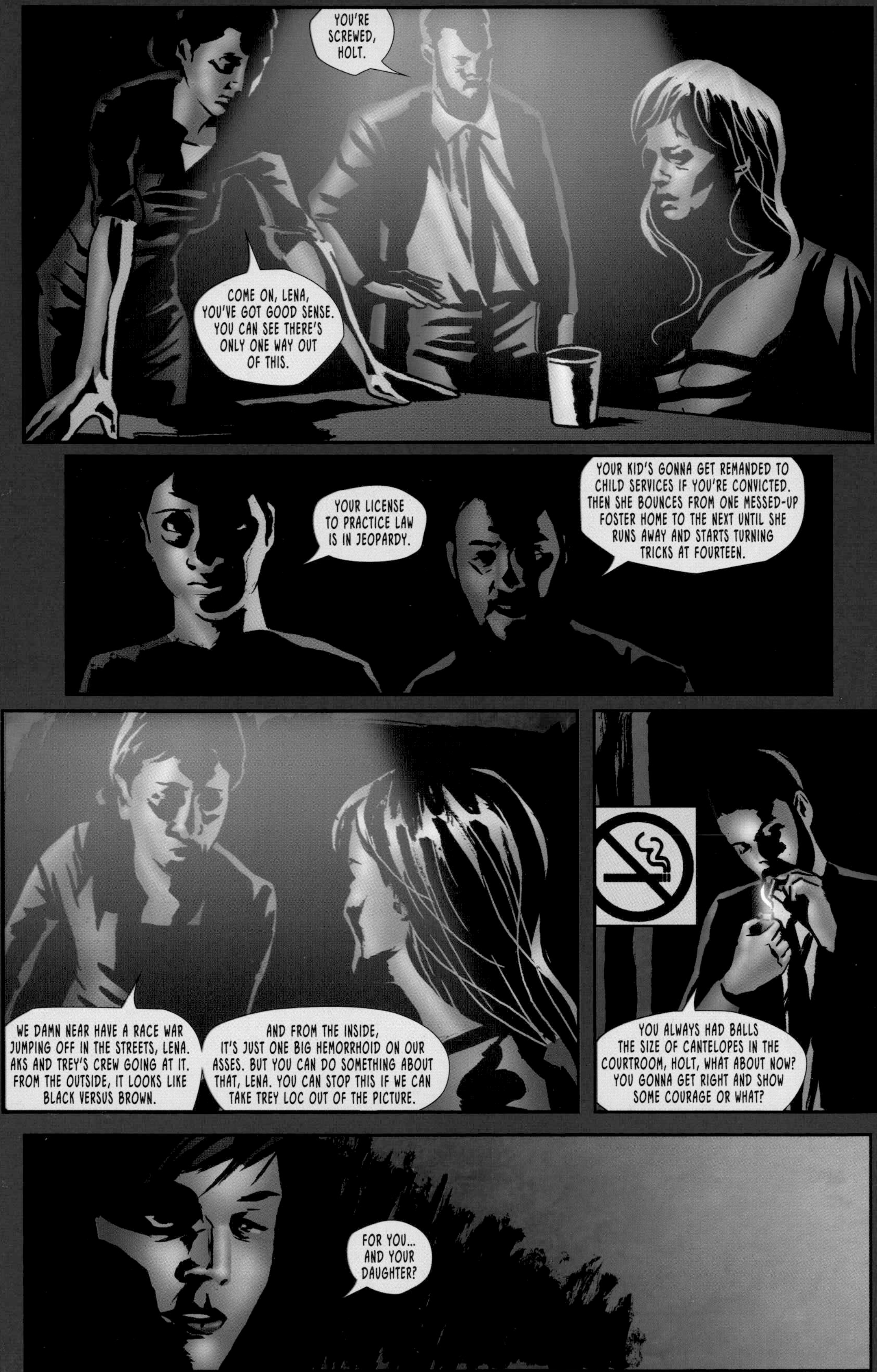
YOU'RE SCREWED, HOLT.
COME ON, LENA, YOU'VE GOT GOOD SENSE. YOU CAN SEE THERE'S ONLY ONE WAY OUT OF THIS.
YOUR LICENSE TO PRACTICE LAW IS IN JEOPARDY.
YOUR KID'S GONNA GET REMANDED TO CHILD SERVICES IF YOU'RE CONVICTED. THEN SHE BOUNCES FROM ONE MESSED-UP FOSTER HOME TO THE NEXT UNTIL SHE RUNS AWAY AND STARTS TURNING TRICKS AT FOURTEEN.
WE DAMN NEAR HAVE A RACE WAR JUMPING OFF IN THE STREETS, LENA. AKS AND TREY'S CREW GOING AT IT. FROM THE OUTSIDE, IT LOOKS LIKE BLACK VERSUS BROWN.
AND FROM THE INSIDE, IT'S JUST ONE BIG HEMORRHOID ON OUR ASSES. BUT YOU CAN DO SOMETHING ABOUT THAT, LENA. YOU CAN STOP THIS IF WE CAN TAKE TREY LOC OUT OF THE PICTURE.
YOU ALWAYS HAD BALLS THE SIZE OF CANTELOPES IN THE COURTROOM, HOLT, WHAT ABOUT NOW? YOU GONNA GET RIGHT AND SHOW SOME COURAGE OR WHAT?
FOR YOU... AND YOUR DAUGHTER?

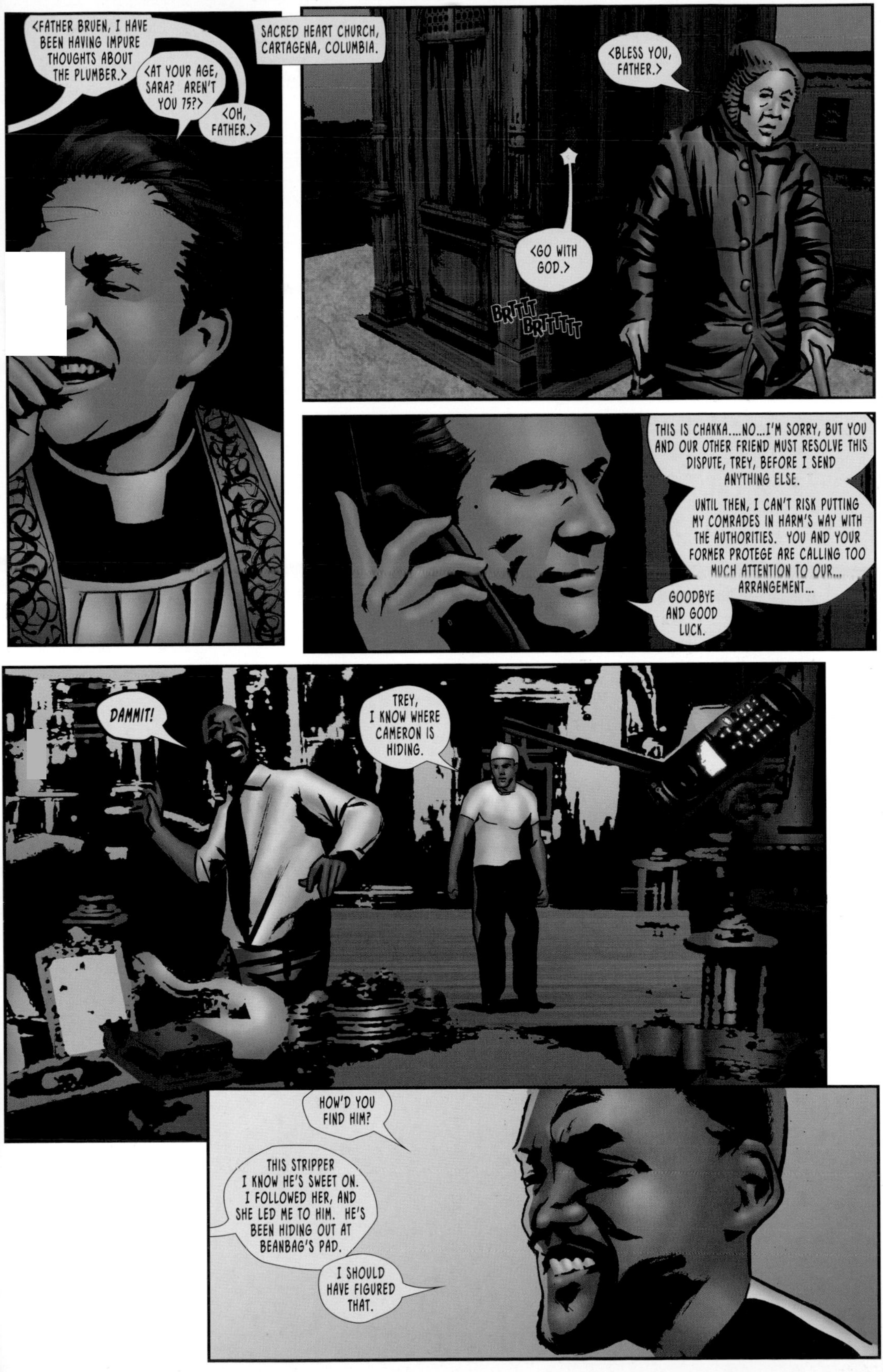
<FATHER BRUEN, I HAVE BEEN HAVING IMPURE THOUGHTS ABOUT THE PLUMBER.>
<AT YOUR AGE, SARA? AREN'T YOU 75?>
<OH, FATHER.>
SACRED HEART CHURCH, CARTAGENA, COLUMBIA.
<BLESS YOU, FATHER.>
<GO WITH GOD.>
BRTTTT BRTTTTTT
THIS IS CHAKKA....NO...I'M SORRY, BUT YOU AND OUR OTHER FRIEND MUST RESOLVE THIS DISPUTE, TREY, BEFORE I SEND ANYTHING ELSE.
UNTIL THEN, I CAN'T RISK PUTTING MY COMRADES IN HARM'S WAY WITH THE AUTHORITIES. YOU AND YOUR FORMER PROTEGE ARE CALLING TOO MUCH ATTENTION TO OUR... ARRANGEMENT...
GOODBYE AND GOOD LUCK.
DAMMIT!
TREY, I KNOW WHERE CAMERON IS HIDING.
HOW'D YOU FIND HIM?
THIS STRIPPER I KNOW HE'S SWEET ON. I FOLLOWED HER, AND SHE LED ME TO HIM. HE'S BEEN HIDING OUT AT BEANBAG'S PAD.
I SHOULD HAVE FIGURED THAT.

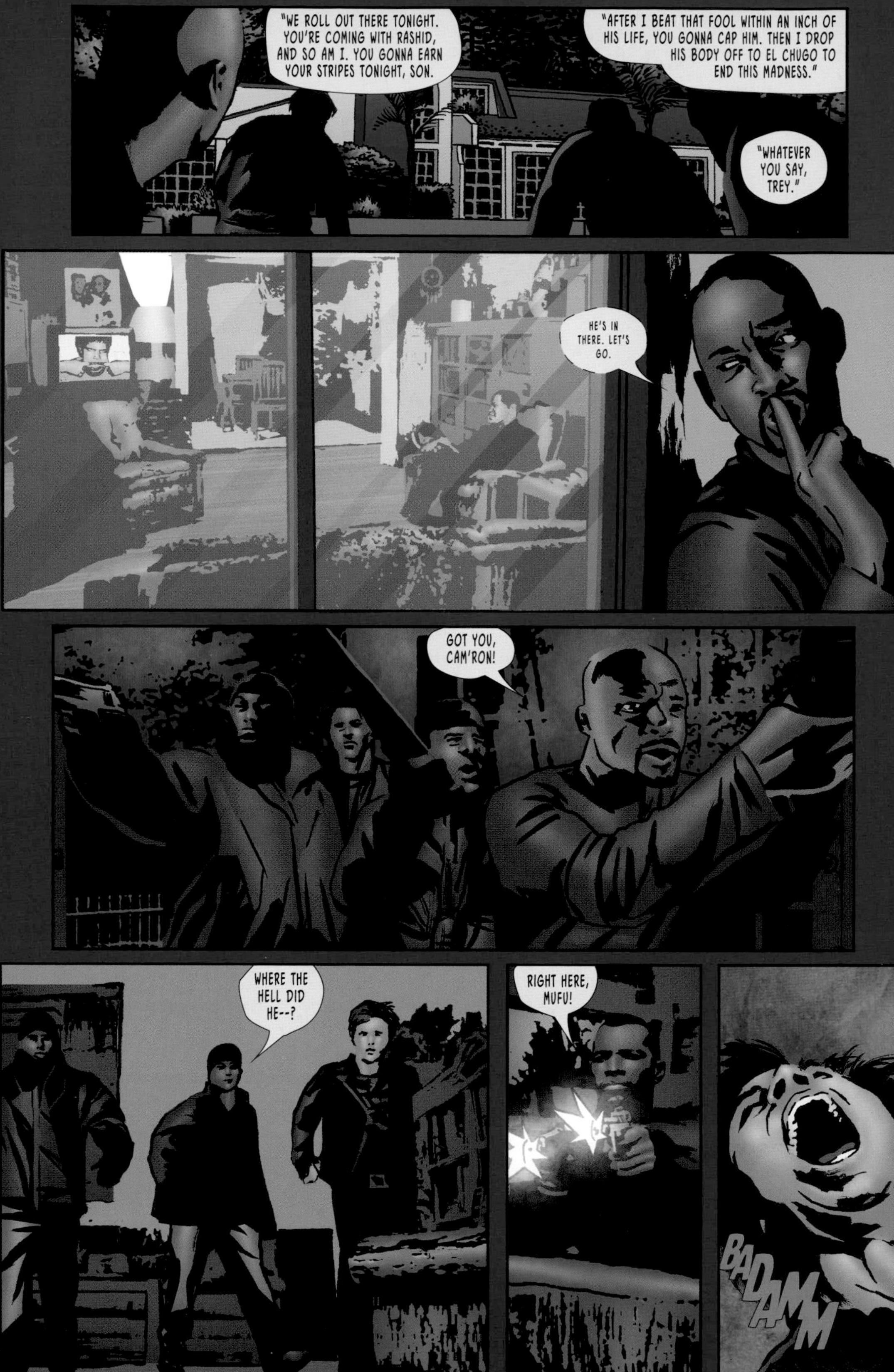
"WE ROLL OUT THERE TONIGHT. YOU'RE COMING WITH RASHID, AND SO AM I. YOU GONNA EARN YOUR STRIPES TONIGHT, SON.
"AFTER I BEAT THAT FOOL WITHIN AN INCH OF HIS LIFE, YOU GONNA CAP HIM. THEN I DROP HIS BODY OFF TO EL CHUGO TO END THIS MADNESS."
"WHATEVER YOU SAY, TREY."
HE'S IN THERE. LET'S GO.
GOT YOU, CAM'RON!
WHERE THE HELL DID HE--?
RIGHT HERE, MUFU!
BADAMMM

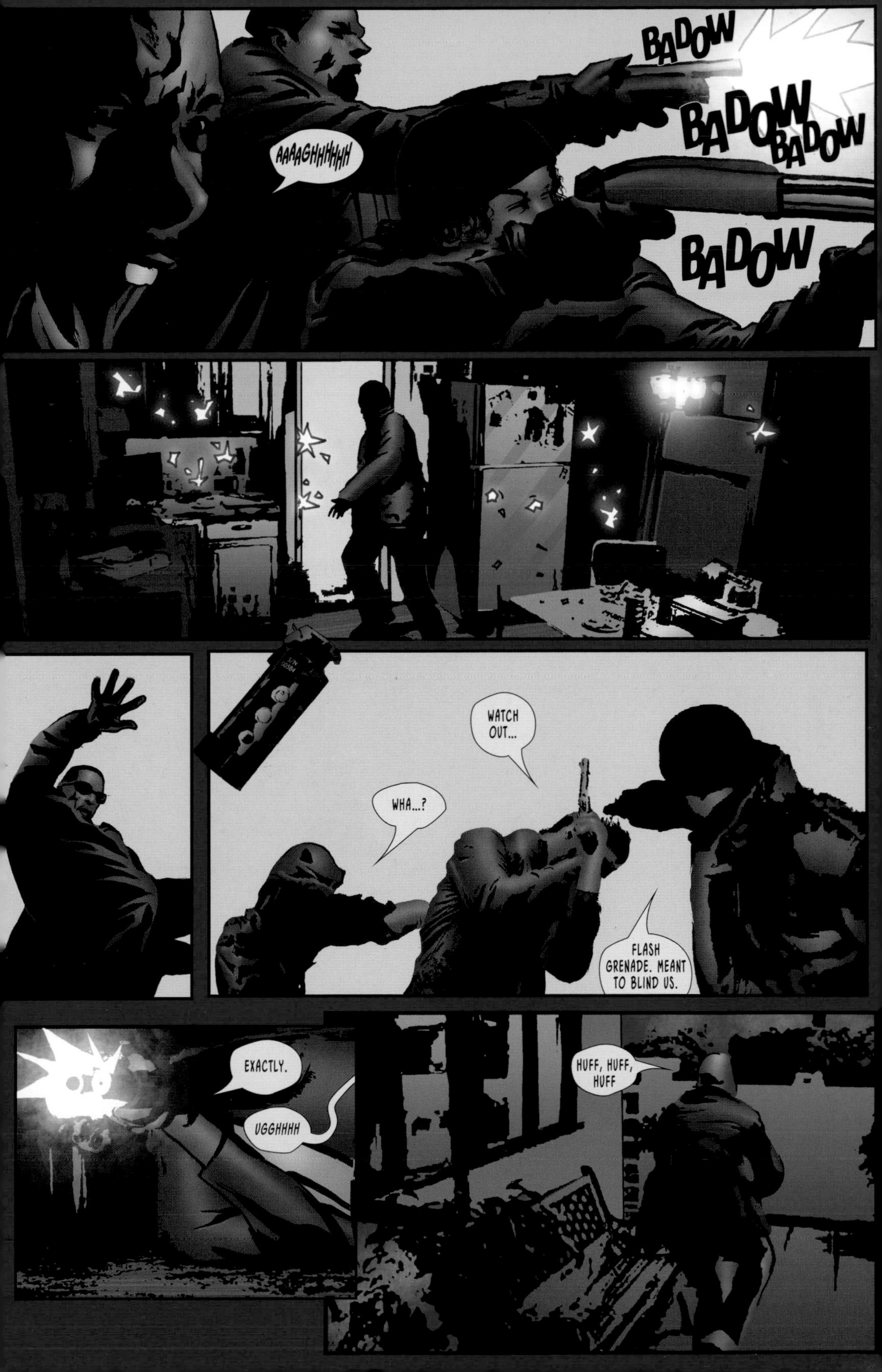
BADOW
AAAAGHHHHHH
BADOW BADOW
BADOW
WATCH OUT...
WHA...?
FLASH GRENADE. MEANT TO BLIND US.
EXACTLY.
UGGHHHH
HUFF, HUFF, HUFF

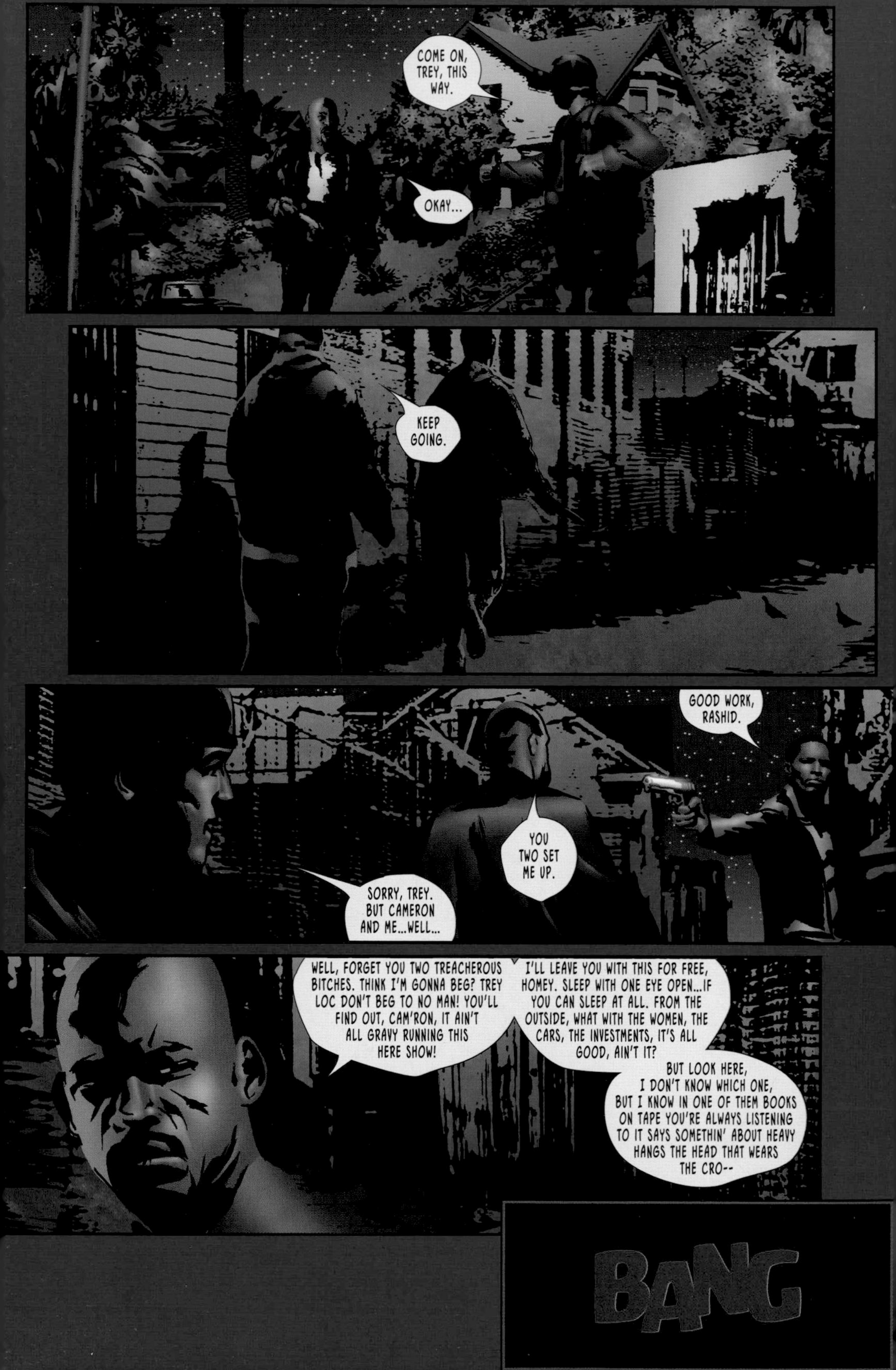
COME ON, TREY, THIS WAY.
OKAY...
KEEP GOING.
GOOD WORK, RASHID.
YOU TWO SET ME UP.
SORRY, TREY. BUT CAMERON AND ME...WELL...
WELL, FORGET YOU TWO TREACHEROUS BITCHES. THINK I'M GONNA BEG? TREY LOC DON'T BEG TO NO MAN! YOU'LL FIND OUT, CAM'RON, IT AIN'T ALL GRAVY RUNNING THIS HERE SHOW!
I'LL LEAVE YOU WITH THIS FOR FREE, HOMEY. SLEEP WITH ONE EYE OPEN...IF YOU CAN SLEEP AT ALL. FROM THE OUTSIDE, WHAT WITH THE WOMEN, THE CARS, THE INVESTMENTS, IT'S ALL GOOD, AIN'T IT?
BUT LOOK HERE, I DON'T KNOW WHICH ONE, BUT I KNOW IN ONE OF THEM BOOKS ON TAPE YOU'RE ALWAYS LISTENING TO IT SAYS SOMETHIN' ABOUT HEAVY HANGS THE HEAD THAT WEARS THE CRO--
BANG

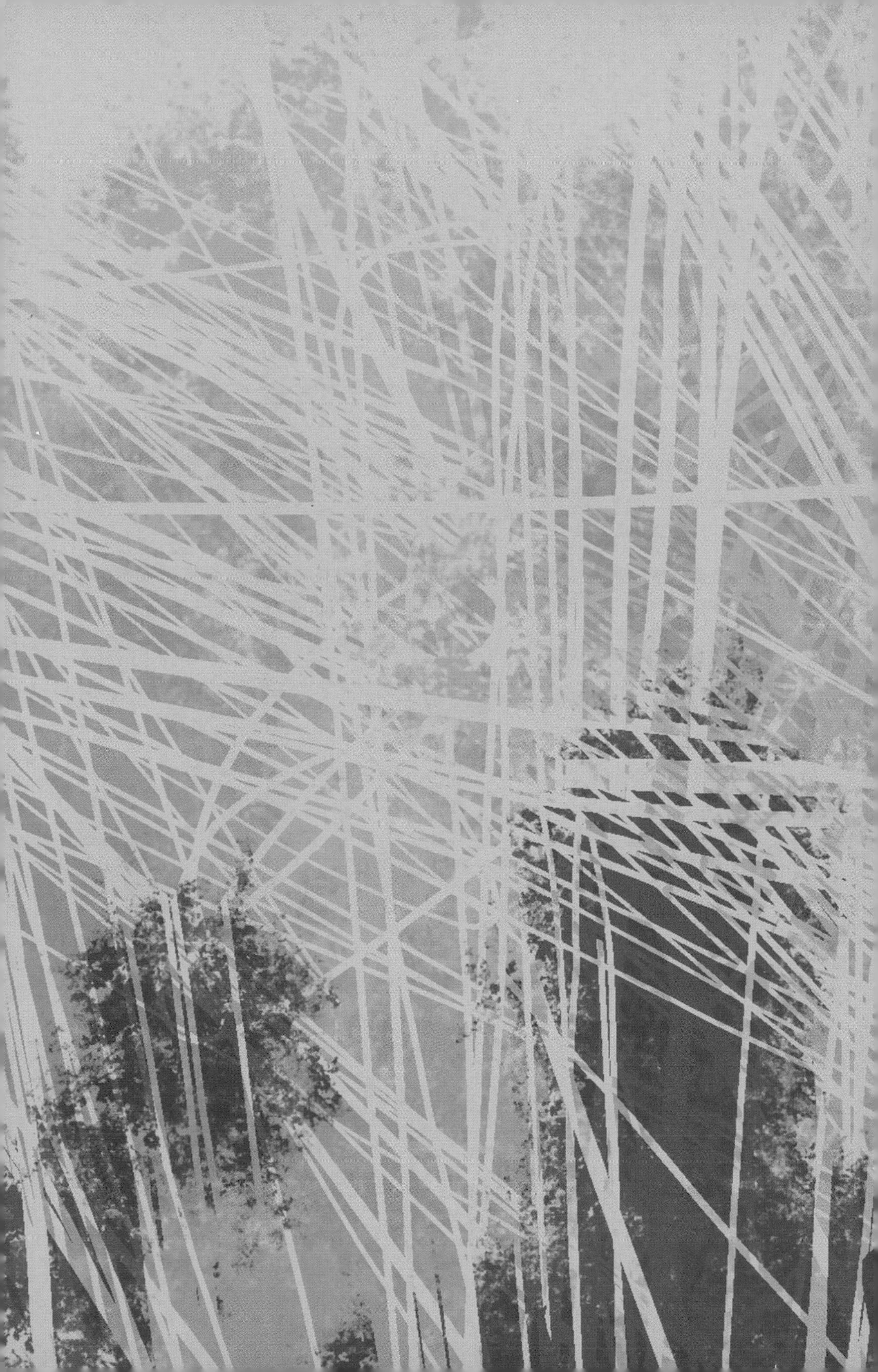

CHAPTER 3

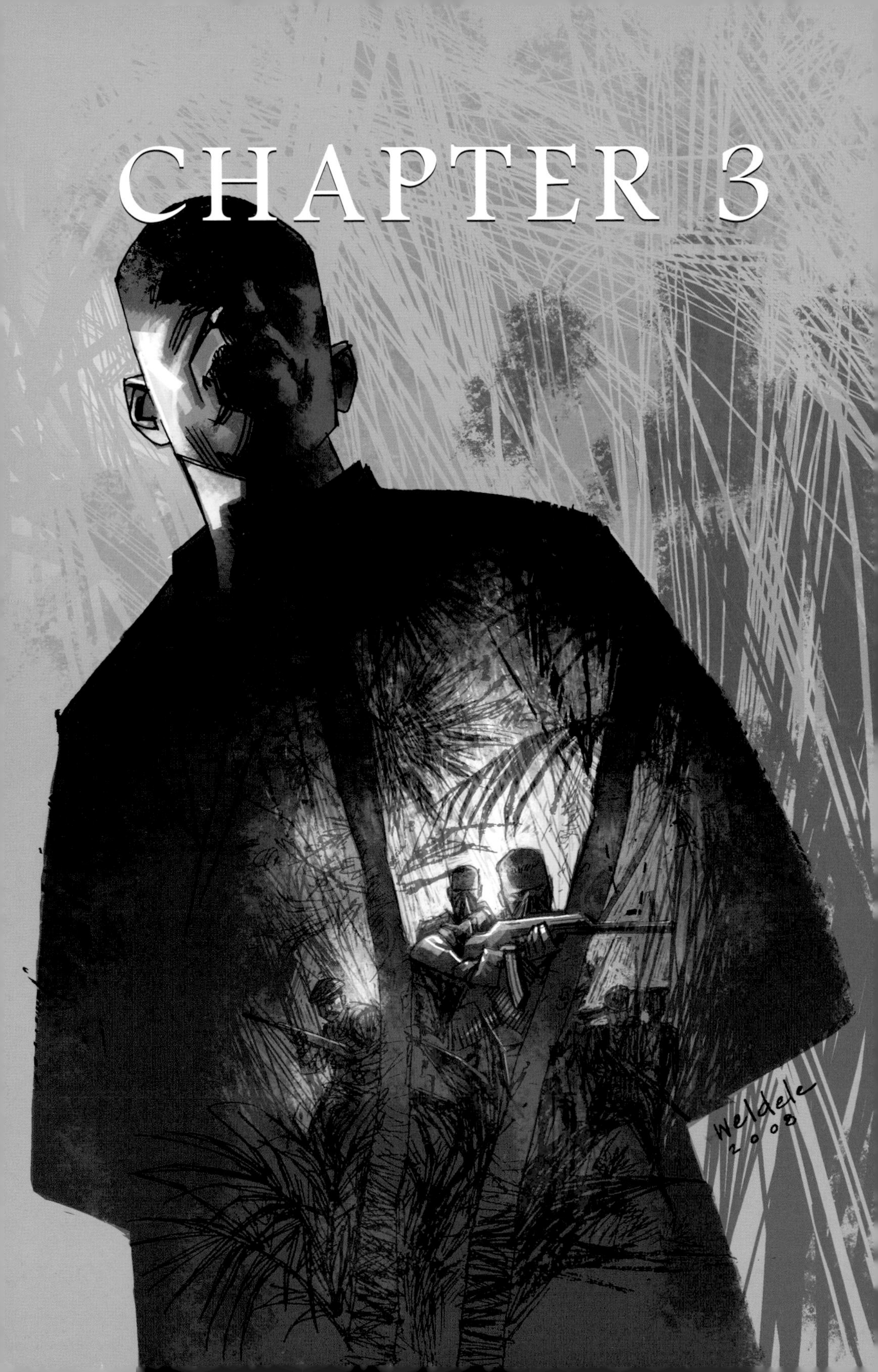
Weldele
2008

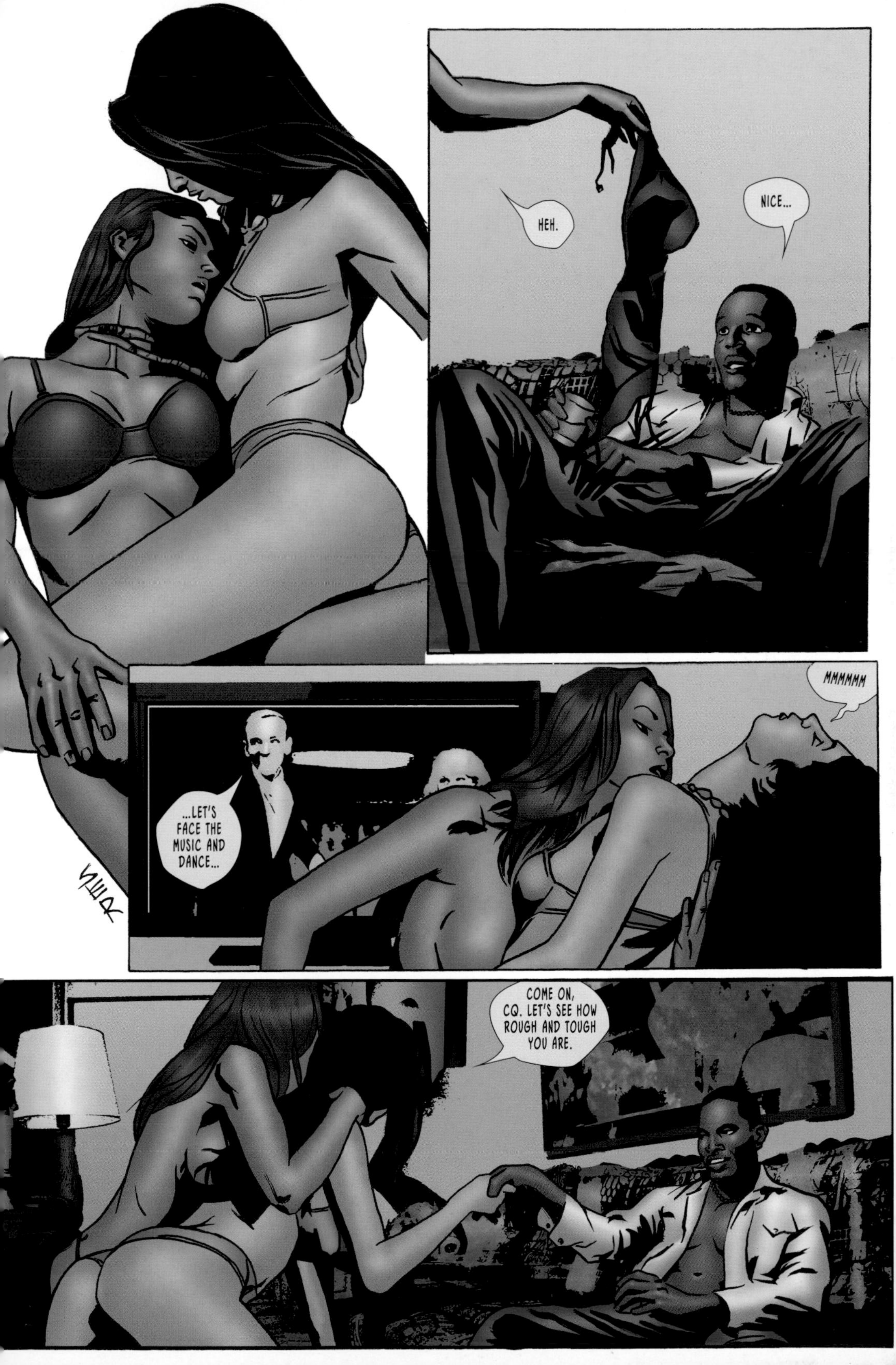
HEH.
NICE...
...LET'S FACE THE MUSIC AND DANCE...
MMMMMM
COME ON, CQ. LET'S SEE HOW ROUGH AND TOUGH YOU ARE.

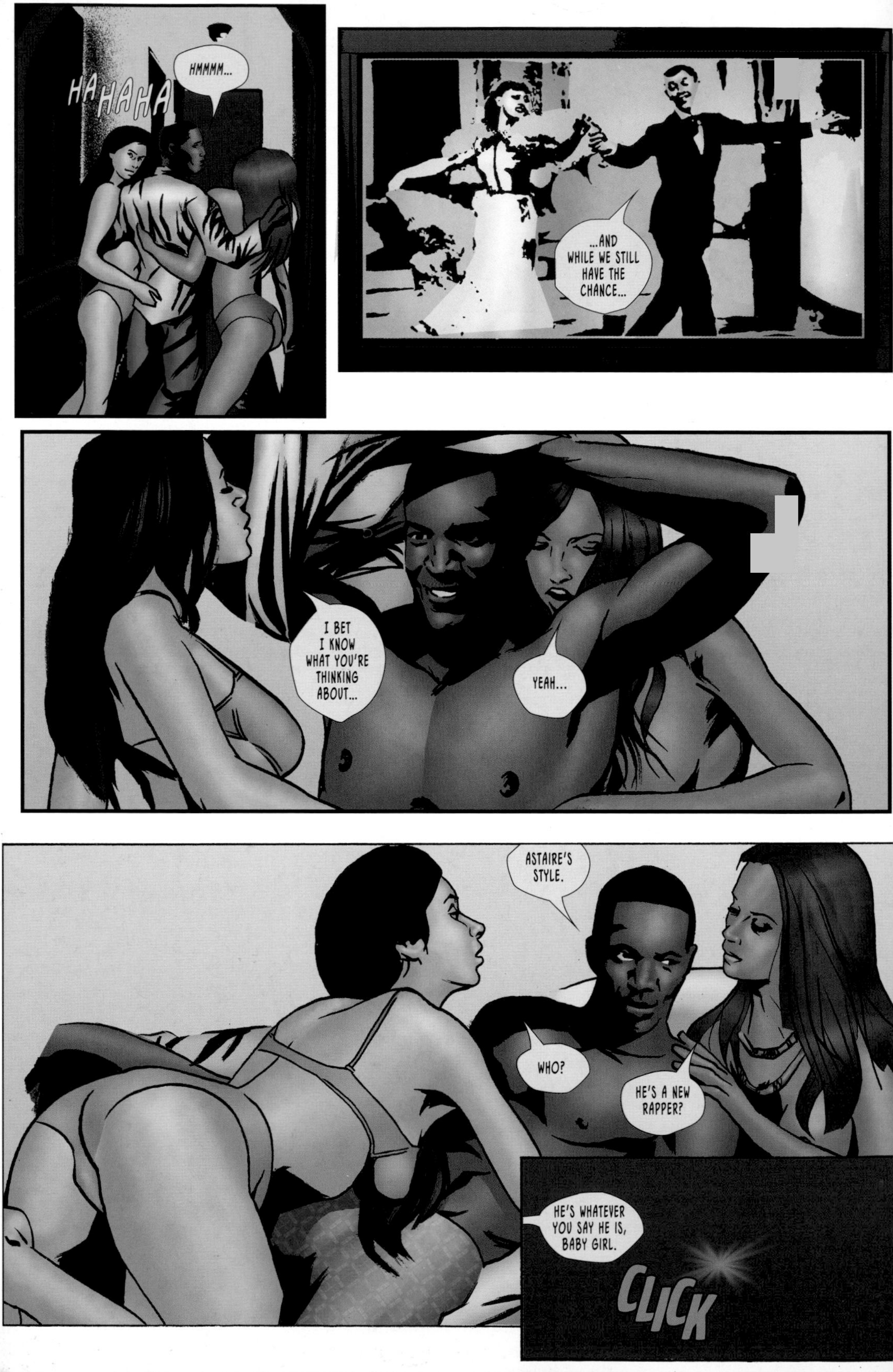
HAHAHA
HMMMM...
...AND WHILE WE STILL HAVE THE CHANCE...
I BET I KNOW WHAT YOU'RE THINKING ABOUT...
YEAH...
ASTAIRE'S STYLE.
WHO?
HE'S A NEW RAPPER?
HE'S WHATEVER YOU SAY HE IS, BABY GIRL.
CLICK

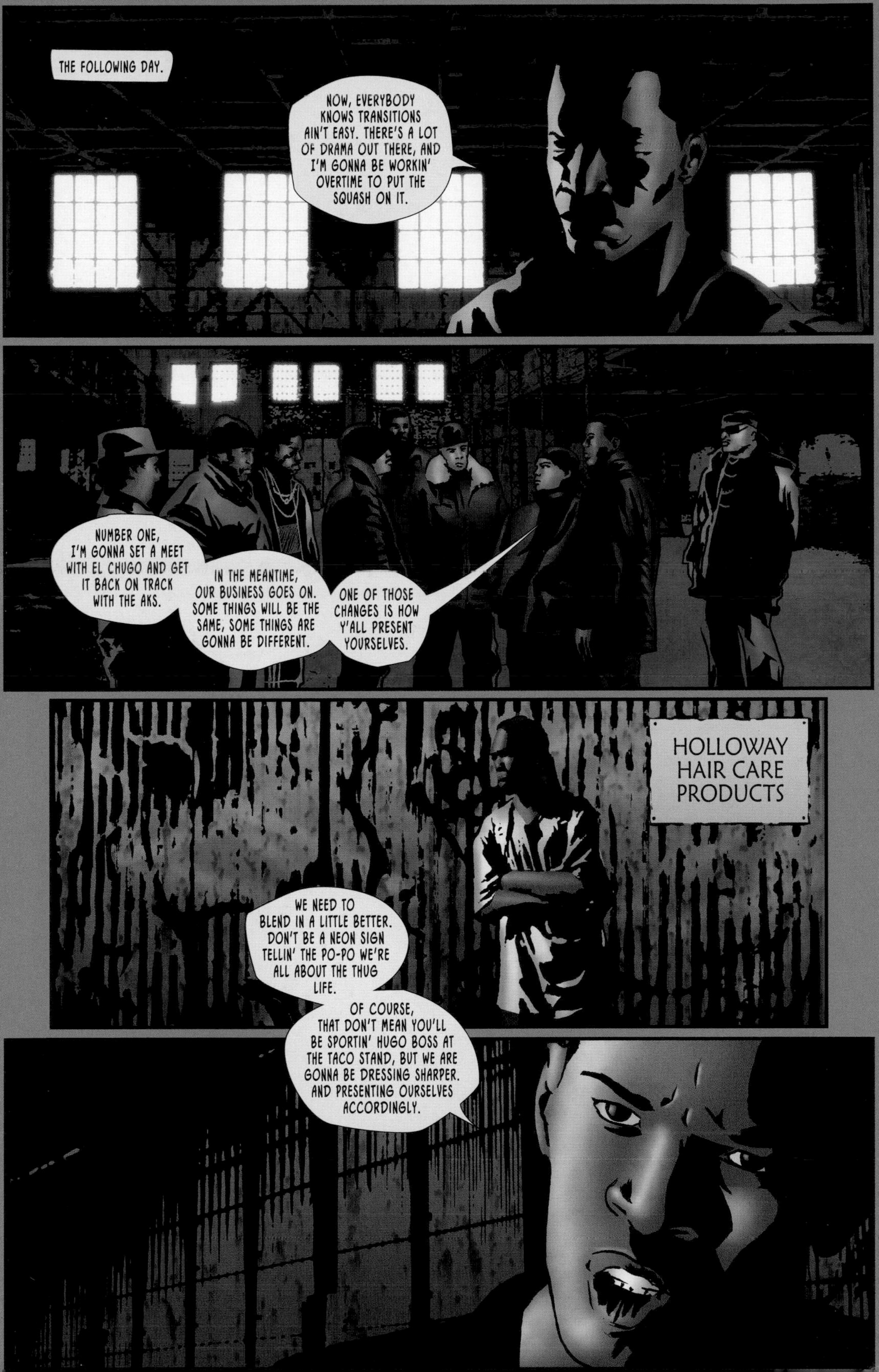
THE FOLLOWING DAY.
NOW, EVERYBODY KNOWS TRANSITIONS AIN'T EASY. THERE'S A LOT OF DRAMA OUT THERE, AND I'M GONNA BE WORKIN' OVERTIME TO PUT THE SQUASH ON IT.
NUMBER ONE, I'M GONNA SET A MEET WITH EL CHUGO AND GET IT BACK ON TRACK WITH THE AKS.
IN THE MEANTIME, OUR BUSINESS GOES ON. SOME THINGS WILL BE THE SAME, SOME THINGS ARE GONNA BE DIFFERENT.
ONE OF THOSE CHANGES IS HOW Y'ALL PRESENT YOURSELVES.
HOLLOWAY HAIR CARE PRODUCTS
WE NEED TO BLEND IN A LITTLE BETTER. DON'T BE A NEON SIGN TELLIN' THE PO-PO WE'RE ALL ABOUT THE THUG LIFE.
OF COURSE, THAT DON'T MEAN YOU'LL BE SPORTIN' HUGO BOSS AT THE TACO STAND, BUT WE ARE GONNA BE DRESSING SHARPER. AND PRESENTING OURSELVES ACCORDINGLY.

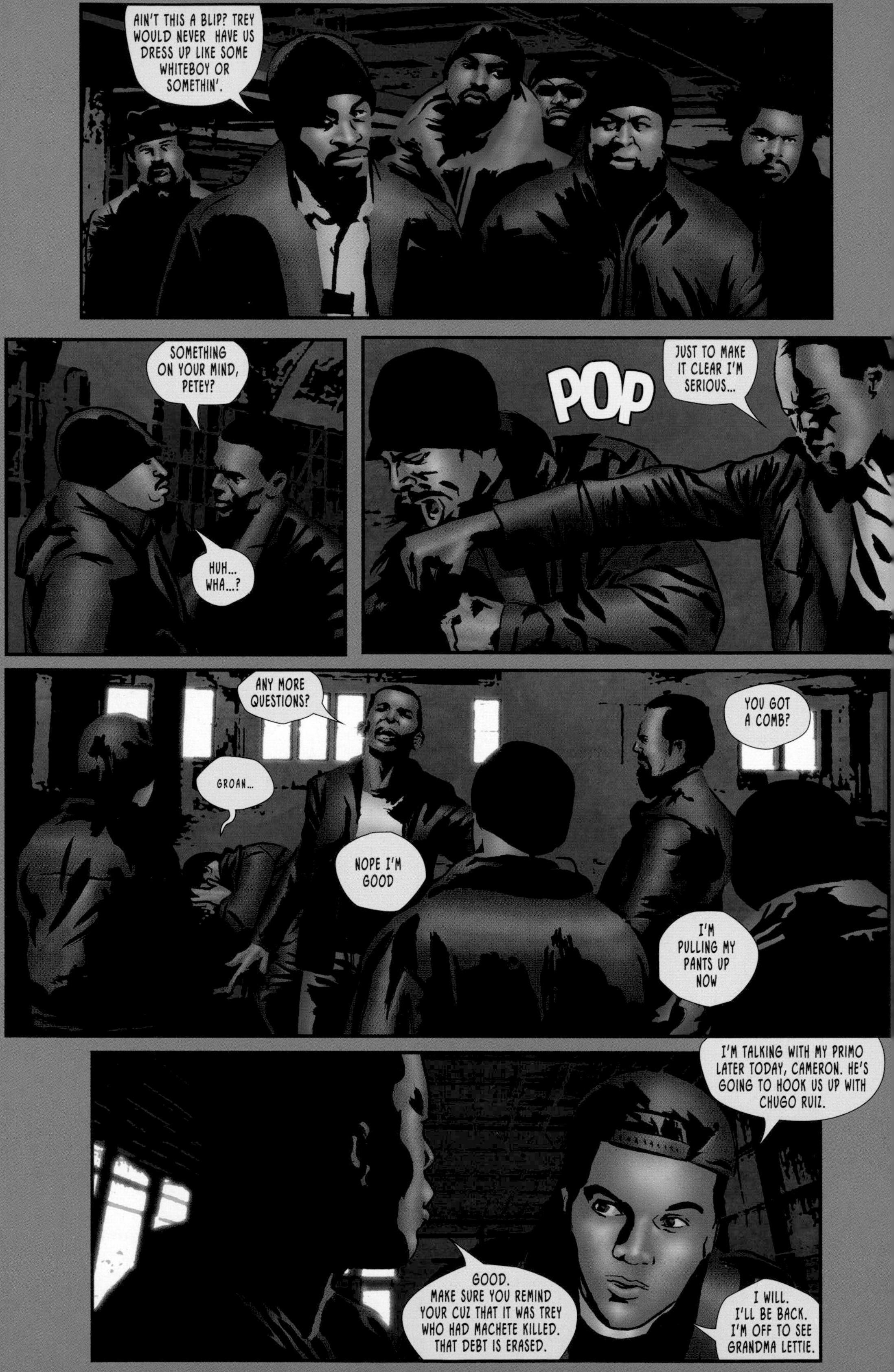
AIN'T THIS A BLIP? TREY WOULD NEVER HAVE US DRESS UP LIKE SOME WHITEBOY OR SOMETHIN'.
SOMETHING ON YOUR MIND, PETEY?
HUH... WHA...?
POP
JUST TO MAKE IT CLEAR I'M SERIOUS...
ANY MORE QUESTIONS?
GROAN...
NOPE I'M GOOD
YOU GOT A COMB?
I'M PULLING MY PANTS UP NOW
I'M TALKING WITH MY PRIMO LATER TODAY, CAMERON. HE'S GOING TO HOOK US UP WITH CHUGO RUIZ.
GOOD. MAKE SURE YOU REMIND YOUR CUZ THAT IT WAS TREY WHO HAD MACHETE KILLED. THAT DEBT IS ERASED.
I WILL. I'LL BE BACK. I'M OFF TO SEE GRANDMA LETTIE.

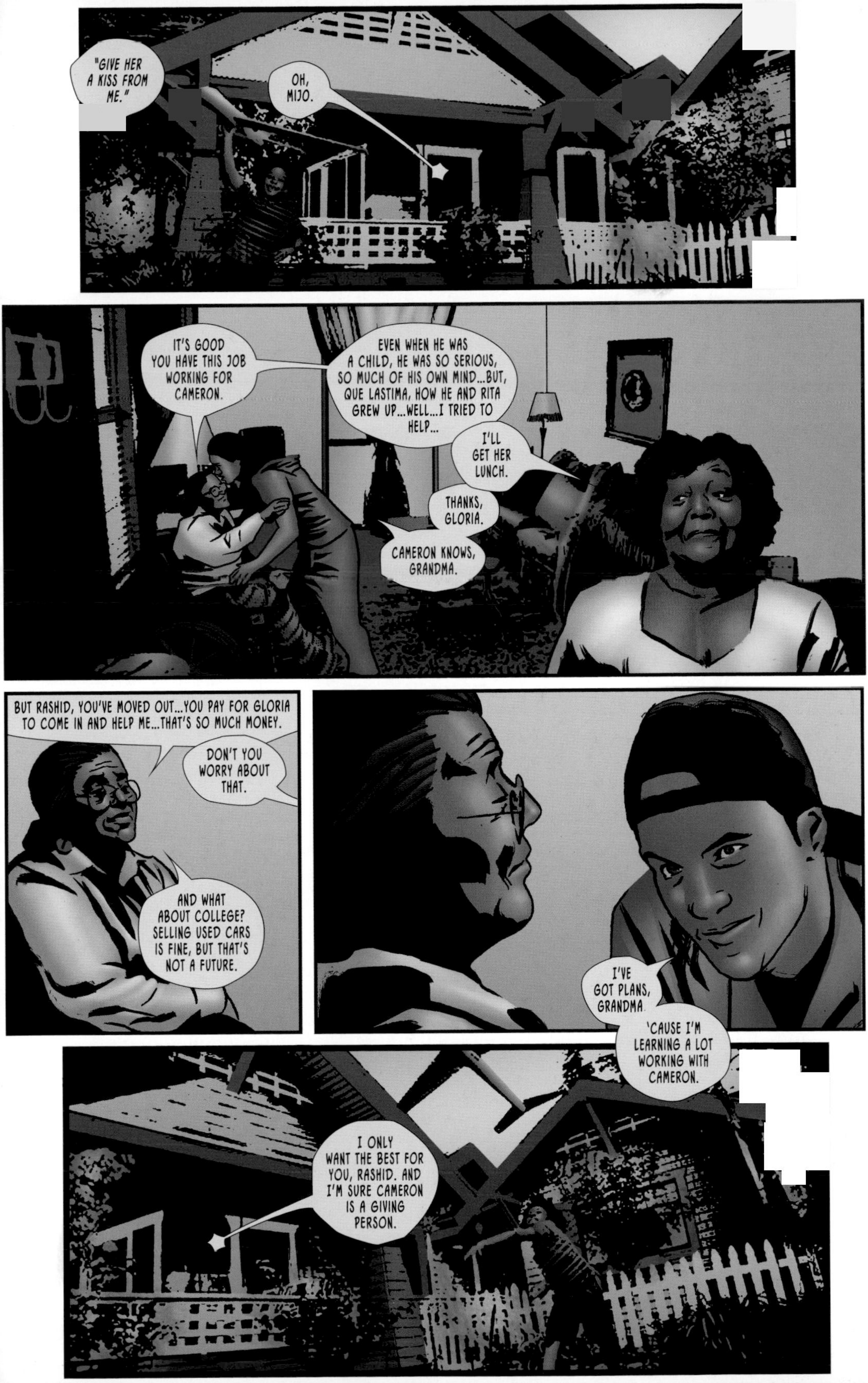
"GIVE HER A KISS FROM ME."
OH, MIJO.
IT'S GOOD YOU HAVE THIS JOB WORKING FOR CAMERON.
EVEN WHEN HE WAS A CHILD, HE WAS SO SERIOUS, SO MUCH OF HIS OWN MIND...BUT, QUE LASTIMA, HOW HE AND RITA GREW UP...WELL...I TRIED TO HELP...
I'LL GET HER LUNCH.
THANKS, GLORIA.
CAMERON KNOWS, GRANDMA.
BUT RASHID, YOU'VE MOVED OUT...YOU PAY FOR GLORIA TO COME IN AND HELP ME...THAT'S SO MUCH MONEY.
DON'T YOU WORRY ABOUT THAT.
AND WHAT ABOUT COLLEGE? SELLING USED CARS IS FINE, BUT THAT'S NOT A FUTURE.
I'VE GOT PLANS, GRANDMA.
'CAUSE I'M LEARNING A LOT WORKING WITH CAMERON.
I ONLY WANT THE BEST FOR YOU, RASHID. AND I'M SURE CAMERON IS A GIVING PERSON.

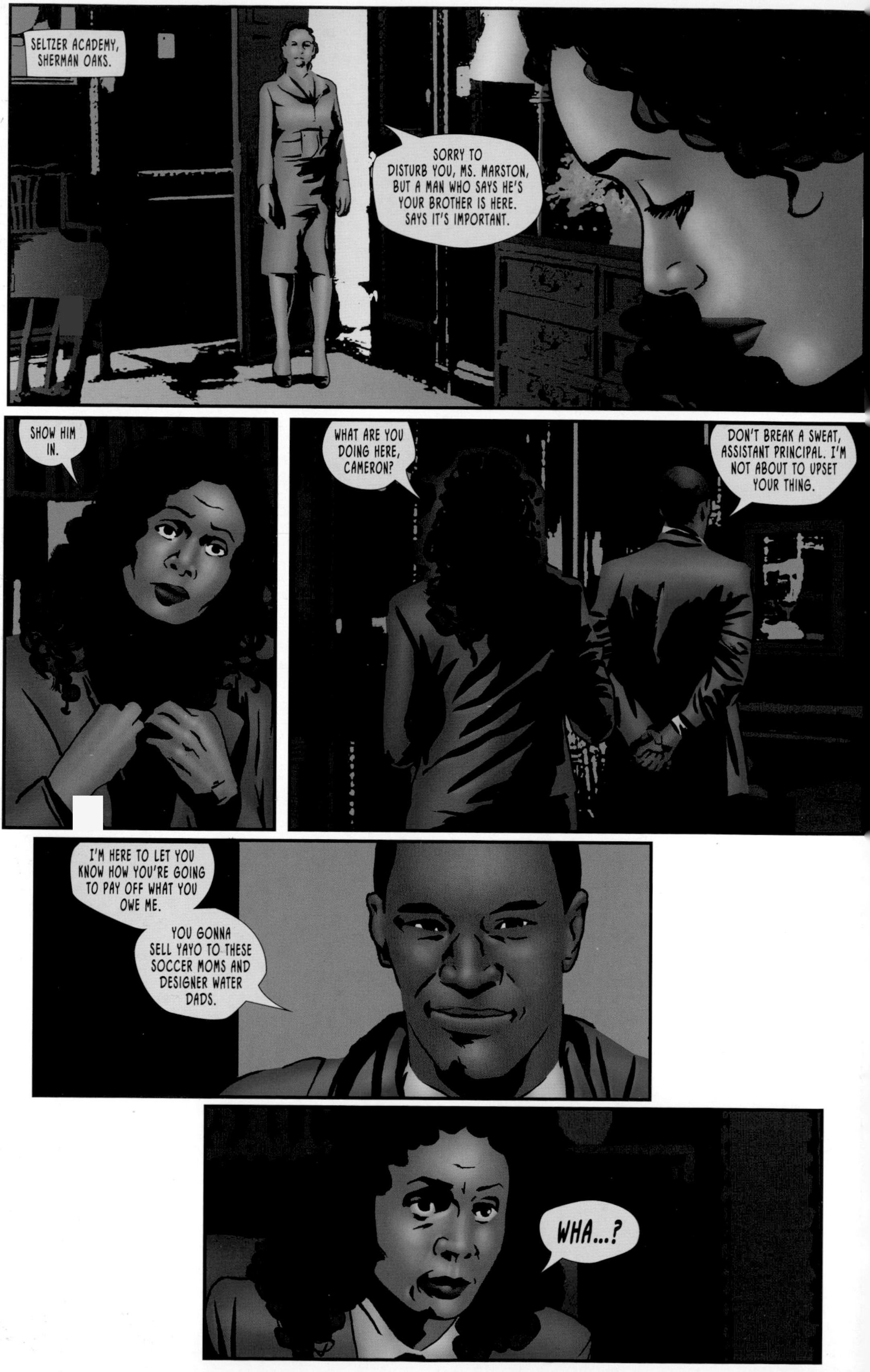
SELTZER ACADEMY, SHERMAN OAKS.
SORRY TO DISTURB YOU, MS. MARSTON, BUT A MAN WHO SAYS HE'S YOUR BROTHER IS HERE. SAYS IT'S IMPORTANT.
SHOW HIM IN.
WHAT ARE YOU DOING HERE, CAMERON?
DON'T BREAK A SWEAT, ASSISTANT PRINCIPAL. I'M NOT ABOUT TO UPSET YOUR THING.
I'M HERE TO LET YOU KNOW HOW YOU'RE GOING TO PAY OFF WHAT YOU OWE ME.
YOU GONNA SELL YAYO TO THESE SOCCER MOMS AND DESIGNER WATER DADS.
WHA...?

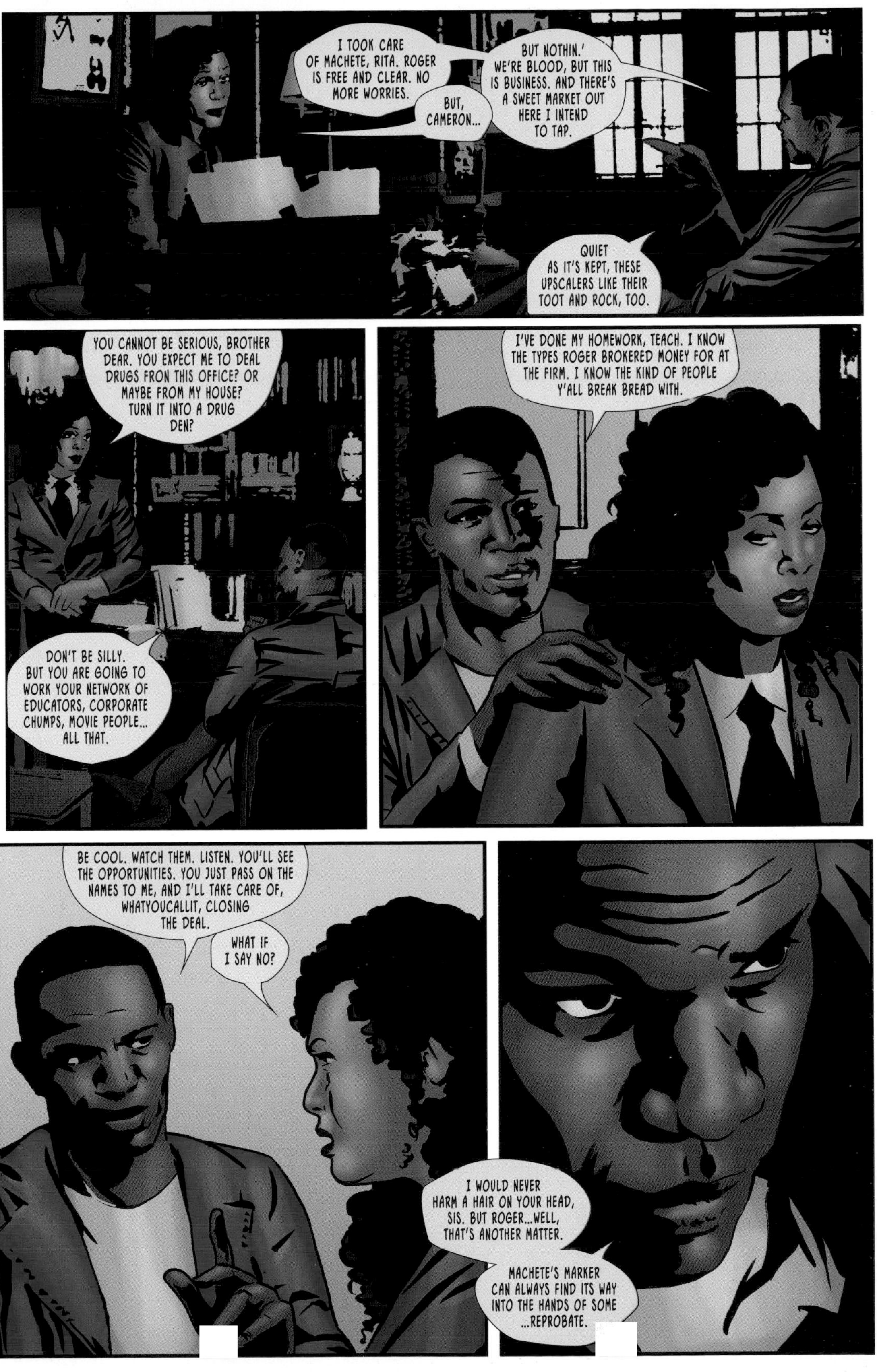

I TOOK CARE OF MACHETE, RITA. ROGER IS FREE AND CLEAR. NO MORE WORRIES.
BUT, CAMERON...
BUT NOTHIN.' WE'RE BLOOD, BUT THIS IS BUSINESS. AND THERE'S A SWEET MARKET OUT HERE I INTEND TO TAP.
QUIET AS IT'S KEPT, THESE UPSCALERS LIKE THEIR TOOT AND ROCK, TOO.
YOU CANNOT BE SERIOUS, BROTHER DEAR. YOU EXPECT ME TO DEAL DRUGS FRON THIS OFFICE? OR MAYBE FROM MY HOUSE? TURN IT INTO A DRUG DEN?
DON'T BE SILLY. BUT YOU ARE GOING TO WORK YOUR NETWORK OF EDUCATORS, CORPORATE CHUMPS, MOVIE PEOPLE... ALL THAT.
I'VE DONE MY HOMEWORK, TEACH. I KNOW THE TYPES ROGER BROKERED MONEY FOR AT THE FIRM. I KNOW THE KIND OF PEOPLE Y'ALL BREAK BREAD WITH.
BE COOL. WATCH THEM. LISTEN. YOU'LL SEE THE OPPORTUNITIES. YOU JUST PASS ON THE NAMES TO ME, AND I'LL TAKE CARE OF, WHATYOUCALLIT, CLOSING THE DEAL.
WHAT IF I SAY NO?
I WOULD NEVER HARM A HAIR ON YOUR HEAD, SIS. BUT ROGER...WELL, THAT'S ANOTHER MATTER.
MACHETE'S MARKER CAN ALWAYS FIND ITS WAY INTO THE HANDS OF SOME ...REPROBATE.

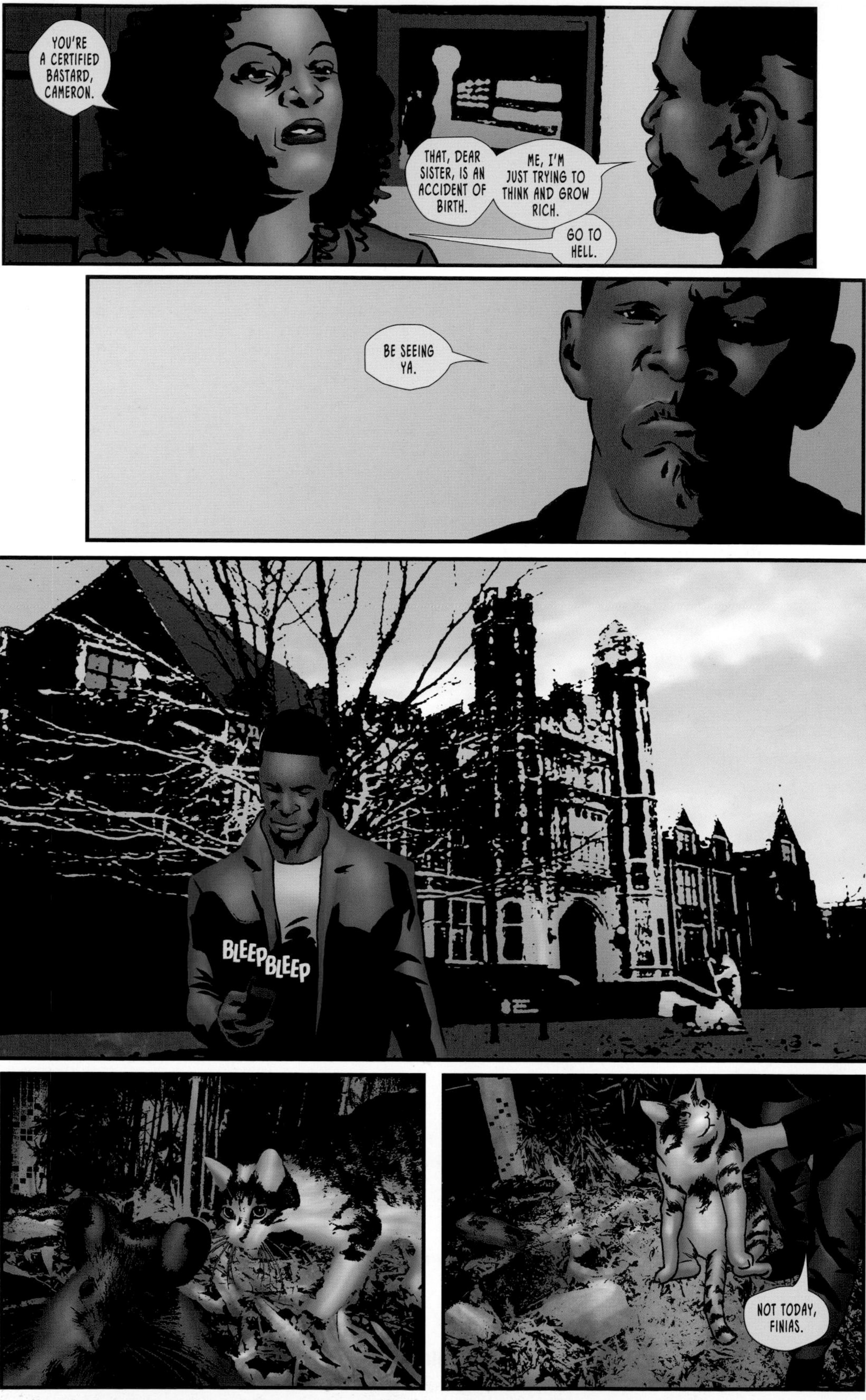
YOU'RE A CERTIFIED BASTARD, CAMERON.
THAT, DEAR SISTER, IS AN ACCIDENT OF BIRTH.
ME, I'M JUST TRYING TO THINK AND GROW RICH.
GO TO HELL.
BE SEEING YA.
BLEEP BLEEP
NOT TODAY, FINIAS.

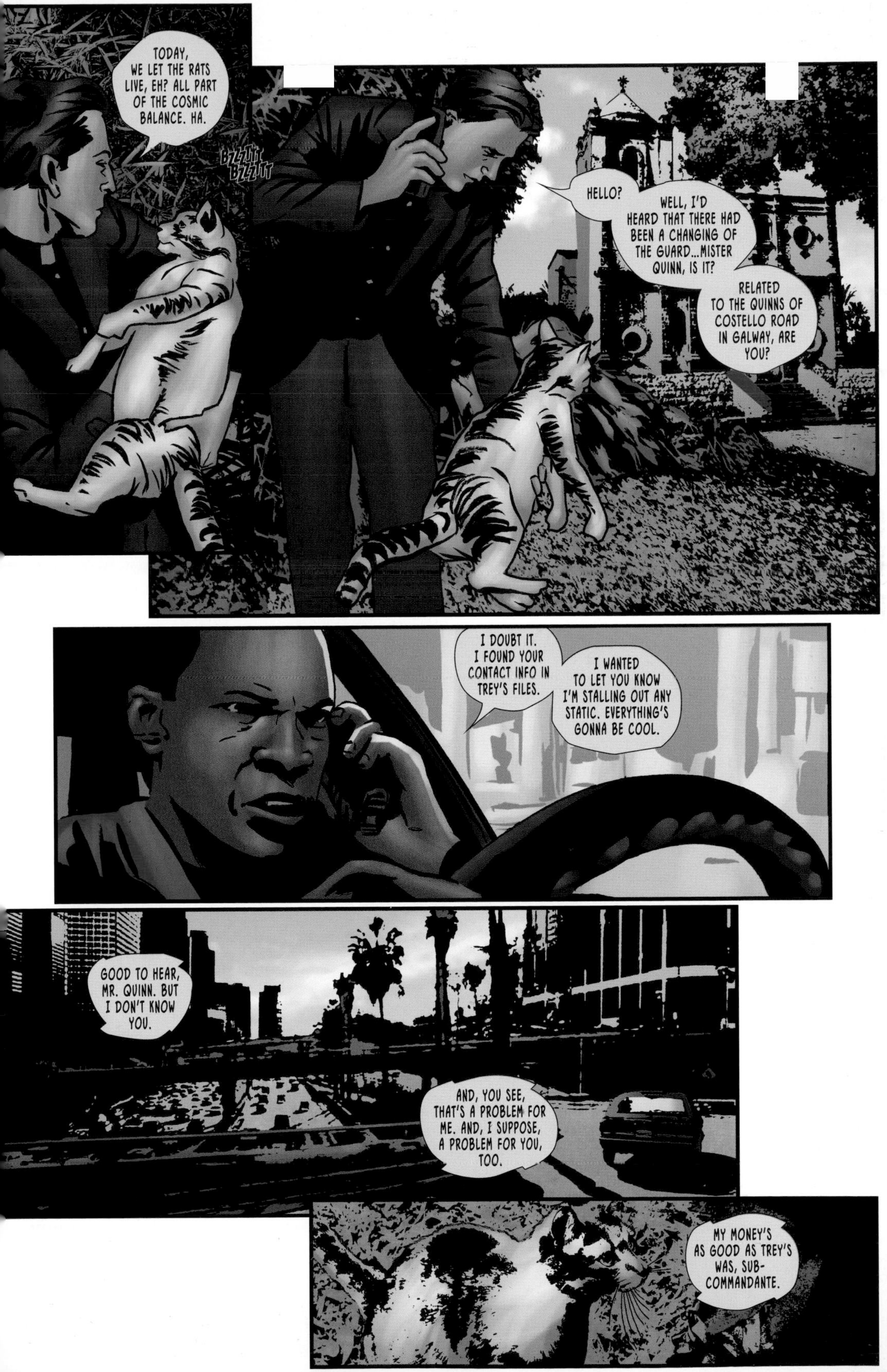
TODAY, WE LET THE RATS LIVE, EH? ALL PART OF THE COSMIC BALANCE. HA.
BZZTTT BZZTTT
HELLO?
WELL, I'D HEARD THAT THERE HAD BEEN A CHANGING OF THE GUARD...MISTER QUINN, IS IT?
RELATED TO THE QUINNS OF COSTELLO ROAD IN GALWAY, ARE YOU?
I DOUBT IT. I FOUND YOUR CONTACT INFO IN TREY'S FILES.
I WANTED TO LET YOU KNOW I'M STALLING OUT ANY STATIC. EVERYTHING'S GONNA BE COOL.
GOOD TO HEAR, MR. QUINN. BUT I DON'T KNOW YOU.
AND, YOU SEE, THAT'S A PROBLEM FOR ME. AND, I SUPPOSE, A PROBLEM FOR YOU, TOO.
MY MONEY'S AS GOOD AS TREY'S WAS, SUB-COMMANDANTE.

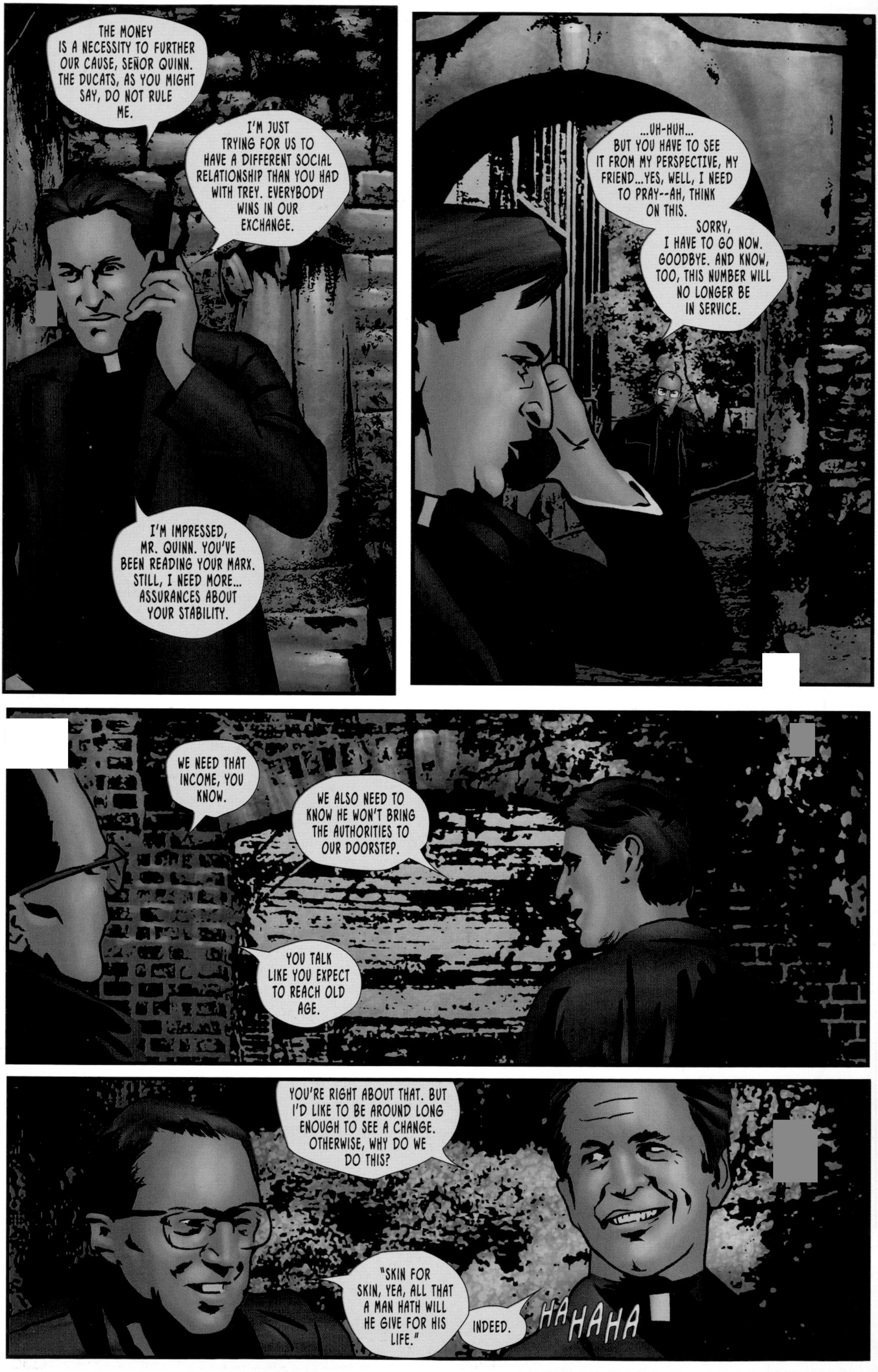
THE MONEY IS A NECESSITY TO FURTHER OUR CAUSE, SEÑOR QUINN. THE DUCATS, AS YOU MIGHT SAY, DO NOT RULE ME.
I'M JUST TRYING FOR US TO HAVE A DIFFERENT SOCIAL RELATIONSHIP THAN YOU HAD WITH TREY. EVERYBODY WINS IN OUR EXCHANGE.
I'M IMPRESSED, MR. QUINN. YOU'VE BEEN READING YOUR MARX. STILL, I NEED MORE... ASSURANCES ABOUT YOUR STABILITY.
...UH-HUH... BUT YOU HAVE TO SEE IT FROM MY PERSPECTIVE, MY FRIEND...YES, WELL, I NEED TO PRAY--AH, THINK ON THIS.
SORRY, I HAVE TO GO NOW. GOODBYE. AND KNOW, TOO, THIS NUMBER WILL NO LONGER BE IN SERVICE.
WE NEED THAT INCOME, YOU KNOW.
WE ALSO NEED TO KNOW HE WON'T BRING THE AUTHORITIES TO OUR DOORSTEP.
YOU TALK LIKE YOU EXPECT TO REACH OLD AGE.
YOU'RE RIGHT ABOUT THAT. BUT I'D LIKE TO BE AROUND LONG ENOUGH TO SEE A CHANGE. OTHERWISE, WHY DO WE DO THIS?
"SKIN FOR SKIN, YEA, ALL THAT A MAN HATH WILL HE GIVE FOR HIS LIFE."
INDEED.
HA HAHAHA

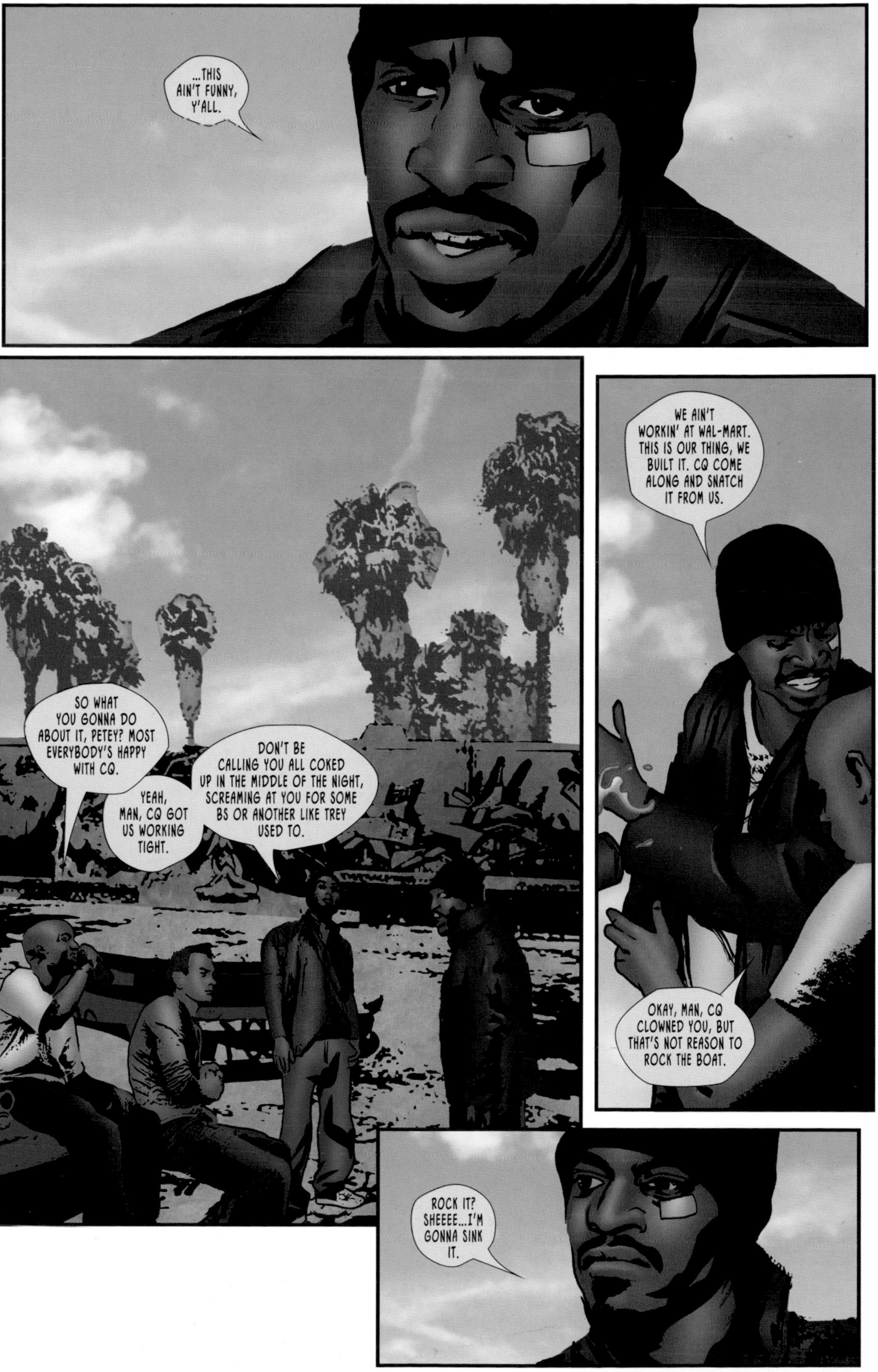
...THIS AIN'T FUNNY, Y'ALL.
SO WHAT YOU GONNA DO ABOUT IT, PETEY? MOST EVERYBODY'S HAPPY WITH CQ.
YEAH, MAN, CQ GOT US WORKING TIGHT.
DON'T BE CALLING YOU ALL COKED UP IN THE MIDDLE OF THE NIGHT, SCREAMING AT YOU FOR SOME BS OR ANOTHER LIKE TREY USED TO.
WE AIN'T WORKIN' AT WAL-MART. THIS IS OUR THING, WE BUILT IT. CQ COME ALONG AND SNATCH IT FROM US.
OKAY, MAN, CQ CLOWNED YOU, BUT THAT'S NOT REASON TO ROCK THE BOAT.
ROCK IT? SHEEEE...I'M GONNA SINK IT.

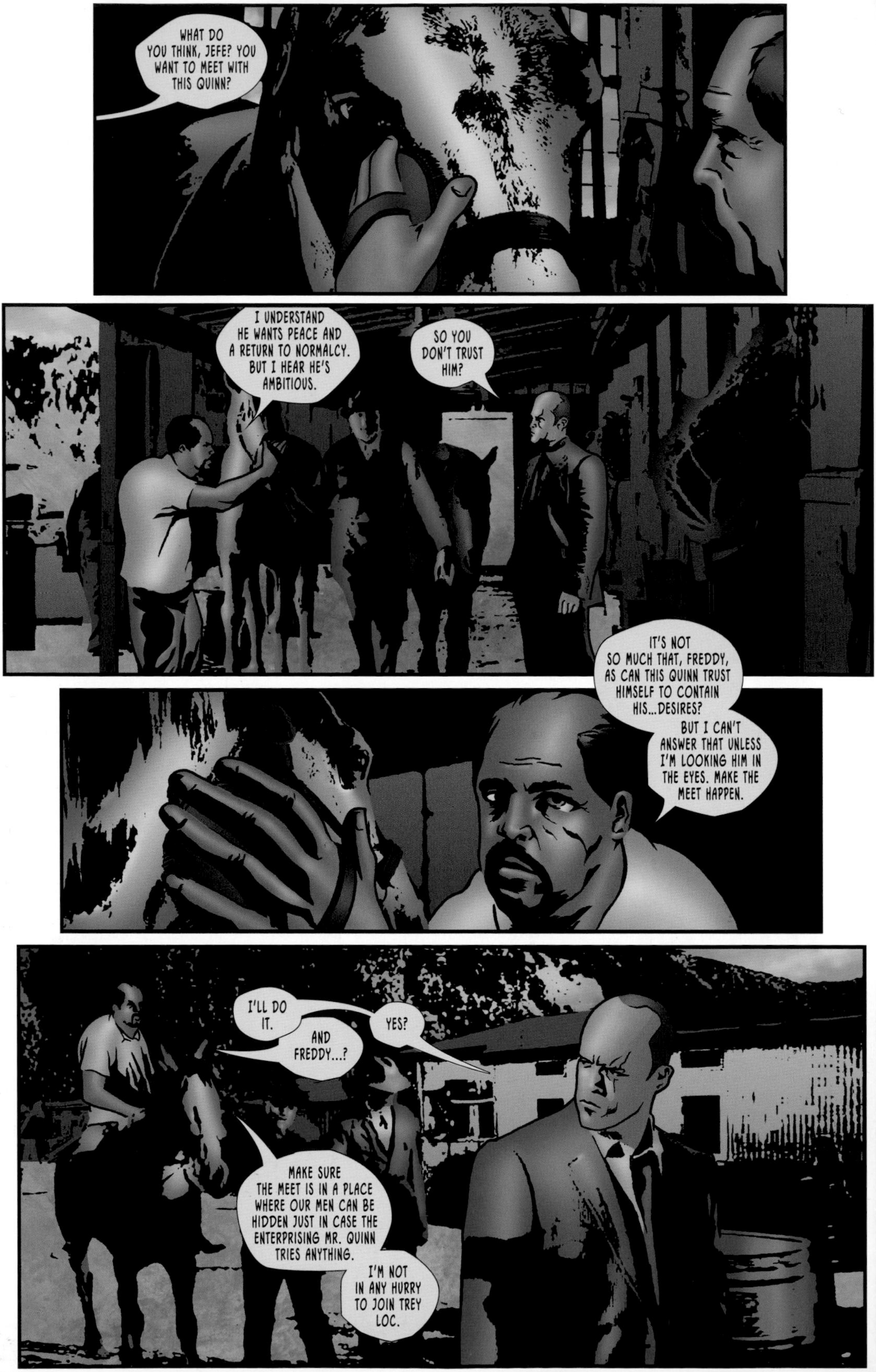
WHAT DO YOU THINK, JEFE? YOU WANT TO MEET WITH THIS QUINN?
I UNDERSTAND HE WANTS PEACE AND A RETURN TO NORMALCY. BUT I HEAR HE'S AMBITIOUS.
SO YOU DON'T TRUST HIM?
IT'S NOT SO MUCH THAT, FREDDY, AS CAN THIS QUINN TRUST HIMSELF TO CONTAIN HIS...DESIRES?
BUT I CAN'T ANSWER THAT UNLESS I'M LOOKING HIM IN THE EYES. MAKE THE MEET HAPPEN.
I'LL DO IT.
AND FREDDY...?
YES?
MAKE SURE THE MEET IS IN A PLACE WHERE OUR MEN CAN BE HIDDEN JUST IN CASE THE ENTERPRISING MR. QUINN TRIES ANYTHING.
I'M NOT IN ANY HURRY TO JOIN TREY LOC.

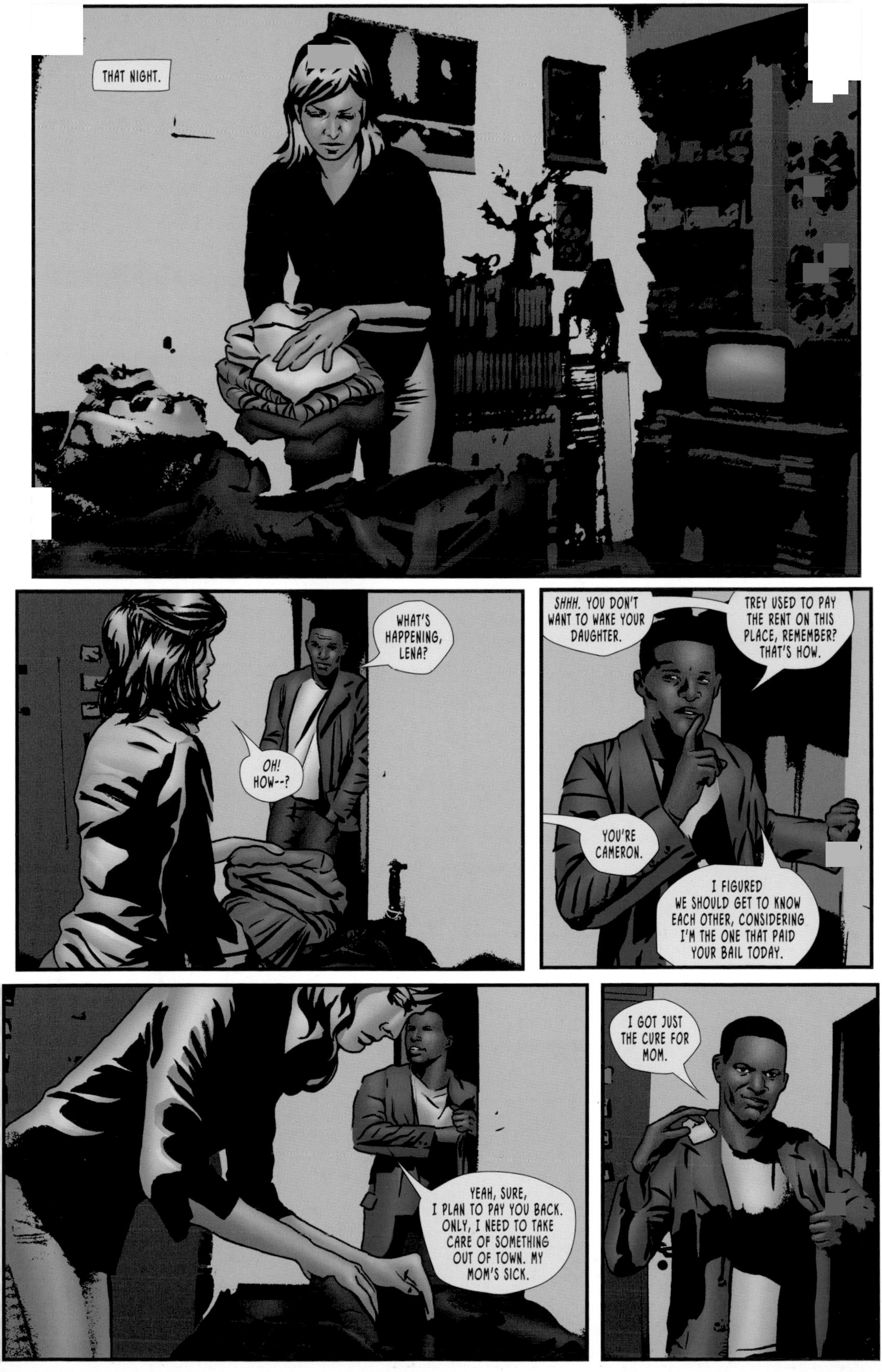
THAT NIGHT.
WHAT'S HAPPENING, LENA?
OH! HOW--?
SHHH. YOU DON'T WANT TO WAKE YOUR DAUGHTER.
TREY USED TO PAY THE RENT ON THIS PLACE, REMEMBER? THAT'S HOW.
YOU'RE CAMERON.
I FIGURED WE SHOULD GET TO KNOW EACH OTHER, CONSIDERING I'M THE ONE THAT PAID YOUR BAIL TODAY.
YEAH, SURE, I PLAN TO PAY YOU BACK. ONLY, I NEED TO TAKE CARE OF SOMETHING OUT OF TOWN. MY MOM'S SICK.
I GOT JUST THE CURE FOR MOM.

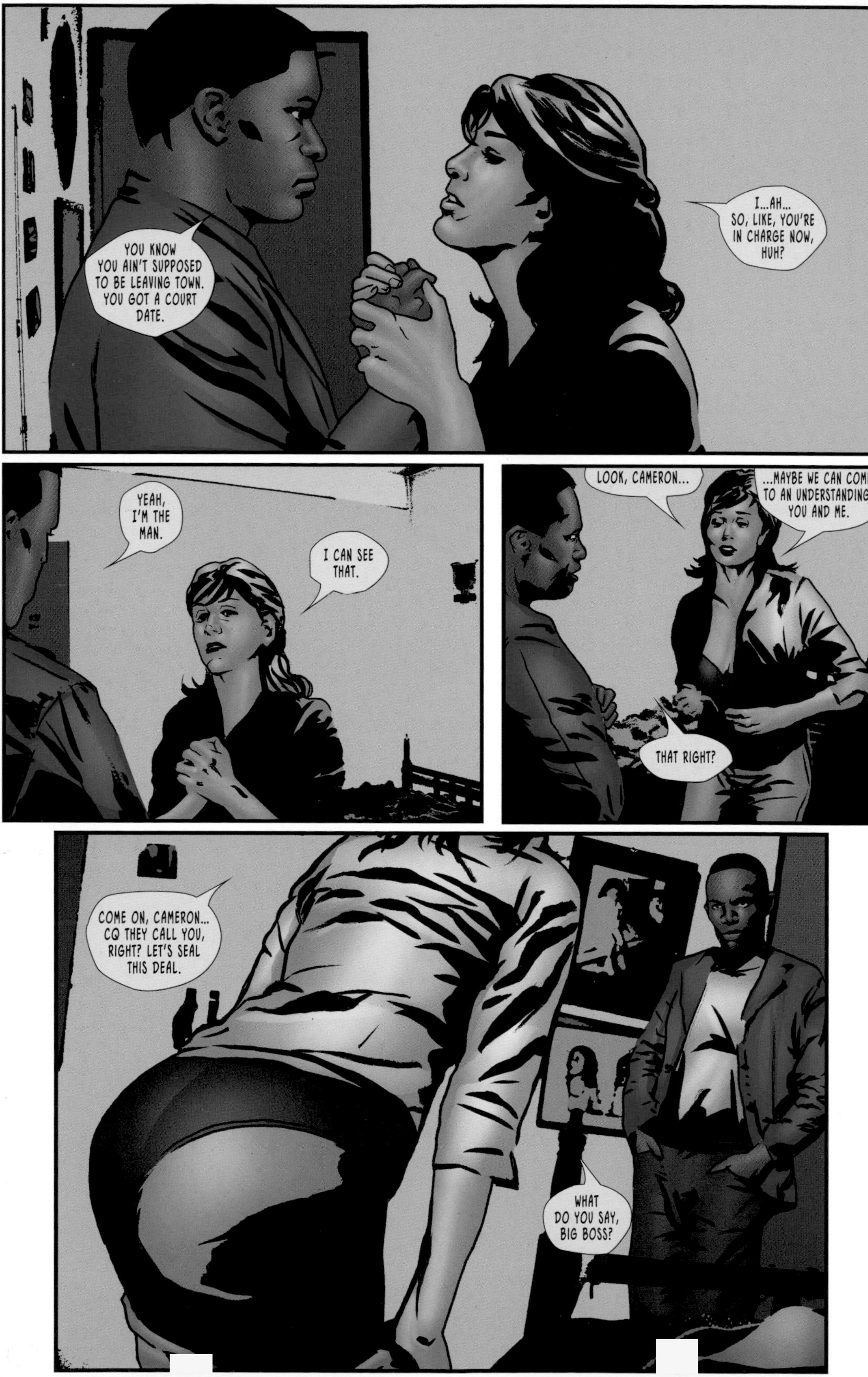
YOU KNOW YOU AIN'T SUPPOSED TO BE LEAVING TOWN. YOU GOT A COURT DATE.
I...AH... SO, LIKE, YOU'RE IN CHARGE NOW, HUH?
YEAH, I'M THE MAN.
I CAN SEE THAT.
LOOK, CAMERON...
...MAYBE WE CAN COME TO AN UNDERSTANDING, YOU AND ME.
THAT RIGHT?
COME ON, CAMERON... CQ THEY CALL YOU, RIGHT? LET'S SEAL THIS DEAL.
WHAT DO YOU SAY, BIG BOSS?

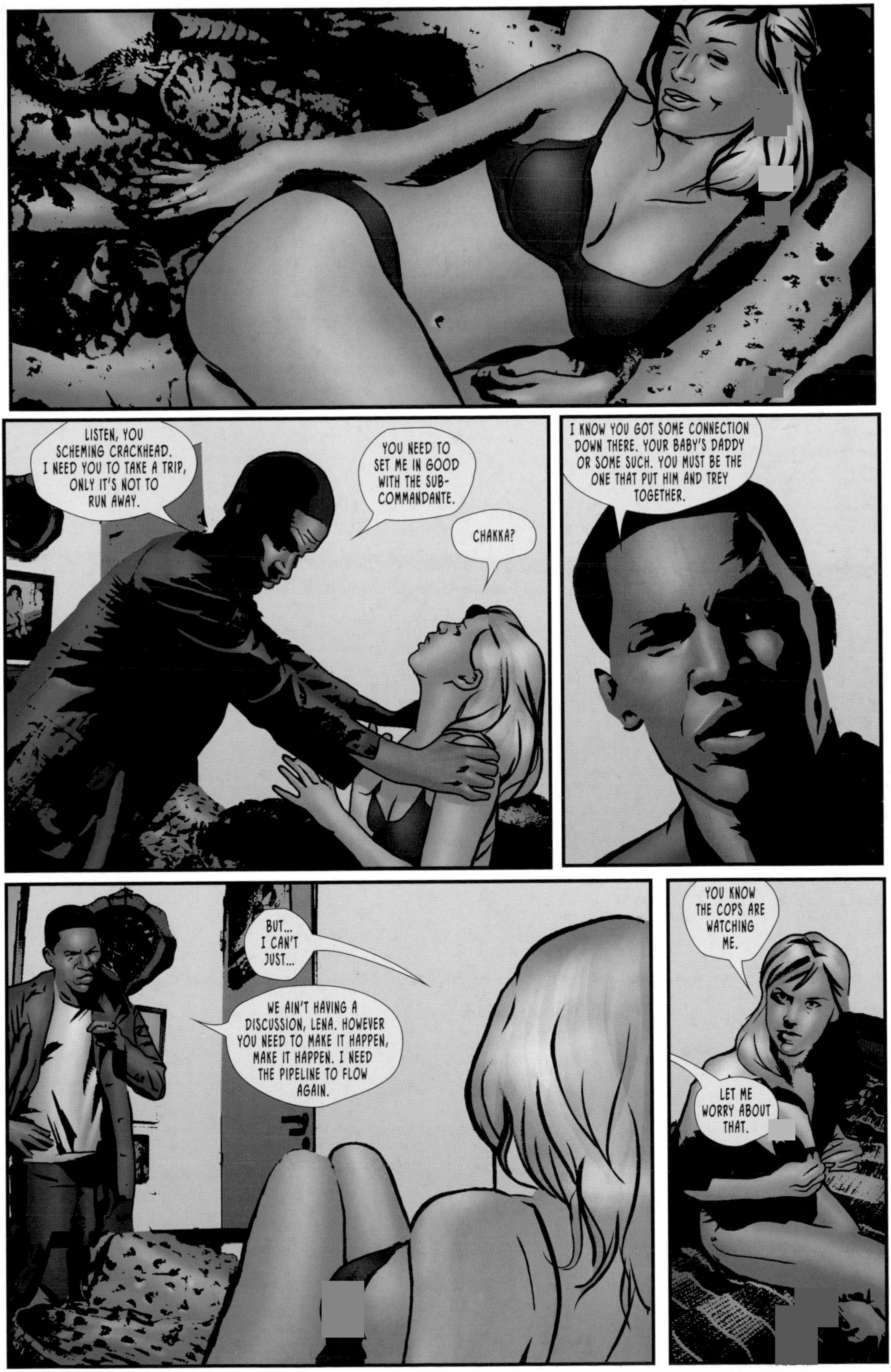
LISTEN, YOU SCHEMING CRACKHEAD. I NEED YOU TO TAKE A TRIP, ONLY IT'S NOT TO RUN AWAY.
YOU NEED TO SET ME IN GOOD WITH THE SUB-COMMANDANTE.
CHAKKA?
I KNOW YOU GOT SOME CONNECTION DOWN THERE. YOUR BABY'S DADDY OR SOME SUCH. YOU MUST BE THE ONE THAT PUT HIM AND TREY TOGETHER.
BUT... I CAN'T JUST...
WE AIN'T HAVING A DISCUSSION, LENA. HOWEVER YOU NEED TO MAKE IT HAPPEN, MAKE IT HAPPEN. I NEED THE PIPELINE TO FLOW AGAIN.
YOU KNOW THE COPS ARE WATCHING ME.
LET ME WORRY ABOUT THAT.

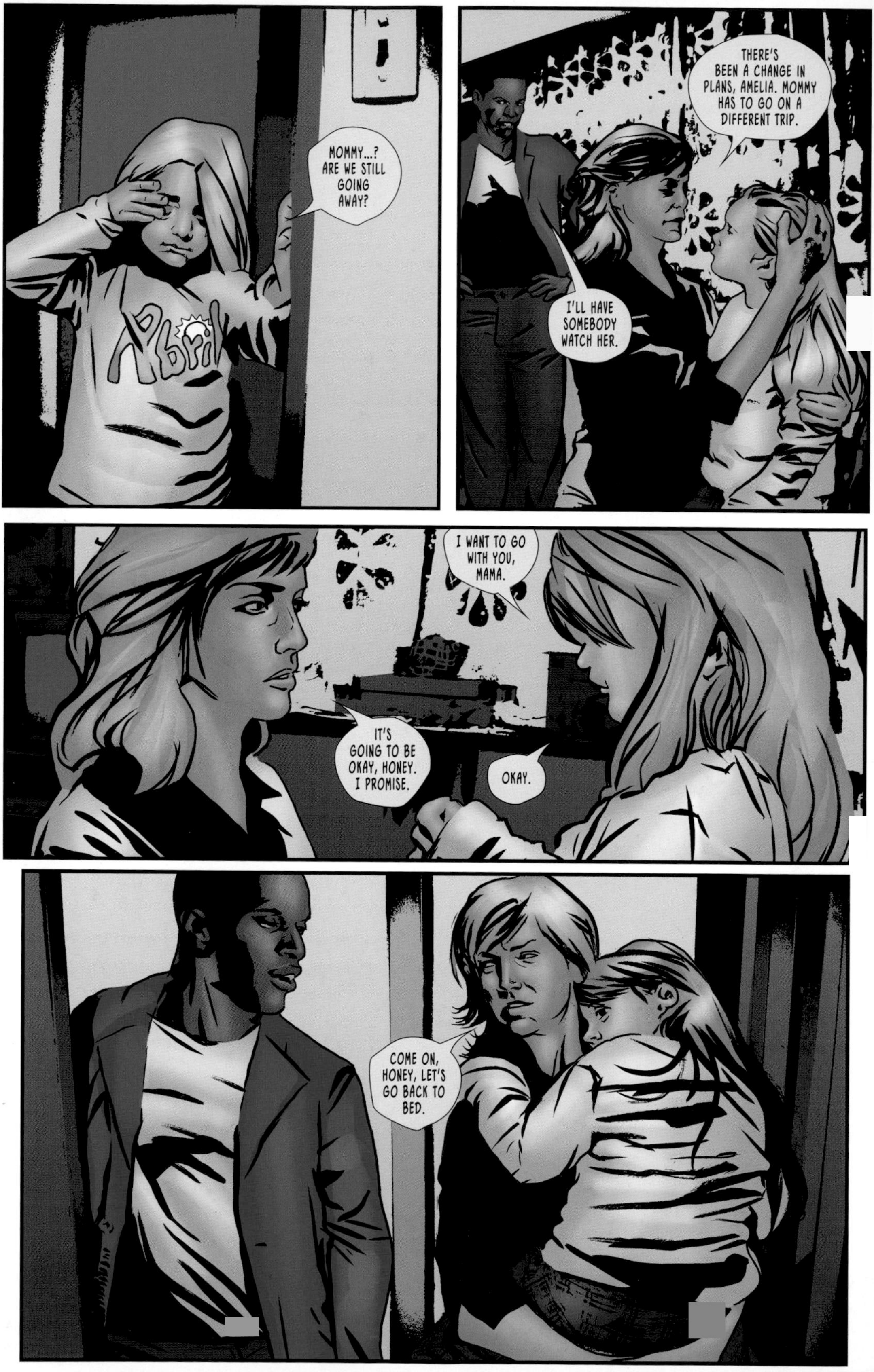
MOMMY...? ARE WE STILL GOING AWAY?
THERE'S BEEN A CHANGE IN PLANS, AMELIA. MOMMY HAS TO GO ON A DIFFERENT TRIP.
I'LL HAVE SOMEBODY WATCH HER.
I WANT TO GO WITH YOU, MAMA.
IT'S GOING TO BE OKAY, HONEY. I PROMISE.
OKAY.
COME ON, HONEY, LET'S GO BACK TO BED.

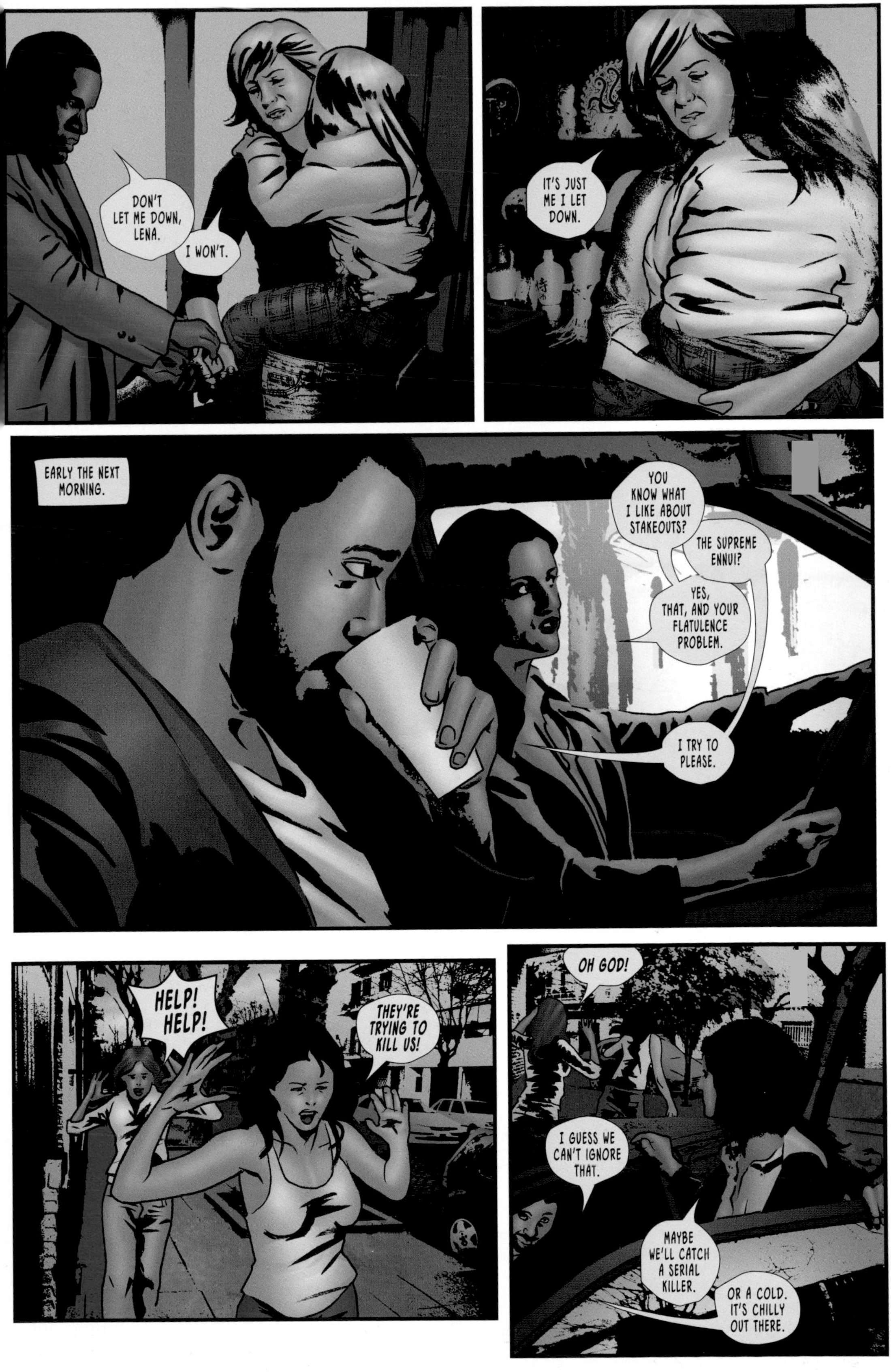
DON'T LET ME DOWN, LENA.
I WON'T.
IT'S JUST ME I LET DOWN.
EARLY THE NEXT MORNING.
YOU KNOW WHAT I LIKE ABOUT STAKEOUTS?
THE SUPREME ENNUI?
YES, THAT, AND YOUR FLATULENCE PROBLEM.
I TRY TO PLEASE.
HELP! HELP!
THEY'RE TRYING TO KILL US!
OH GOD!
I GUESS WE CAN'T IGNORE THAT.
MAYBE WE'LL CATCH A SERIAL KILLER.
OR A COLD. IT'S CHILLY OUT THERE.

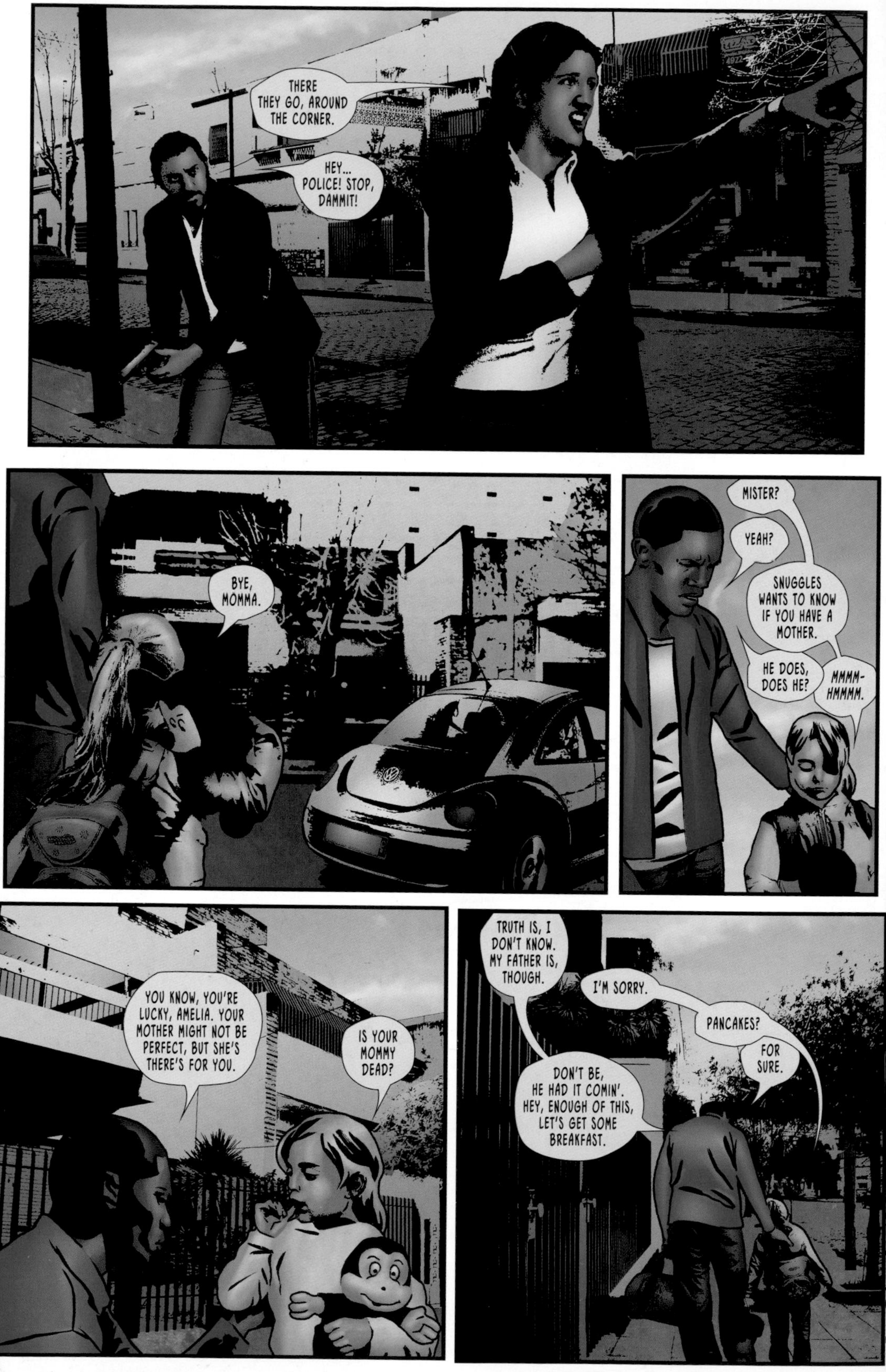
THERE THEY GO, AROUND THE CORNER.
HEY... POLICE! STOP, DAMMIT!
BYE, MOMMA.
MISTER?
YEAH?
SNUGGLES WANTS TO KNOW IF YOU HAVE A MOTHER.
HE DOES, DOES HE?
MMMM-HMMMM.
YOU KNOW, YOU'RE LUCKY, AMELIA. YOUR MOTHER MIGHT NOT BE PERFECT, BUT SHE'S THERE'S FOR YOU.
IS YOUR MOMMY DEAD?
TRUTH IS, I DON'T KNOW. MY FATHER IS, THOUGH.
I'M SORRY.
DON'T BE, HE HAD IT COMIN'. HEY, ENOUGH OF THIS, LET'S GET SOME BREAKFAST.
PANCAKES?
FOR SURE.

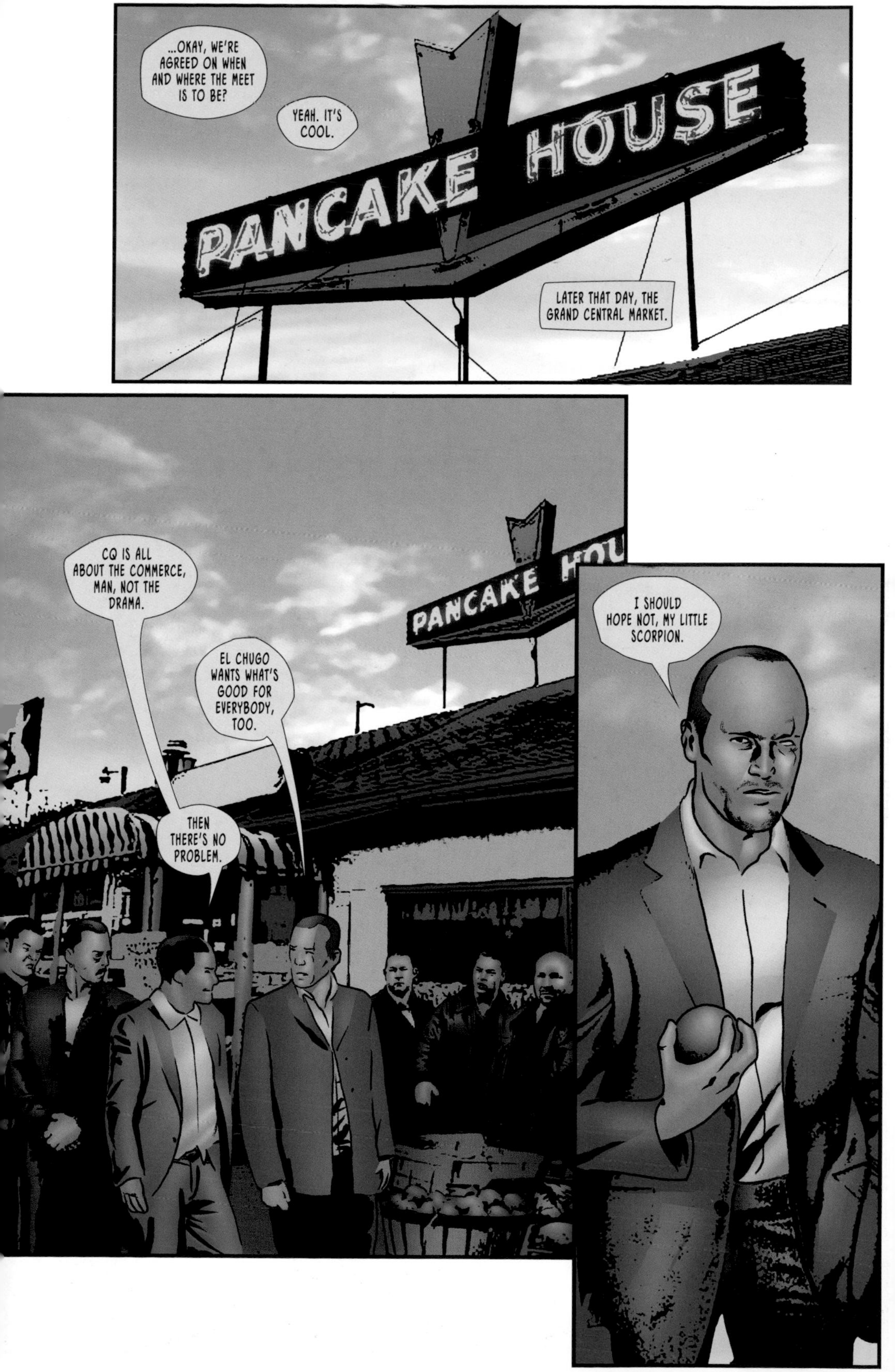
...OKAY, WE'RE AGREED ON WHEN AND WHERE THE MEET IS TO BE?
YEAH. IT'S COOL.
PANCAKE HOUSE
LATER THAT DAY, THE GRAND CENTRAL MARKET.
CQ IS ALL ABOUT THE COMMERCE, MAN, NOT THE DRAMA.
EL CHUGO WANTS WHAT'S GOOD FOR EVERYBODY, TOO.
THEN THERE'S NO PROBLEM.
I SHOULD HOPE NOT, MY LITTLE SCORPION.

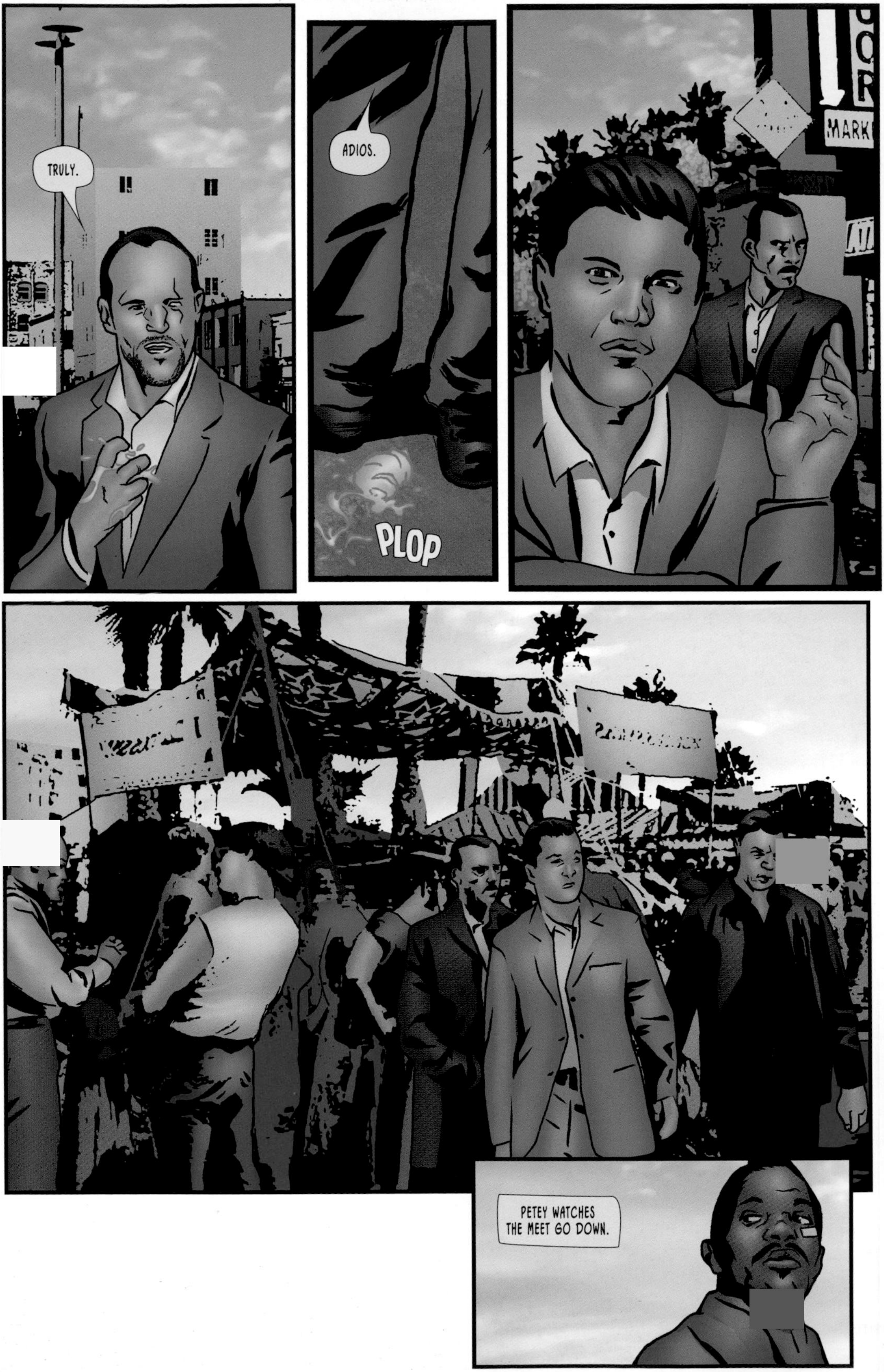
TRULY.
ADIOS.
PLOP
PETEY WATCHES THE MEET GO DOWN.

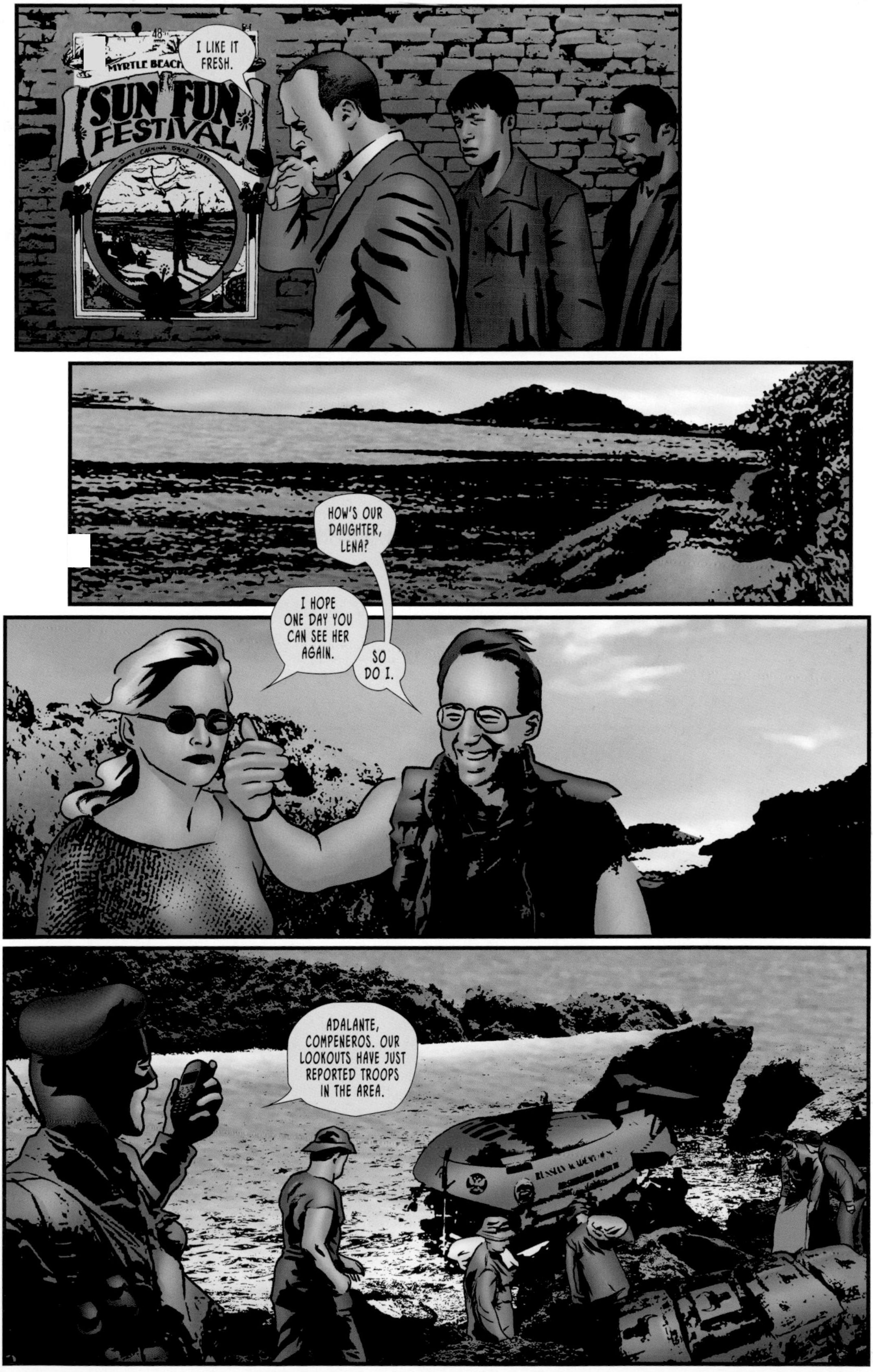
MYRTLE BEACH
SUN FUN FESTIVAL
I LIKE IT FRESH.
HOW'S OUR DAUGHTER, LENA?
I HOPE ONE DAY YOU CAN SEE HER AGAIN.
SO DO I.
ADALANTE, COMPENEROS. OUR LOOKOUTS HAVE JUST REPORTED TROOPS IN THE AREA.

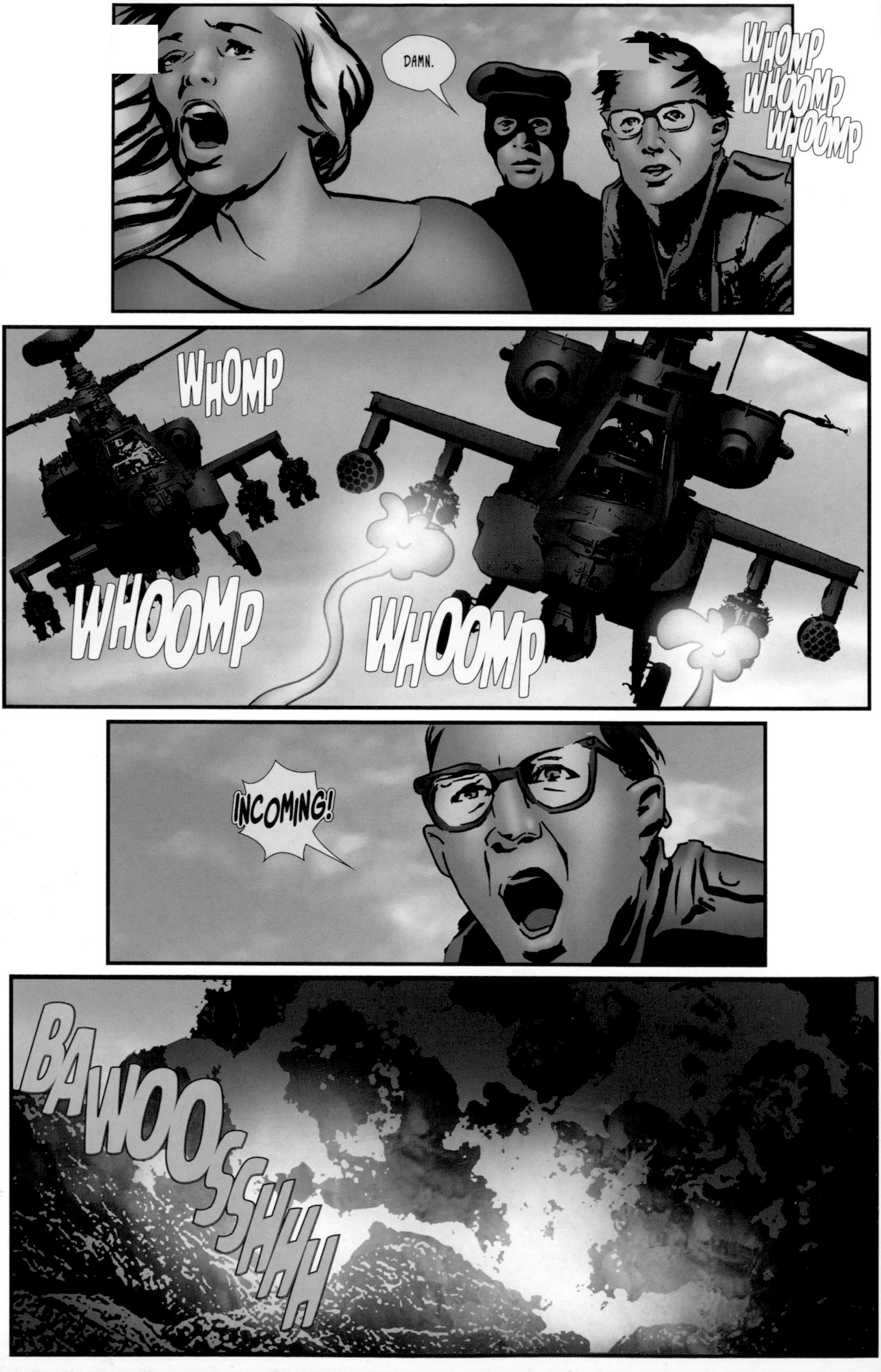
DAMN.
WHOMP
WHOOMP
WHOOMP
WHOMP
WHOOMP
WHOOMP
INCOMING!
BAWOOSSHHH

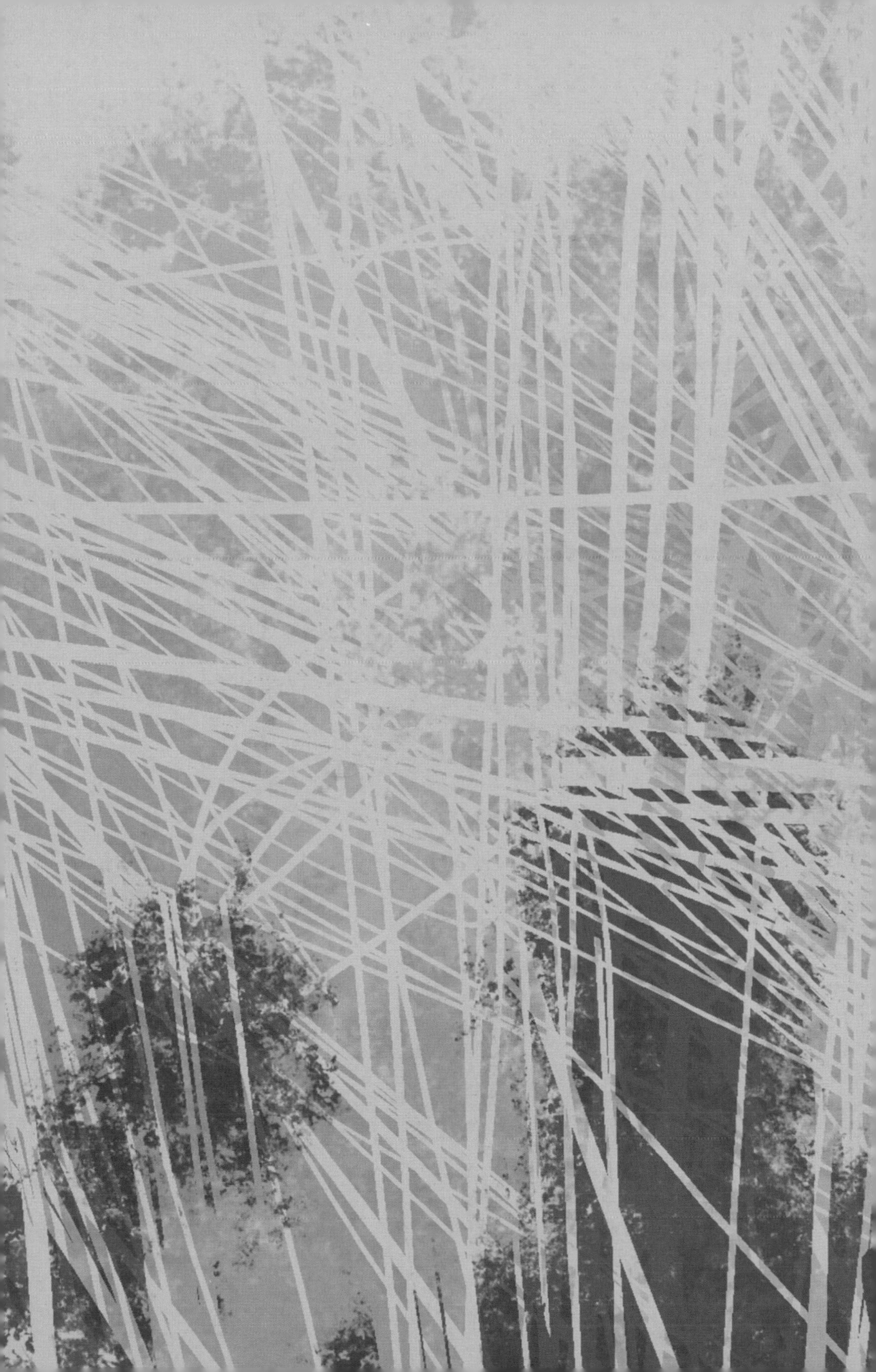

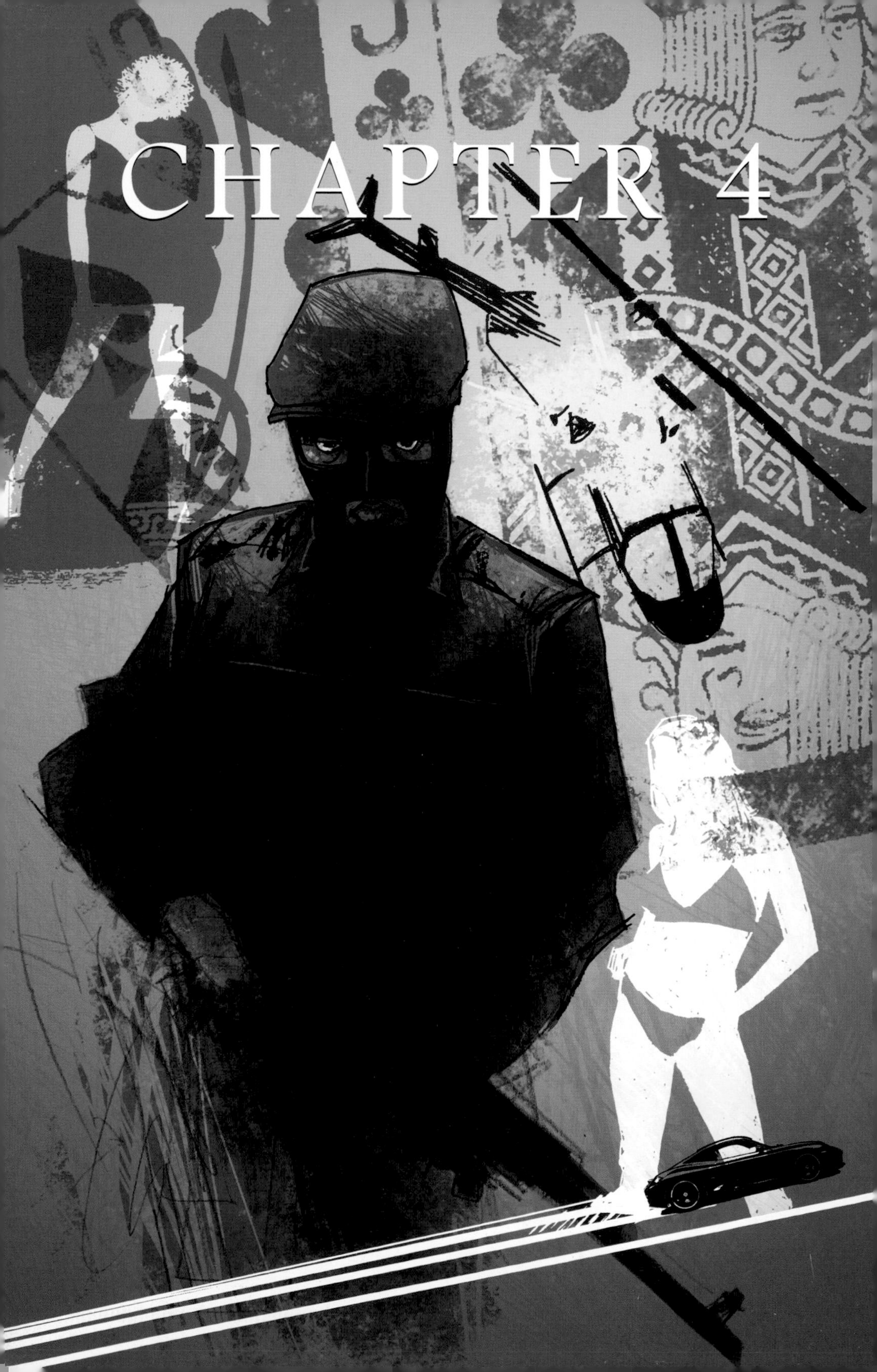
CHAPTER 4

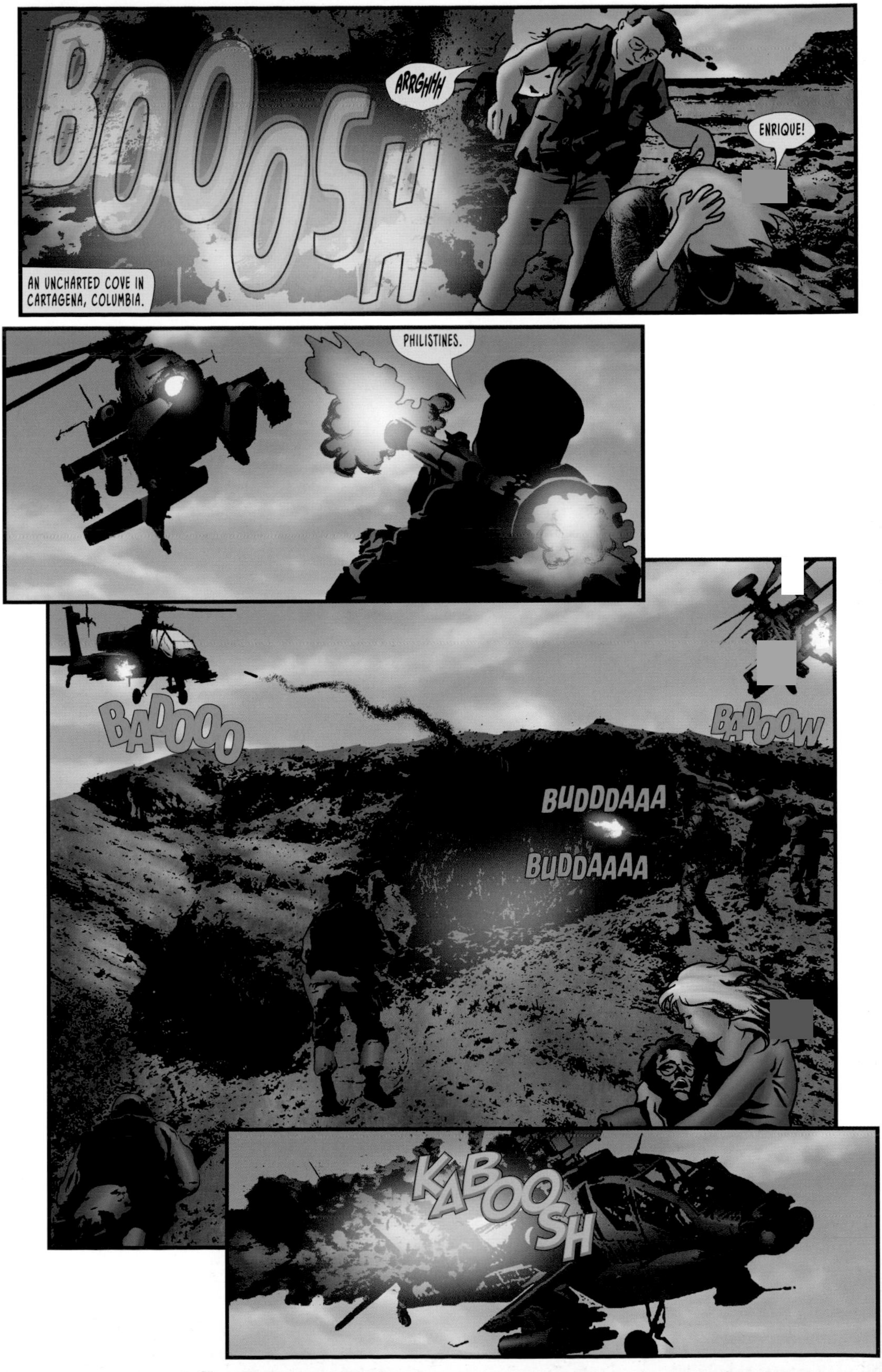
BOOOOSH
ARRGHHH
ENRIQUE!
AN UNCHARTED COVE IN CARTAGENA, COLUMBIA.
PHILISTINES.
BADOOO
BADOOW
BUDDDAAA
BUDDAAAA
KABOOOSH

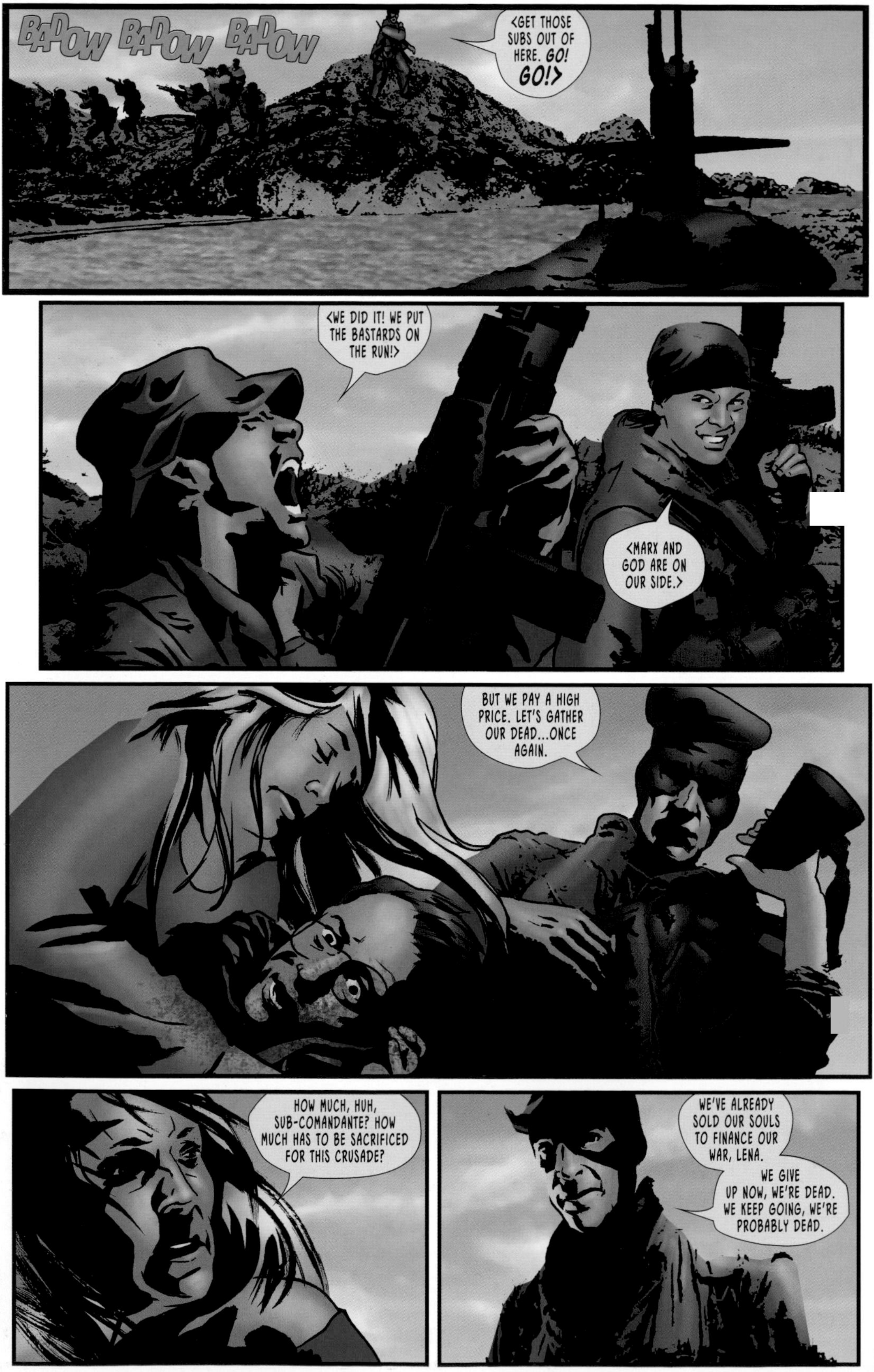
BAPOW BAPOW BAPOW
<GET THOSE SUBS OUT OF HERE. GO! GO!>
<WE DID IT! WE PUT THE BASTARDS ON THE RUN!>
<MARX AND GOD ARE ON OUR SIDE.>
BUT WE PAY A HIGH PRICE. LET'S GATHER OUR DEAD...ONCE AGAIN.
HOW MUCH, HUH, SUB-COMANDANTE? HOW MUCH HAS TO BE SACRIFICED FOR THIS CRUSADE?
WE'VE ALREADY SOLD OUR SOULS TO FINANCE OUR WAR, LENA.
WE GIVE UP NOW, WE'RE DEAD. WE KEEP GOING, WE'RE PROBABLY DEAD.

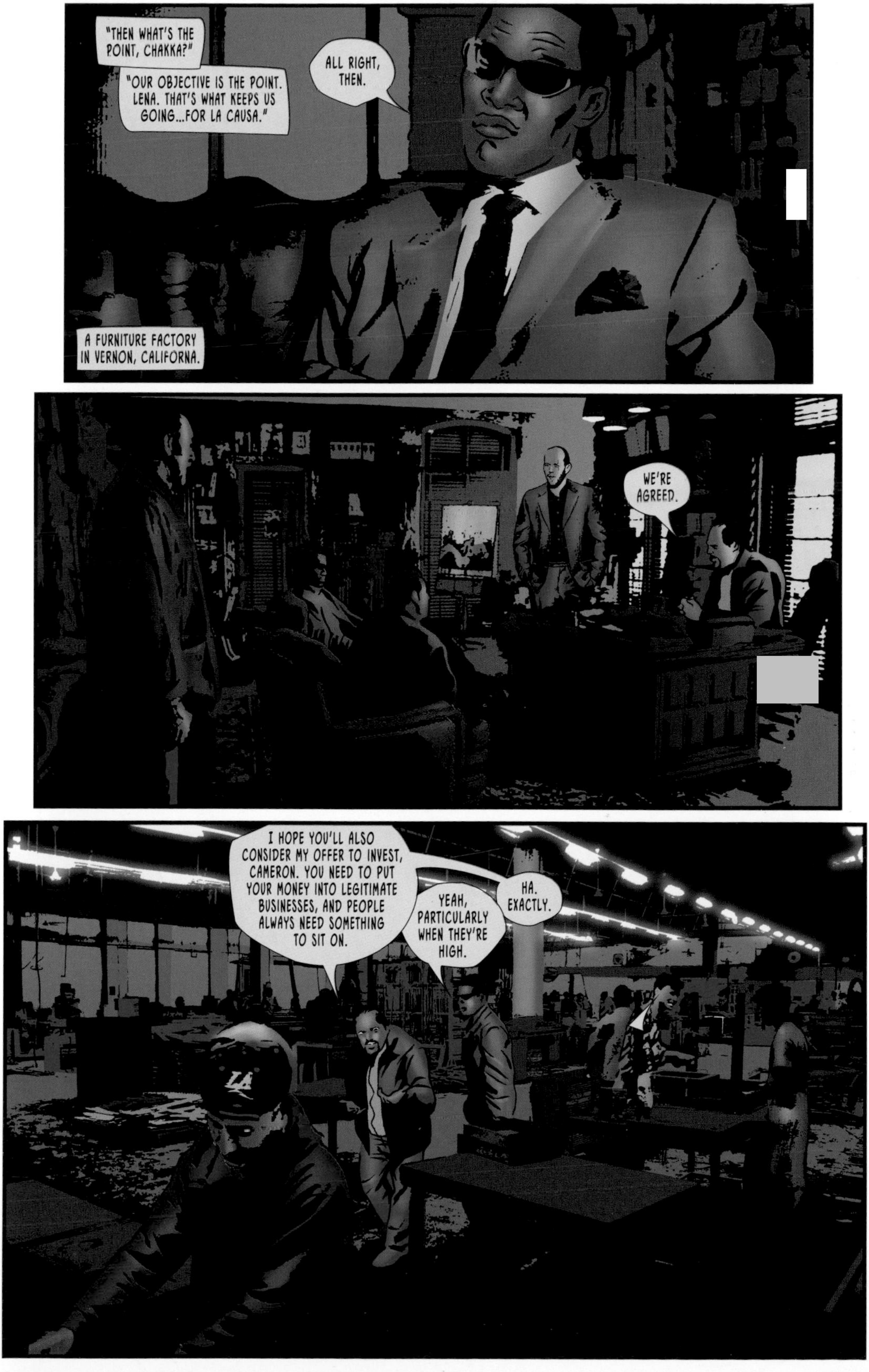
"THEN WHAT'S THE POINT, CHAKKA?"
"OUR OBJECTIVE IS THE POINT. LENA. THAT'S WHAT KEEPS US GOING...FOR LA CAUSA."
ALL RIGHT, THEN.
A FURNITURE FACTORY IN VERNON, CALIFORNA.
WE'RE AGREED.
I HOPE YOU'LL ALSO CONSIDER MY OFFER TO INVEST, CAMERON. YOU NEED TO PUT YOUR MONEY INTO LEGITIMATE BUSINESSES, AND PEOPLE ALWAYS NEED SOMETHING TO SIT ON.
YEAH, PARTICULARLY WHEN THEY'RE HIGH.
HA. EXACTLY.

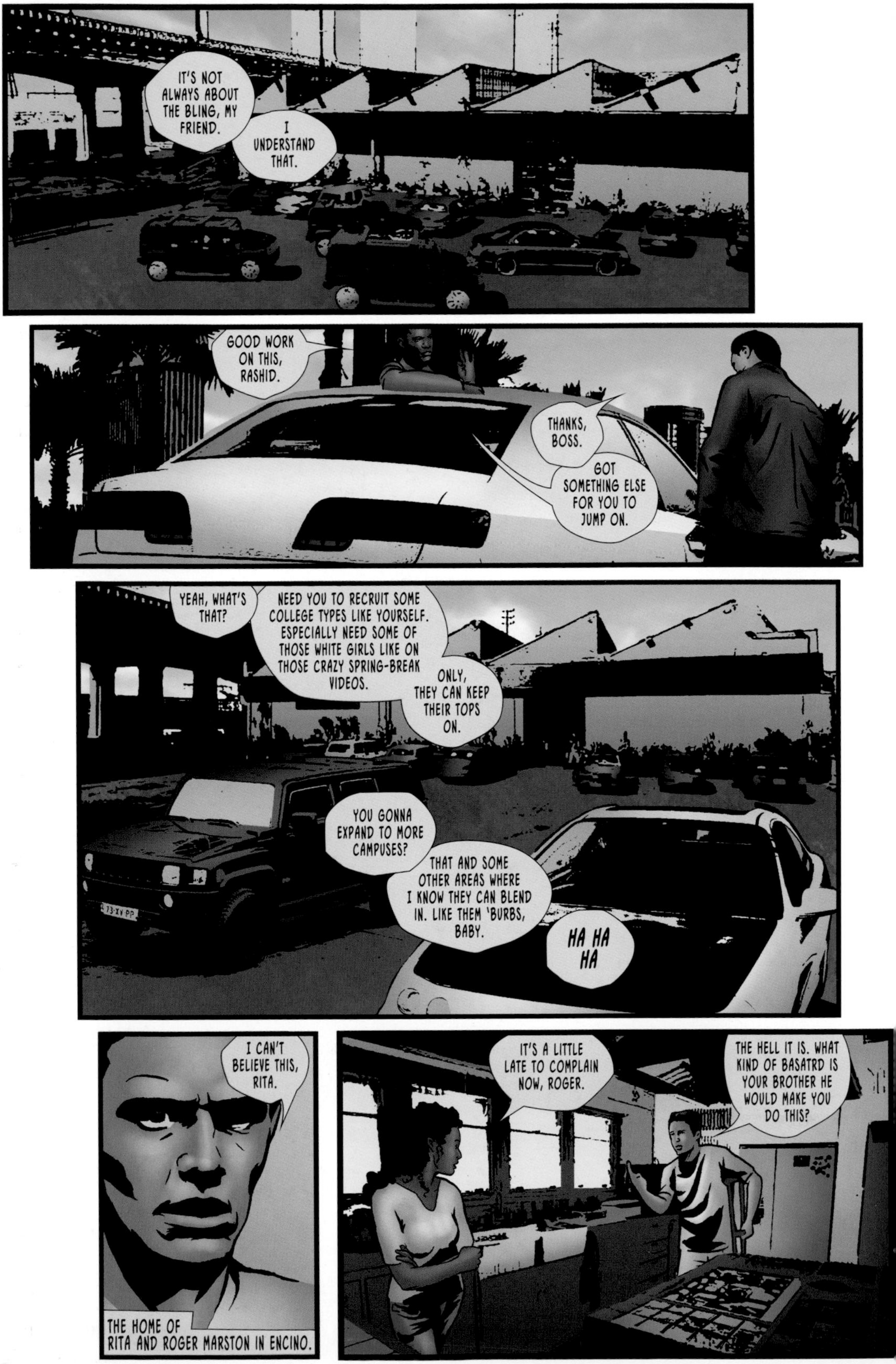
IT'S NOT ALWAYS ABOUT THE BLING, MY FRIEND.
I UNDERSTAND THAT.
GOOD WORK ON THIS, RASHID.
THANKS, BOSS.
GOT SOMETHING ELSE FOR YOU TO JUMP ON.
YEAH, WHAT'S THAT?
NEED YOU TO RECRUIT SOME COLLEGE TYPES LIKE YOURSELF. ESPECIALLY NEED SOME OF THOSE WHITE GIRLS LIKE ON THOSE CRAZY SPRING-BREAK VIDEOS.
ONLY, THEY CAN KEEP THEIR TOPS ON.
YOU GONNA EXPAND TO MORE CAMPUSES?
THAT AND SOME OTHER AREAS WHERE I KNOW THEY CAN BLEND IN. LIKE THEM 'BURBS, BABY.
HA HA HA
I CAN'T BELIEVE THIS, RITA.
THE HOME OF RITA AND ROGER MARSTON IN ENCINO.
IT'S A LITTLE LATE TO COMPLAIN NOW, ROGER.
THE HELL IT IS. WHAT KIND OF BASATRD IS YOUR BROTHER HE WOULD MAKE YOU DO THIS?

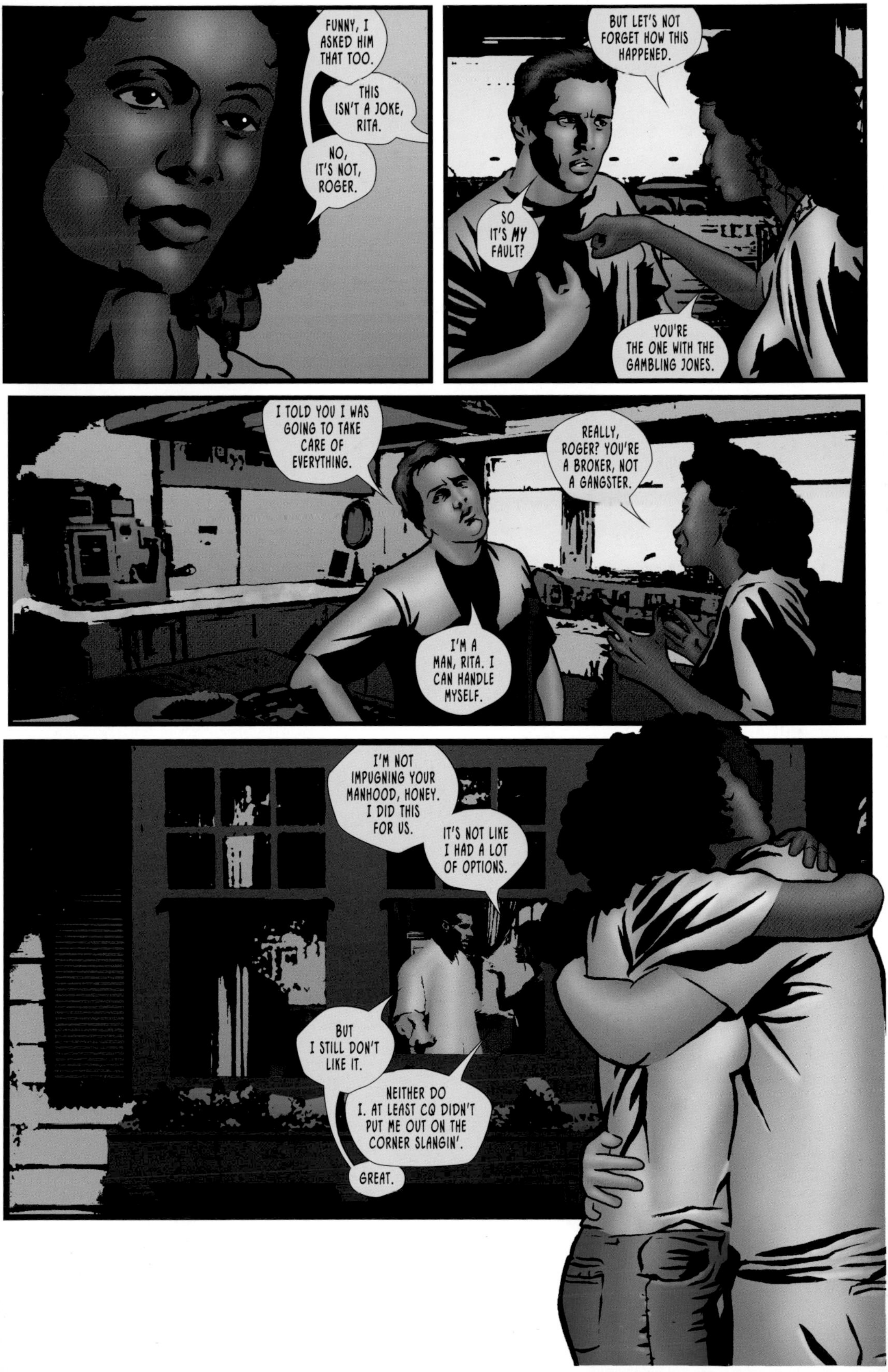
FUNNY, I ASKED HIM THAT TOO.
THIS ISN'T A JOKE, RITA.
NO, IT'S NOT, ROGER.
BUT LET'S NOT FORGET HOW THIS HAPPENED.
SO IT'S MY FAULT?
YOU'RE THE ONE WITH THE GAMBLING JONES.
I TOLD YOU I WAS GOING TO TAKE CARE OF EVERYTHING.
REALLY, ROGER? YOU'RE A BROKER, NOT A GANGSTER.
I'M A MAN, RITA. I CAN HANDLE MYSELF.
I'M NOT IMPUGNING YOUR MANHOOD, HONEY. I DID THIS FOR US.
IT'S NOT LIKE I HAD A LOT OF OPTIONS.
BUT I STILL DON'T LIKE IT.
NEITHER DO I. AT LEAST CQ DIDN'T PUT ME OUT ON THE CORNER SLANGIN'.
GREAT.

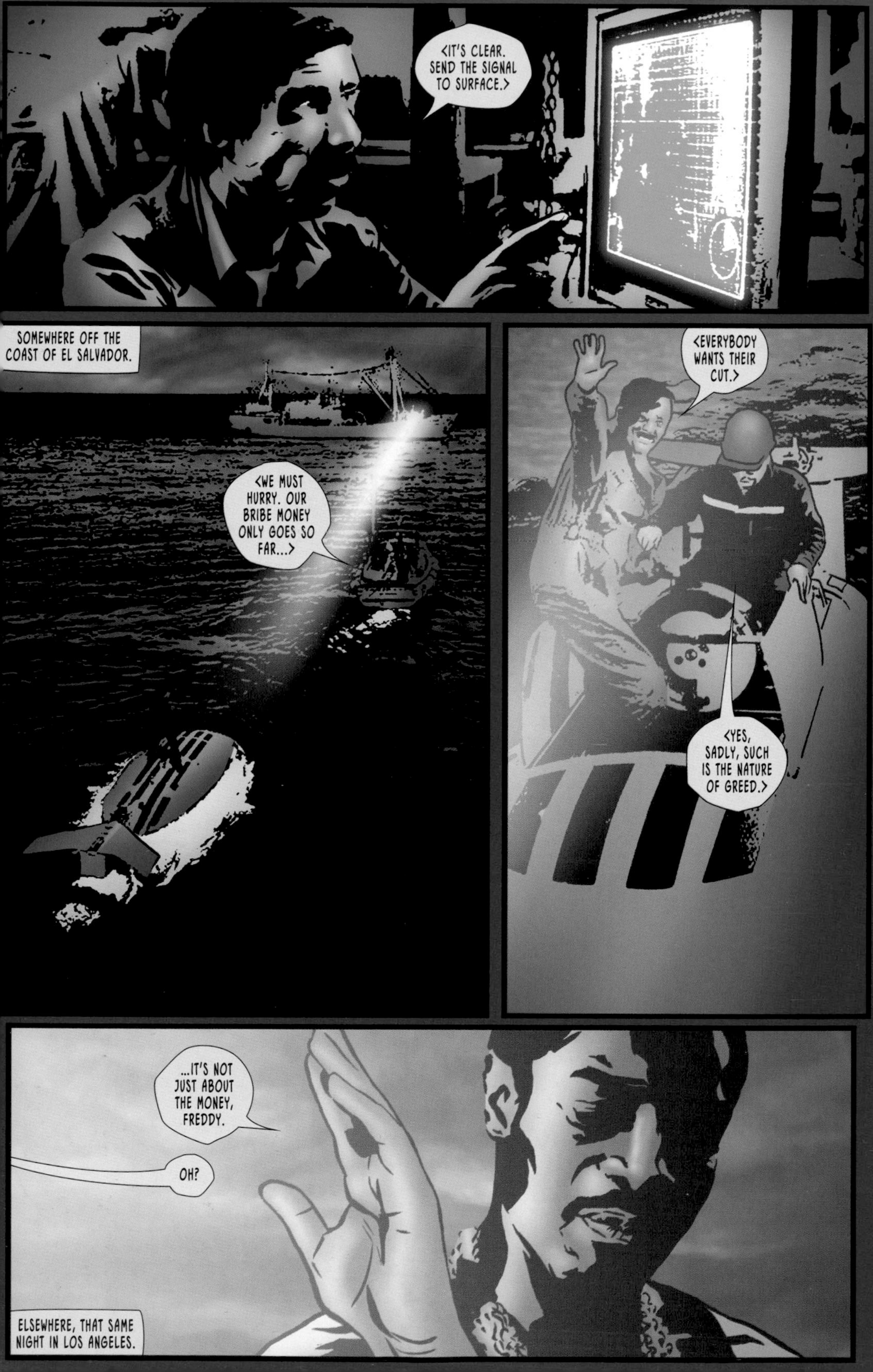
<IT'S CLEAR. SEND THE SIGNAL TO SURFACE.>
SOMEWHERE OFF THE COAST OF EL SALVADOR.
<WE MUST HURRY. OUR BRIBE MONEY ONLY GOES SO FAR...>
<EVERYBODY WANTS THEIR CUT.>
<YES, SADLY, SUCH IS THE NATURE OF GREED.>
...IT'S NOT JUST ABOUT THE MONEY, FREDDY.
OH?
ELSEWHERE, THAT SAME NIGHT IN LOS ANGELES.

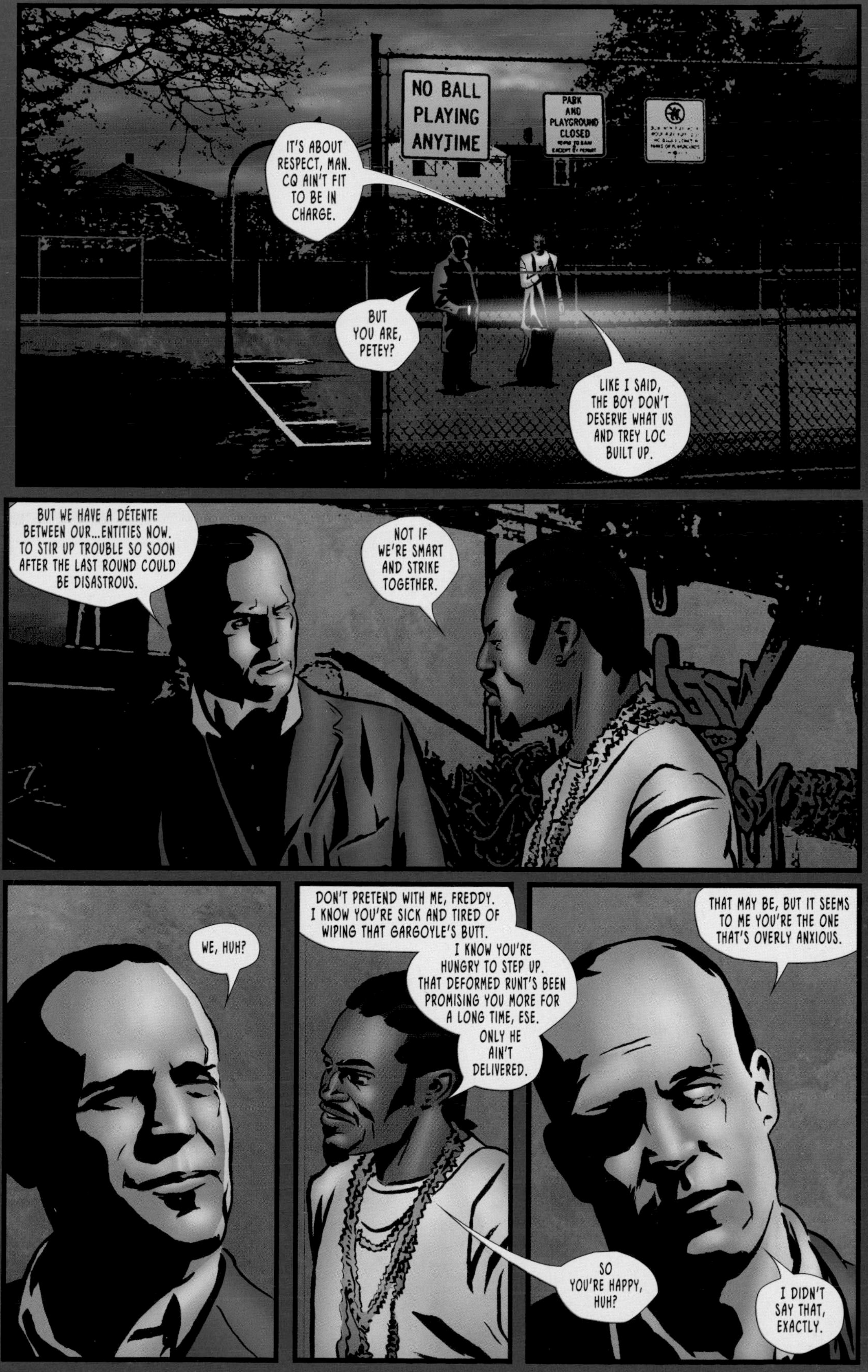
NO BALL PLAYING ANYTIME
PARK AND PLAYGROUND CLOSED
IT'S ABOUT RESPECT, MAN. CQ AIN'T FIT TO BE IN CHARGE.
BUT YOU ARE, PETEY?
LIKE I SAID, THE BOY DON'T DESERVE WHAT US AND TREY LOC BUILT UP.
BUT WE HAVE A DÉTENTE BETWEEN OUR...ENTITIES NOW. TO STIR UP TROUBLE SO SOON AFTER THE LAST ROUND COULD BE DISASTROUS.
NOT IF WE'RE SMART AND STRIKE TOGETHER.
WE, HUH?
DON'T PRETEND WITH ME, FREDDY. I KNOW YOU'RE SICK AND TIRED OF WIPING THAT GARGOYLE'S BUTT.
I KNOW YOU'RE HUNGRY TO STEP UP. THAT DEFORMED RUNT'S BEEN PROMISING YOU MORE FOR A LONG TIME, ESE.
ONLY HE AIN'T DELIVERED.
SO YOU'RE HAPPY, HUH?
THAT MAY BE, BUT IT SEEMS TO ME YOU'RE THE ONE THAT'S OVERLY ANXIOUS.
I DIDN'T SAY THAT, EXACTLY.

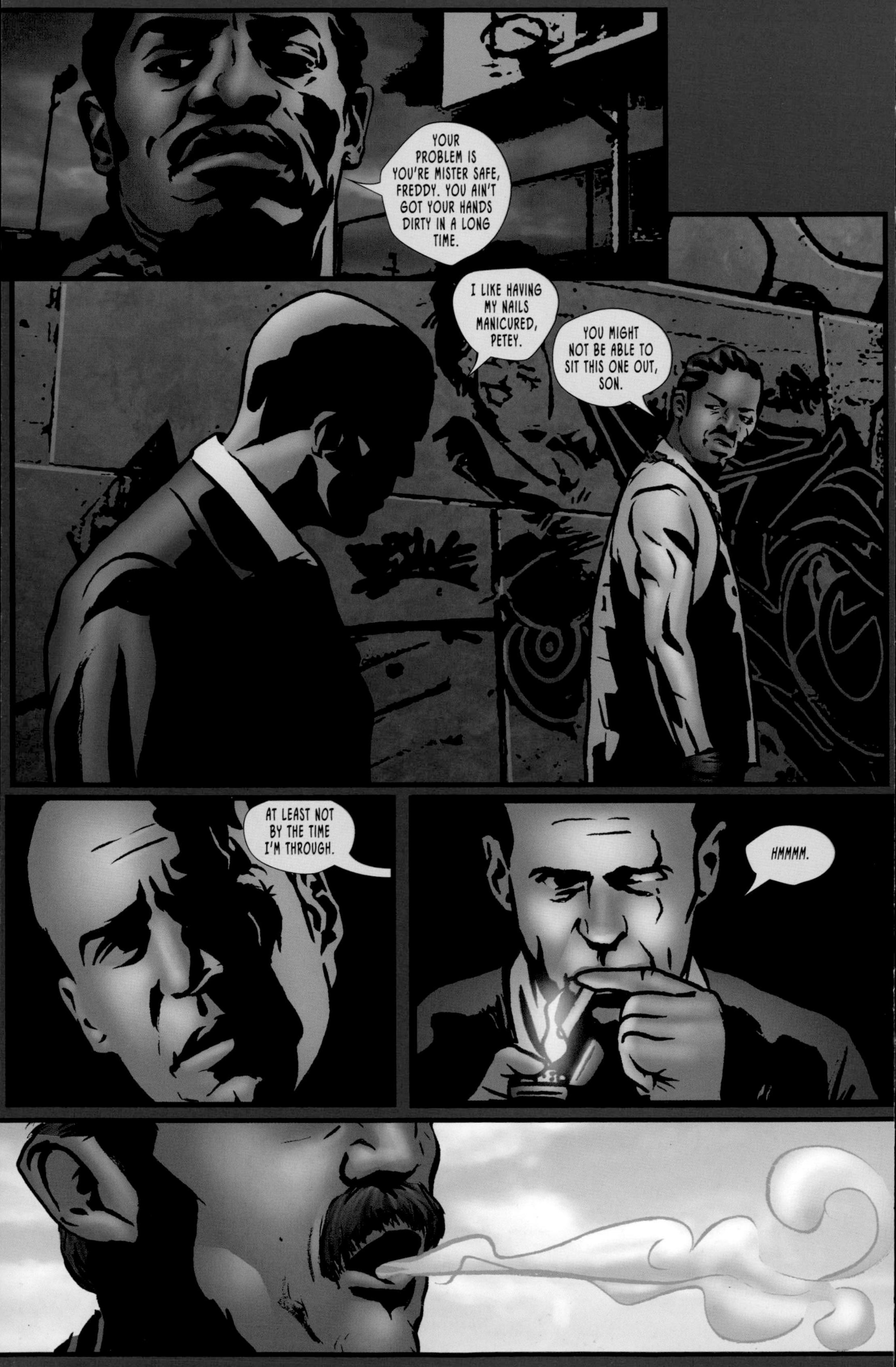
YOUR PROBLEM IS YOU'RE MISTER SAFE, FREDDY. YOU AIN'T GOT YOUR HANDS DIRTY IN A LONG TIME.
I LIKE HAVING MY NAILS MANICURED, PETEY.
YOU MIGHT NOT BE ABLE TO SIT THIS ONE OUT, SON.
AT LEAST NOT BY THE TIME I'M THROUGH.
HMMMM.

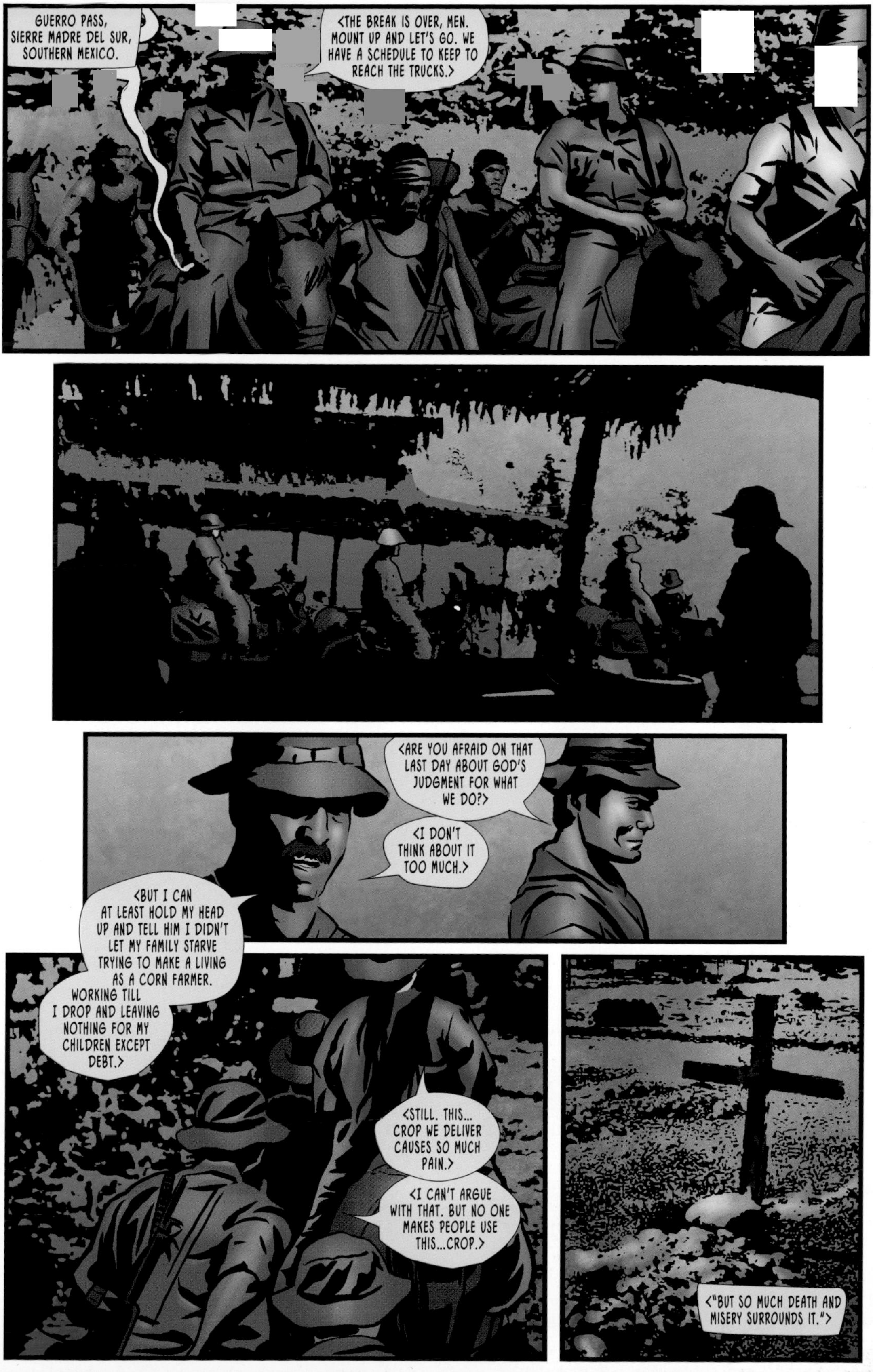
GUERRO PASS, SIERRE MADRE DEL SUR, SOUTHERN MEXICO.
<THE BREAK IS OVER, MEN. MOUNT UP AND LET'S GO. WE HAVE A SCHEDULE TO KEEP TO REACH THE TRUCKS.>
<ARE YOU AFRAID ON THAT LAST DAY ABOUT GOD'S JUDGMENT FOR WHAT WE DO?>
<I DON'T THINK ABOUT IT TOO MUCH.>
<BUT I CAN AT LEAST HOLD MY HEAD UP AND TELL HIM I DIDN'T LET MY FAMILY STARVE TRYING TO MAKE A LIVING AS A CORN FARMER.
WORKING TILL I DROP AND LEAVING NOTHING FOR MY CHILDREN EXCEPT DEBT.>
<STILL. THIS... CROP WE DELIVER CAUSES SO MUCH PAIN.>
<I CAN'T ARGUE WITH THAT. BUT NO ONE MAKES PEOPLE USE THIS...CROP.>
<"BUT SO MUCH DEATH AND MISERY SURROUNDS IT.">

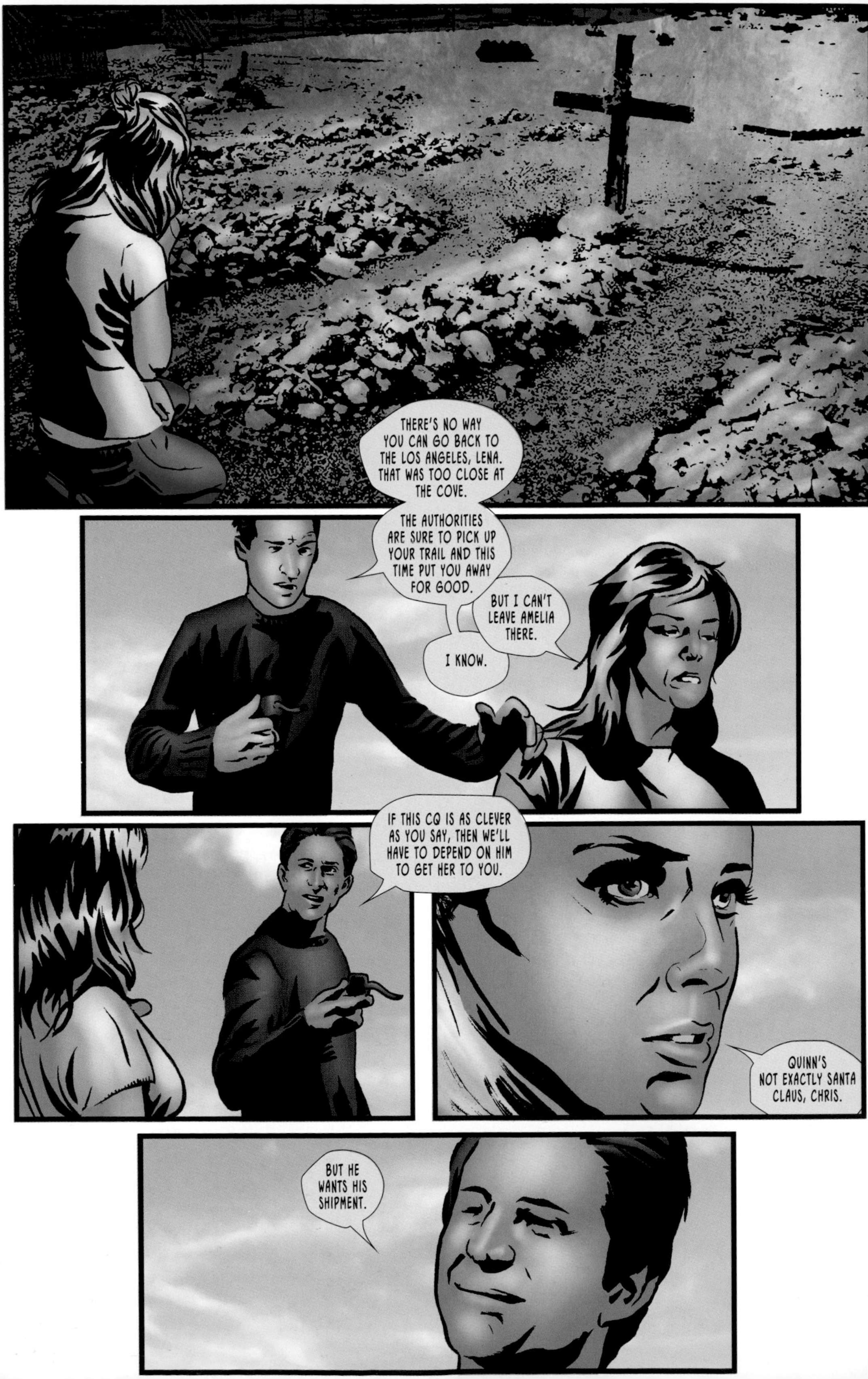
THERE'S NO WAY YOU CAN GO BACK TO THE LOS ANGELES, LENA. THAT WAS TOO CLOSE AT THE COVE.
THE AUTHORITIES ARE SURE TO PICK UP YOUR TRAIL AND THIS TIME PUT YOU AWAY FOR GOOD.
BUT I CAN'T LEAVE AMELIA THERE.
I KNOW.
IF THIS CQ IS AS CLEVER AS YOU SAY, THEN WE'LL HAVE TO DEPEND ON HIM TO GET HER TO YOU.
QUINN'S NOT EXACTLY SANTA CLAUS, CHRIS.
BUT HE WANTS HIS SHIPMENT.

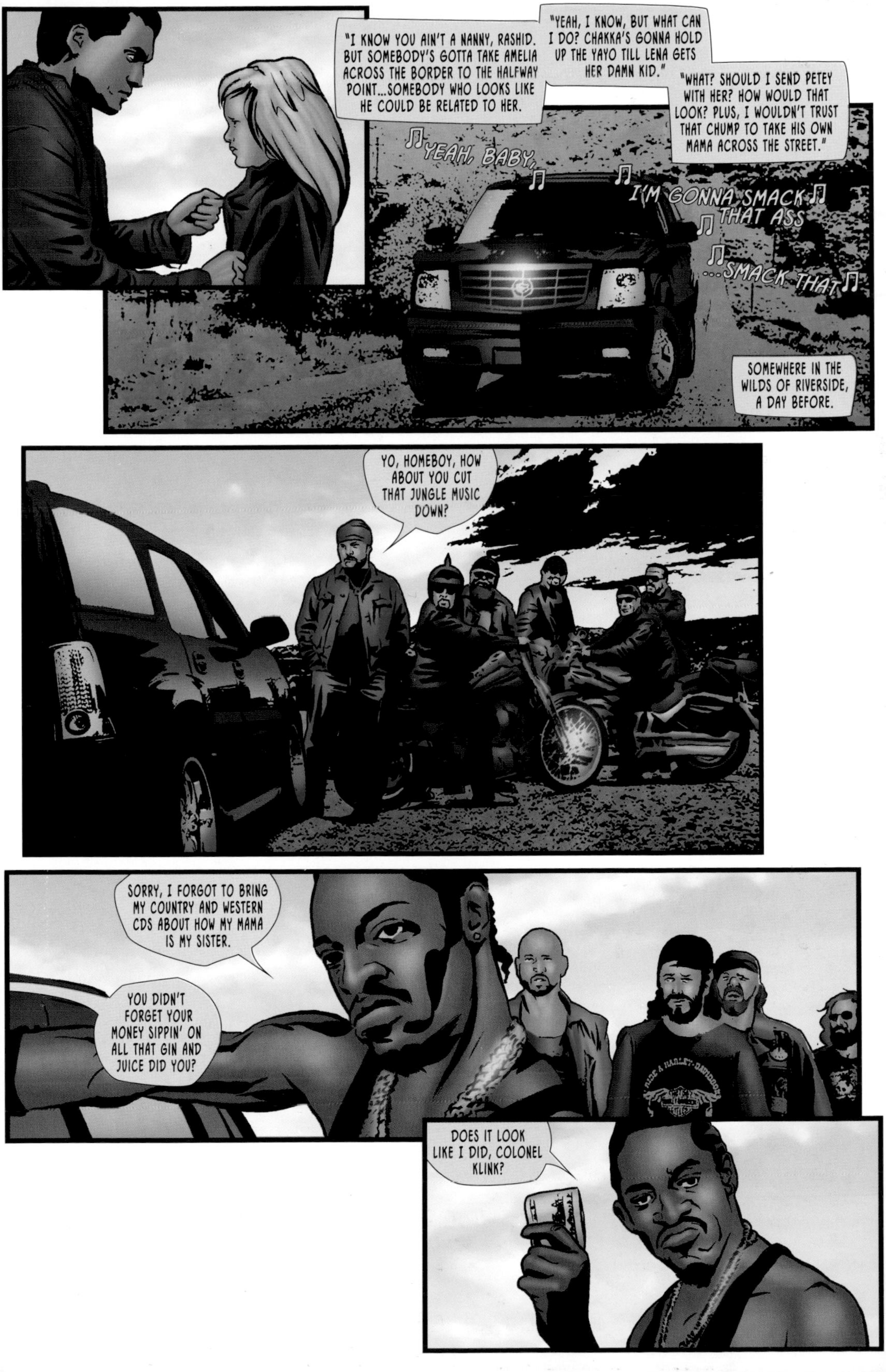
"I KNOW YOU AIN'T A NANNY, RASHID. BUT SOMEBODY'S GOTTA TAKE AMELIA ACROSS THE BORDER TO THE HALFWAY POINT...SOMEBODY WHO LOOKS LIKE HE COULD BE RELATED TO HER.
"YEAH, I KNOW, BUT WHAT CAN I DO? CHAKKA'S GONNA HOLD UP THE YAYO TILL LENA GETS HER DAMN KID."
"WHAT? SHOULD I SEND PETEY WITH HER? HOW WOULD THAT LOOK? PLUS, I WOULDN'T TRUST THAT CHUMP TO TAKE HIS OWN MAMA ACROSS THE STREET."
♫YEAH, BABY,♫
♫I'M GONNA SMACK♫
♫THAT ASS
♫...SMACK THAT♫
SOMEWHERE IN THE WILDS OF RIVERSIDE, A DAY BEFORE.
YO, HOMEBOY, HOW ABOUT YOU CUT THAT JUNGLE MUSIC DOWN?
SORRY, I FORGOT TO BRING MY COUNTRY AND WESTERN CDS ABOUT HOW MY MAMA IS MY SISTER.
YOU DIDN'T FORGET YOUR MONEY SIPPIN' ON ALL THAT GIN AND JUICE DID YOU?
DOES IT LOOK LIKE I DID, COLONEL KLINK?

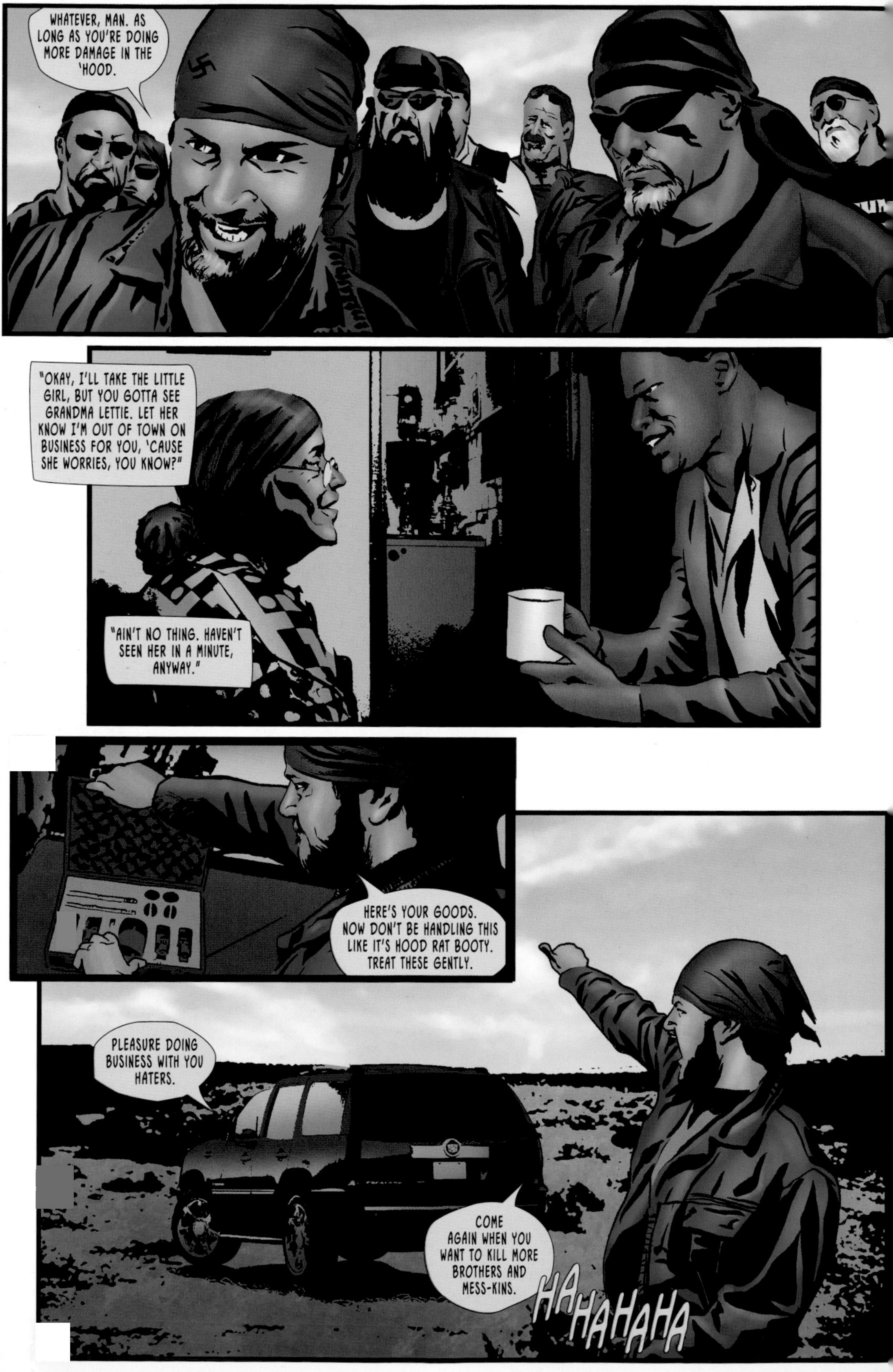
WHATEVER, MAN. AS LONG AS YOU'RE DOING MORE DAMAGE IN THE 'HOOD.
"OKAY, I'LL TAKE THE LITTLE GIRL, BUT YOU GOTTA SEE GRANDMA LETTIE. LET HER KNOW I'M OUT OF TOWN ON BUSINESS FOR YOU, 'CAUSE SHE WORRIES, YOU KNOW?"
"AIN'T NO THING. HAVEN'T SEEN HER IN A MINUTE, ANYWAY."
HERE'S YOUR GOODS. NOW DON'T BE HANDLING THIS LIKE IT'S HOOD RAT BOOTY. TREAT THESE GENTLY.
PLEASURE DOING BUSINESS WITH YOU HATERS.
COME AGAIN WHEN YOU WANT TO KILL MORE BROTHERS AND MESS-KINS.
HAHAHAHAHA

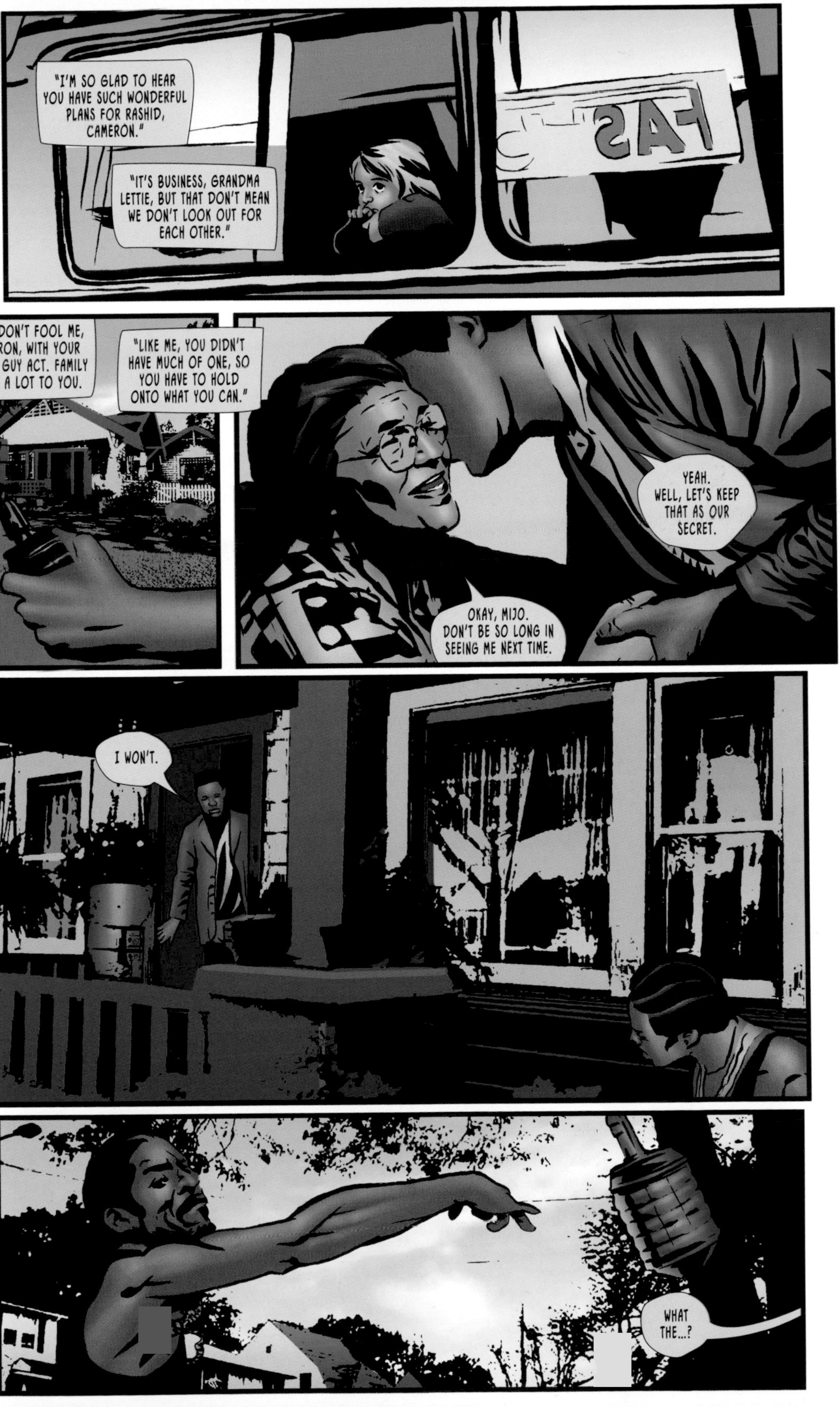
"I'M SO GLAD TO HEAR YOU HAVE SUCH WONDERFUL PLANS FOR RASHID, CAMERON."
"IT'S BUSINESS, GRANDMA LETTIE, BUT THAT DON'T MEAN WE DON'T LOOK OUT FOR EACH OTHER."
"YOU DON'T FOOL ME, CAMERON, WITH YOUR TOUGH GUY ACT. FAMILY MEANS A LOT TO YOU.
"LIKE ME, YOU DIDN'T HAVE MUCH OF ONE, SO YOU HAVE TO HOLD ONTO WHAT YOU CAN."
YEAH. WELL, LET'S KEEP THAT AS OUR SECRET.
OKAY, MIJO. DON'T BE SO LONG IN SEEING ME NEXT TIME.
I WON'T.
WHAT THE...?

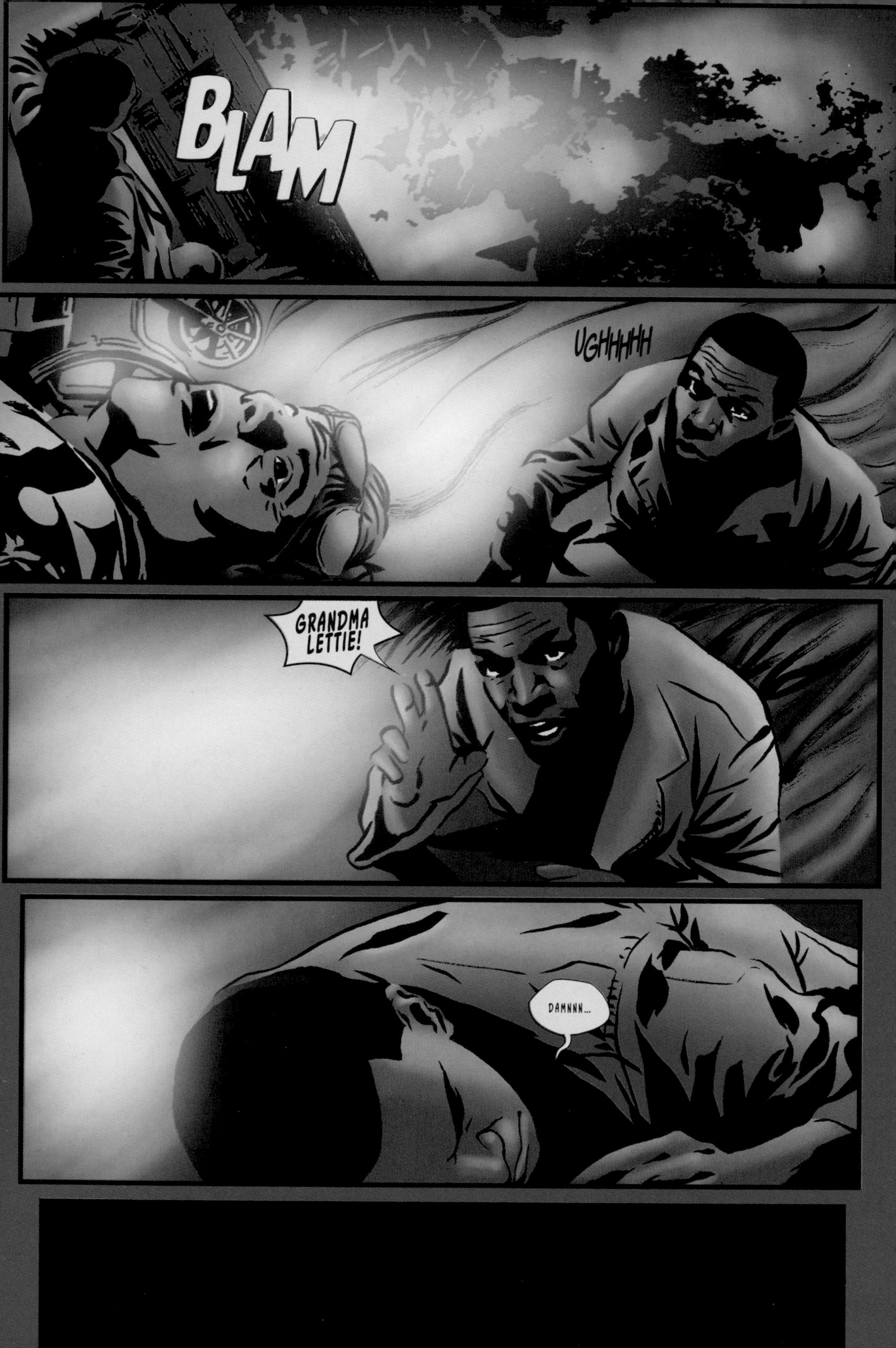
BLAM
UGHHHHH
GRANDMA LETTIE!
DAMNNN...

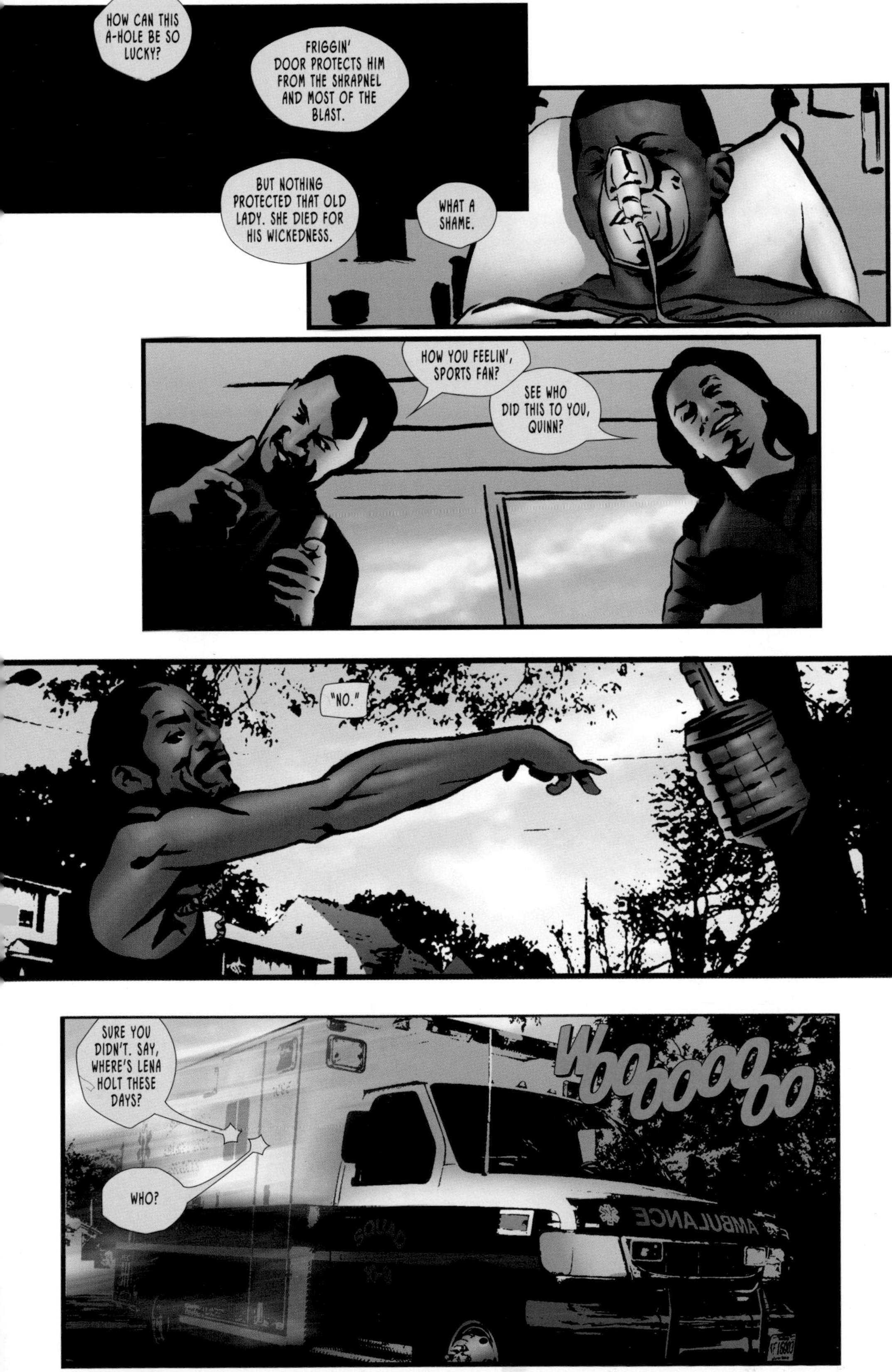
HOW CAN THIS A-HOLE BE SO LUCKY?
FRIGGIN' DOOR PROTECTS HIM FROM THE SHRAPNEL AND MOST OF THE BLAST.
BUT NOTHING PROTECTED THAT OLD LADY. SHE DIED FOR HIS WICKEDNESS.
WHAT A SHAME.
HOW YOU FEELIN', SPORTS FAN?
SEE WHO DID THIS TO YOU, QUINN?
"NO."
SURE YOU DIDN'T. SAY, WHERE'S LENA HOLT THESE DAYS?
WHO?
WOOOOOOO
AMBULANCE

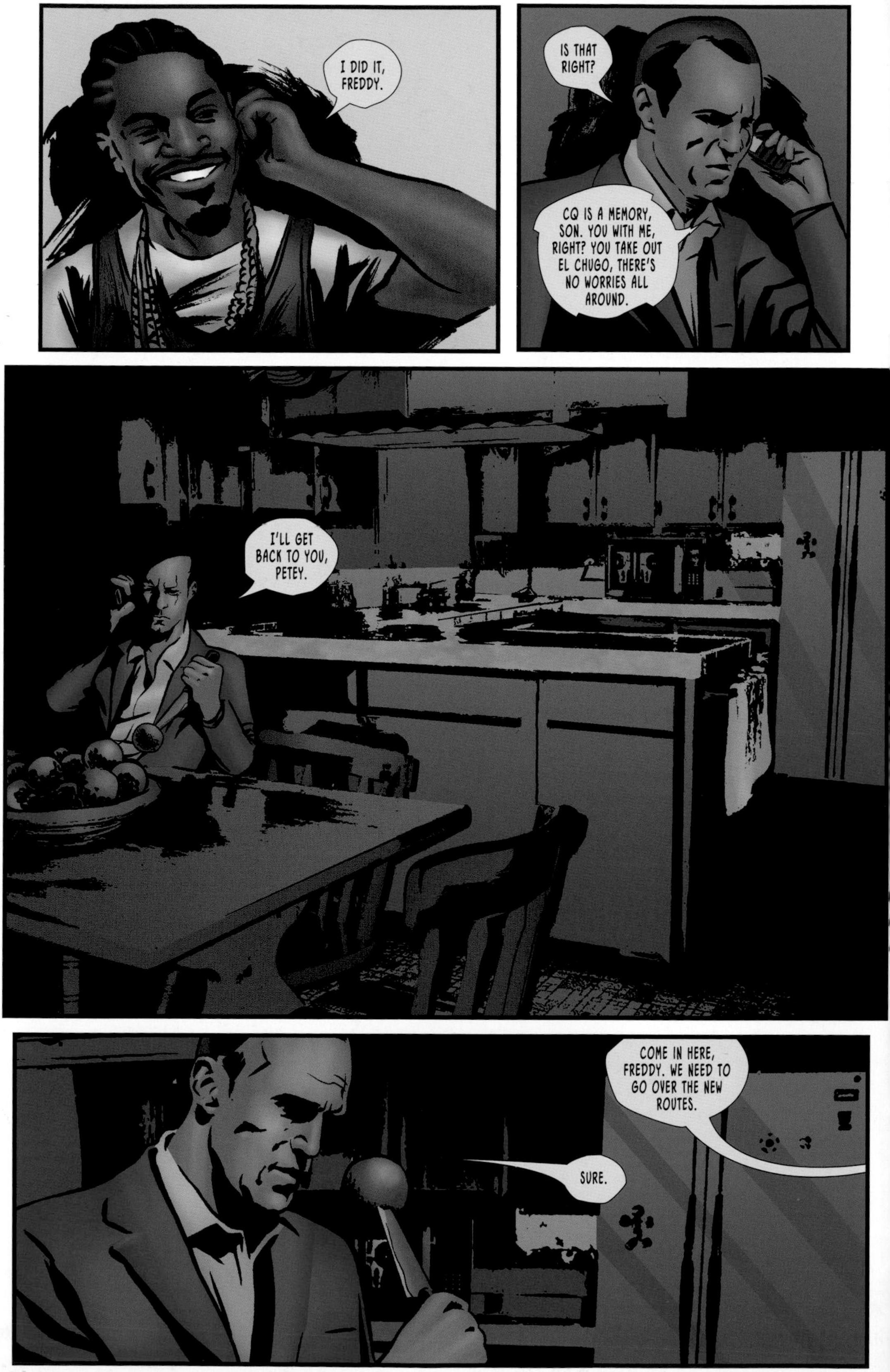
I DID IT, FREDDY.
IS THAT RIGHT?
CQ IS A MEMORY, SON. YOU WITH ME, RIGHT? YOU TAKE OUT EL CHUGO, THERE'S NO WORRIES ALL AROUND.
I'LL GET BACK TO YOU, PETEY.
COME IN HERE, FREDDY. WE NEED TO GO OVER THE NEW ROUTES.
SURE.

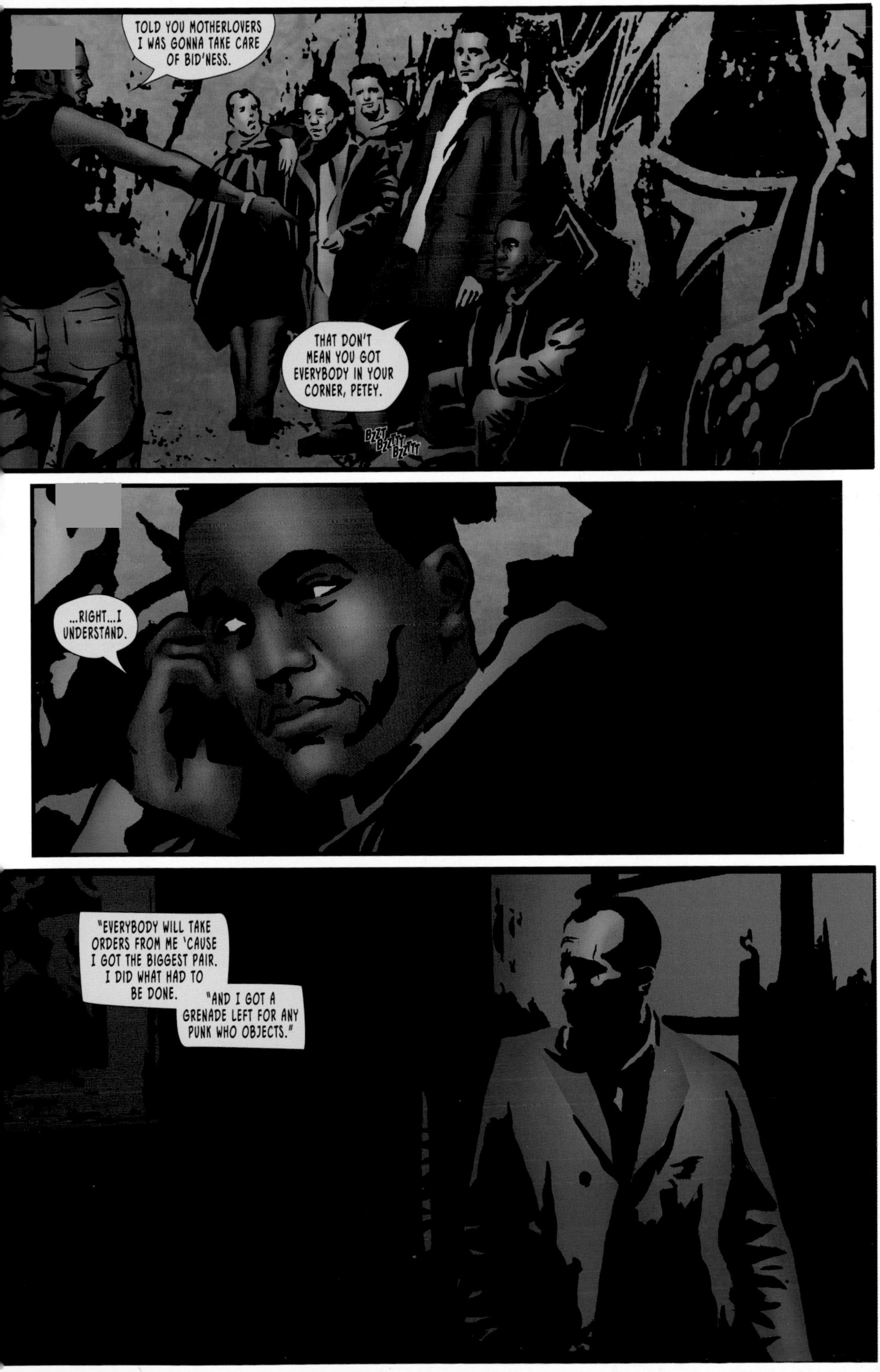
TOLD YOU MOTHERLOVERS I WAS GONNA TAKE CARE OF BID'NESS.
THAT DON'T MEAN YOU GOT EVERYBODY IN YOUR CORNER, PETEY.
BZZT BZZTTT BZZTTT
...RIGHT...I UNDERSTAND.
"EVERYBODY WILL TAKE ORDERS FROM ME 'CAUSE I GOT THE BIGGEST PAIR. I DID WHAT HAD TO BE DONE.
"AND I GOT A GRENADE LEFT FOR ANY PUNK WHO OBJECTS."

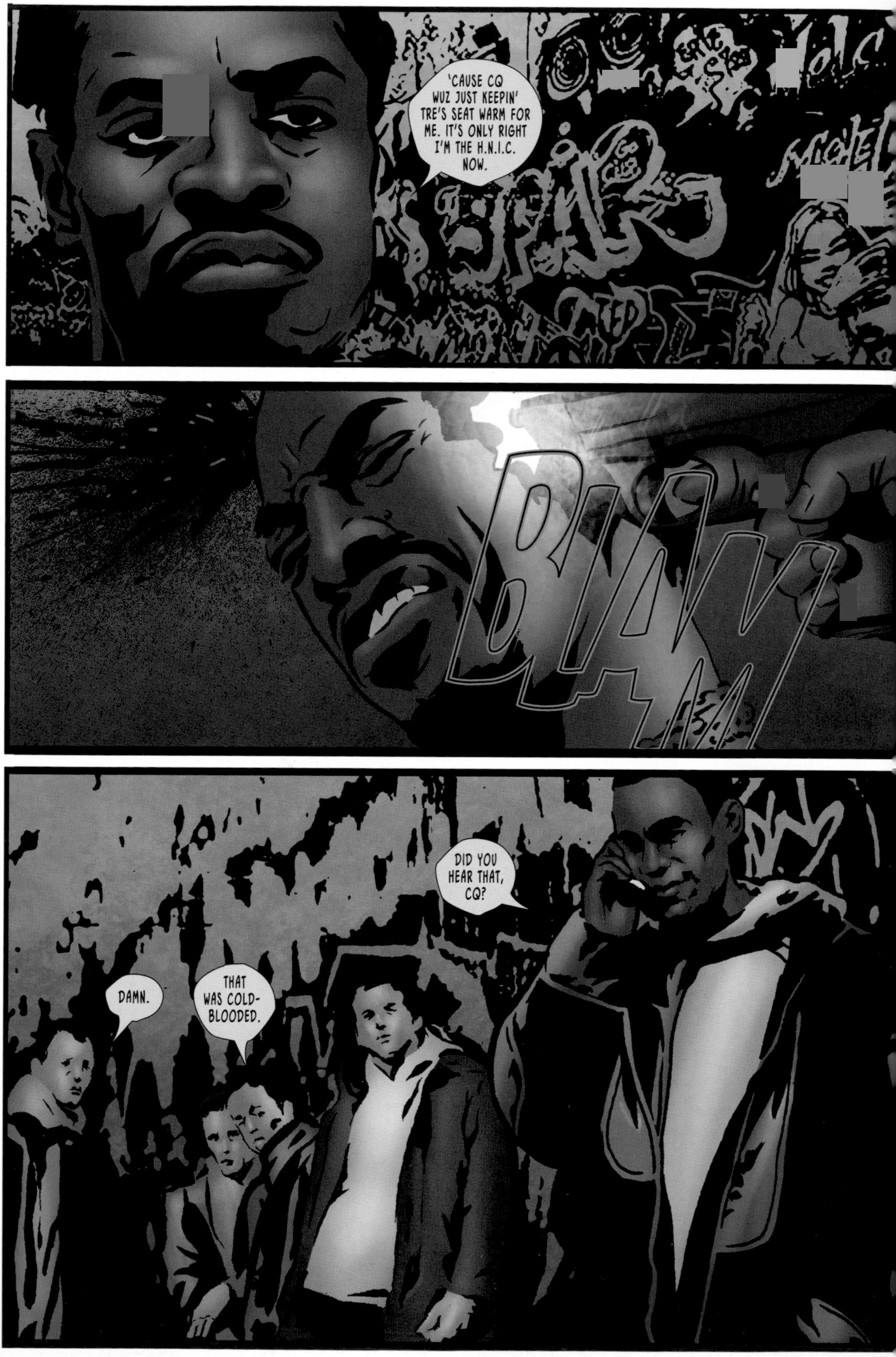
'CAUSE CQ WUZ JUST KEEPIN' TRE'S SEAT WARM FOR ME. IT'S ONLY RIGHT I'M THE H.N.I.C. NOW.
BLAM
DID YOU HEAR THAT, CQ?
DAMN.
THAT WAS COLD-BLOODED.

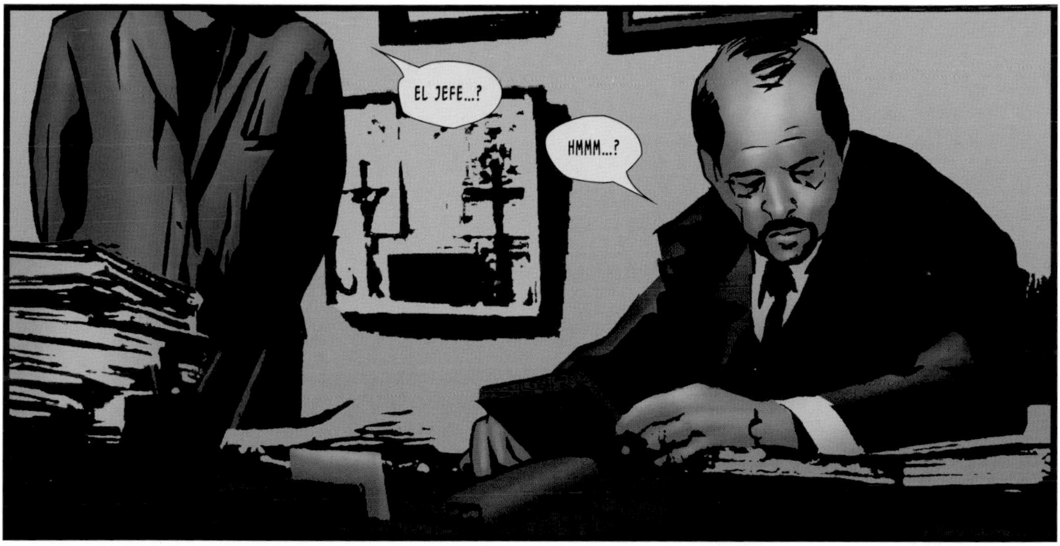
EL JEFE...?
HMMM...?

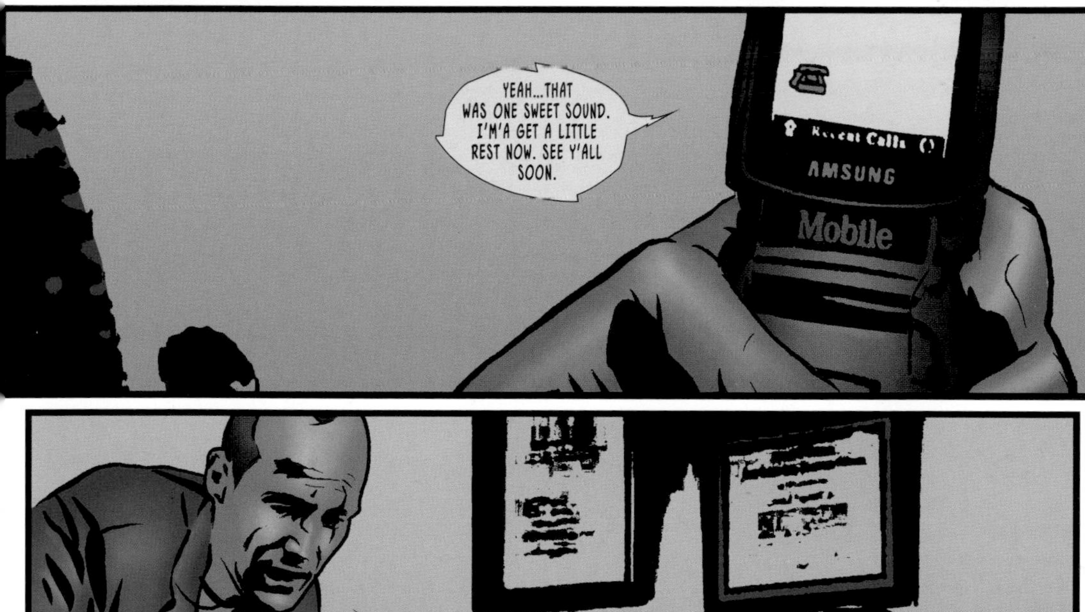
YEAH...THAT WAS ONE SWEET SOUND. I'M'A GET A LITTLE REST NOW. SEE Y'ALL SOON.
AMSUNG
Mobile

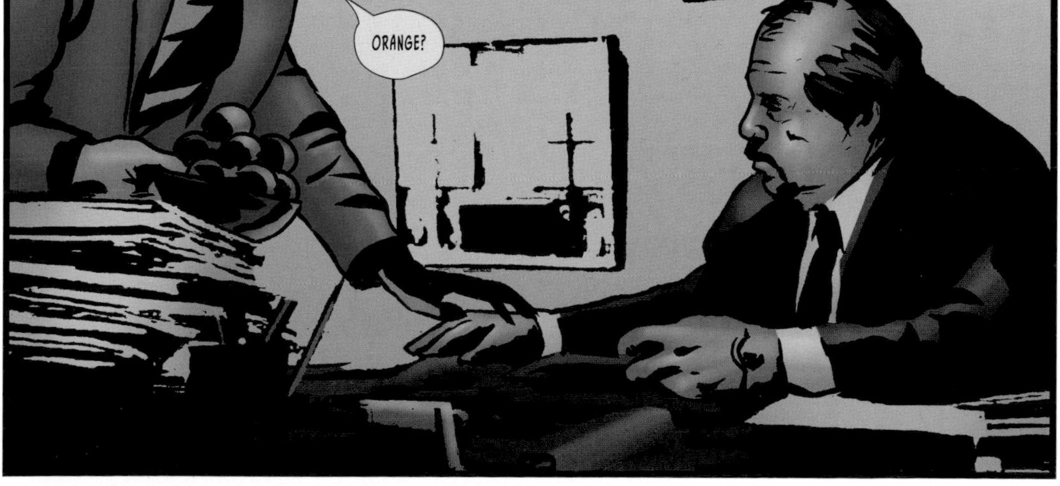
ORANGE?

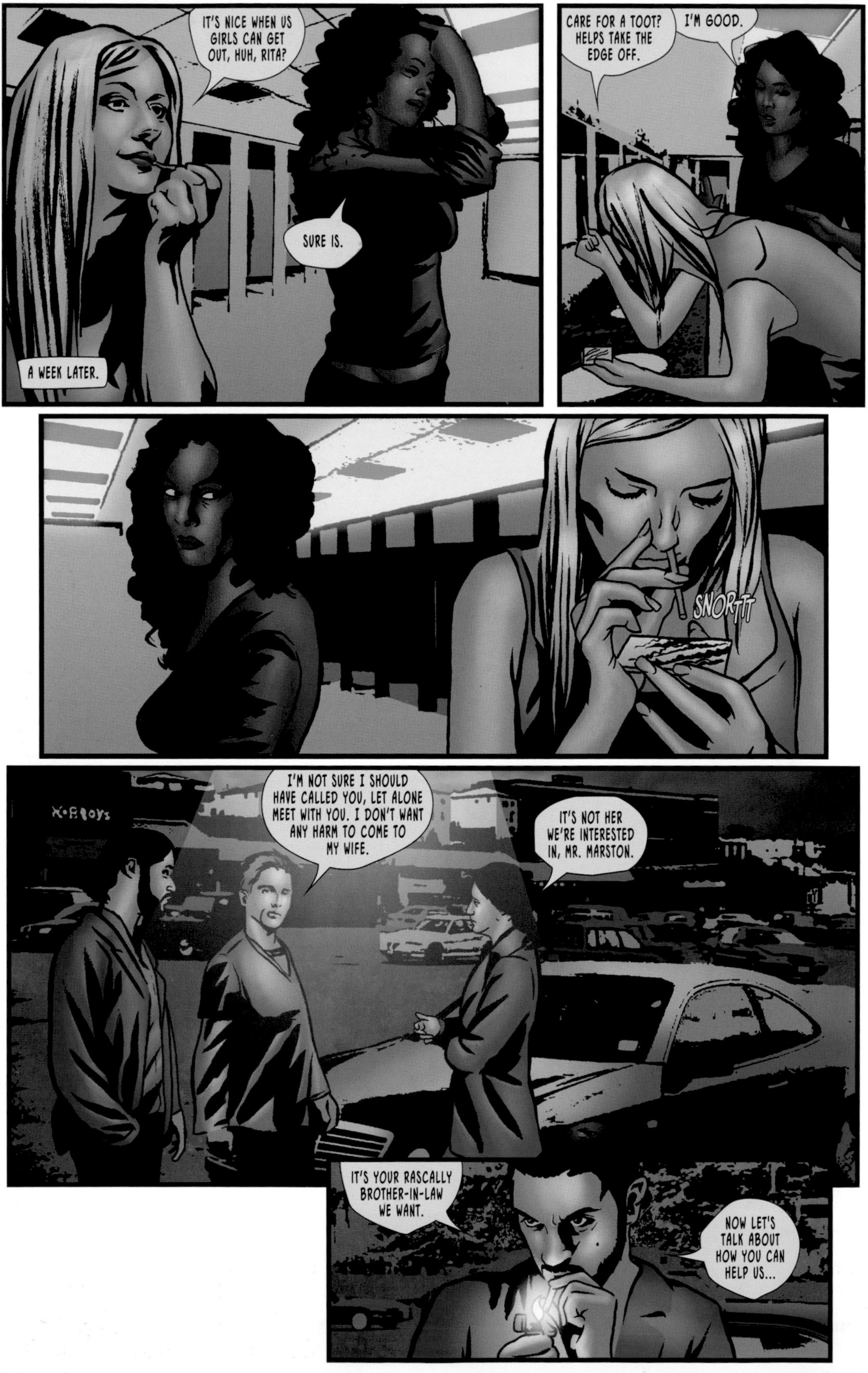
IT'S NICE WHEN US GIRLS CAN GET OUT, HUH, RITA?
SURE IS.
A WEEK LATER.
CARE FOR A TOOT? HELPS TAKE THE EDGE OFF.
I'M GOOD.
SNORTTT
I'M NOT SURE I SHOULD HAVE CALLED YOU, LET ALONE MEET WITH YOU. I DON'T WANT ANY HARM TO COME TO MY WIFE.
IT'S NOT HER WE'RE INTERESTED IN, MR. MARSTON.
IT'S YOUR RASCALLY BROTHER-IN-LAW WE WANT.
NOW LET'S TALK ABOUT HOW YOU CAN HELP US...

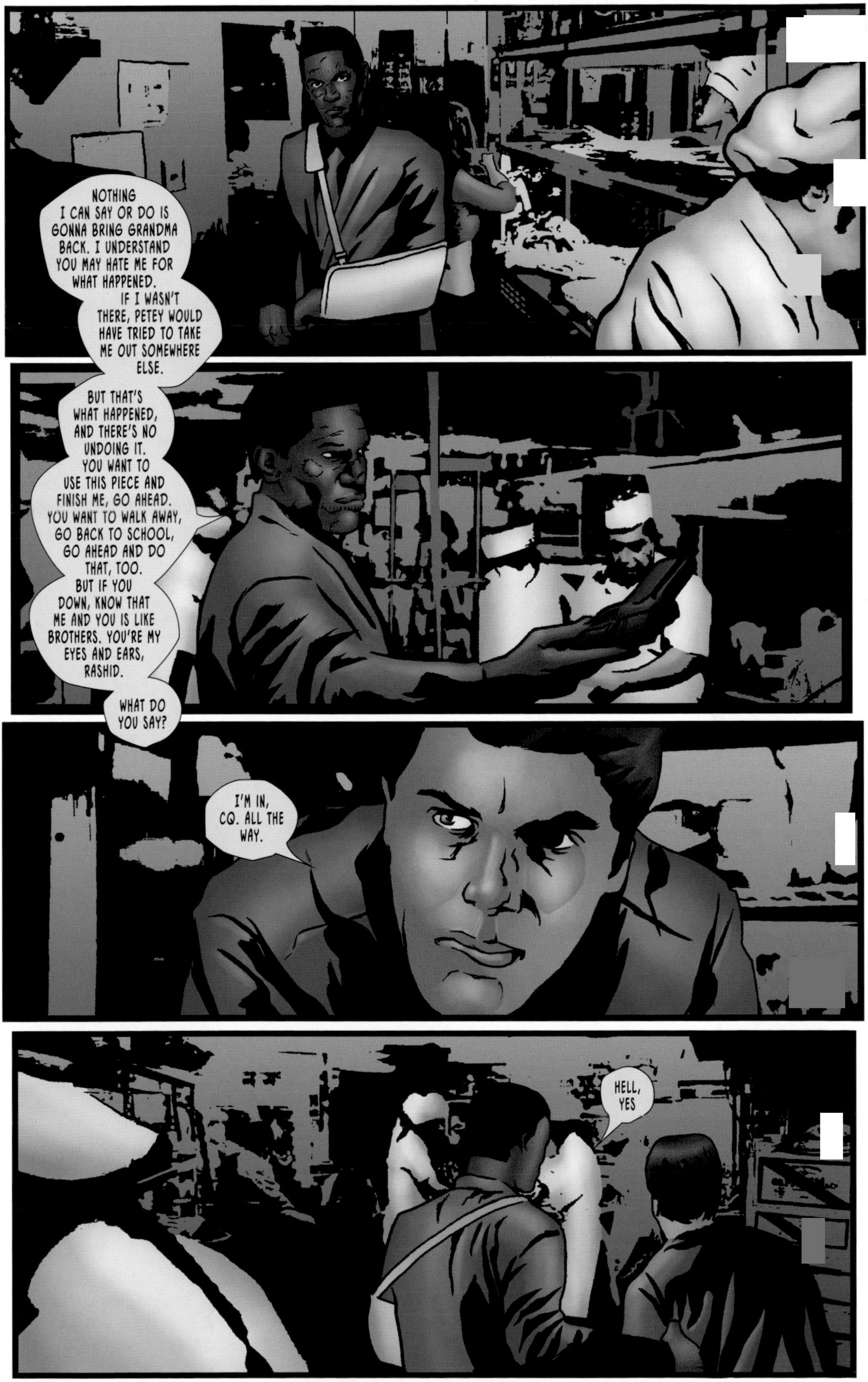
NOTHING I CAN SAY OR DO IS GONNA BRING GRANDMA BACK. I UNDERSTAND YOU MAY HATE ME FOR WHAT HAPPENED.
IF I WASN'T THERE, PETEY WOULD HAVE TRIED TO TAKE ME OUT SOMEWHERE ELSE.
BUT THAT'S WHAT HAPPENED, AND THERE'S NO UNDOING IT. YOU WANT TO USE THIS PIECE AND FINISH ME, GO AHEAD. YOU WANT TO WALK AWAY, GO BACK TO SCHOOL, GO AHEAD AND DO THAT, TOO. BUT IF YOU DOWN, KNOW THAT ME AND YOU IS LIKE BROTHERS. YOU'RE MY EYES AND EARS, RASHID.
WHAT DO YOU SAY?
I'M IN, CQ. ALL THE WAY.
HELL, YES

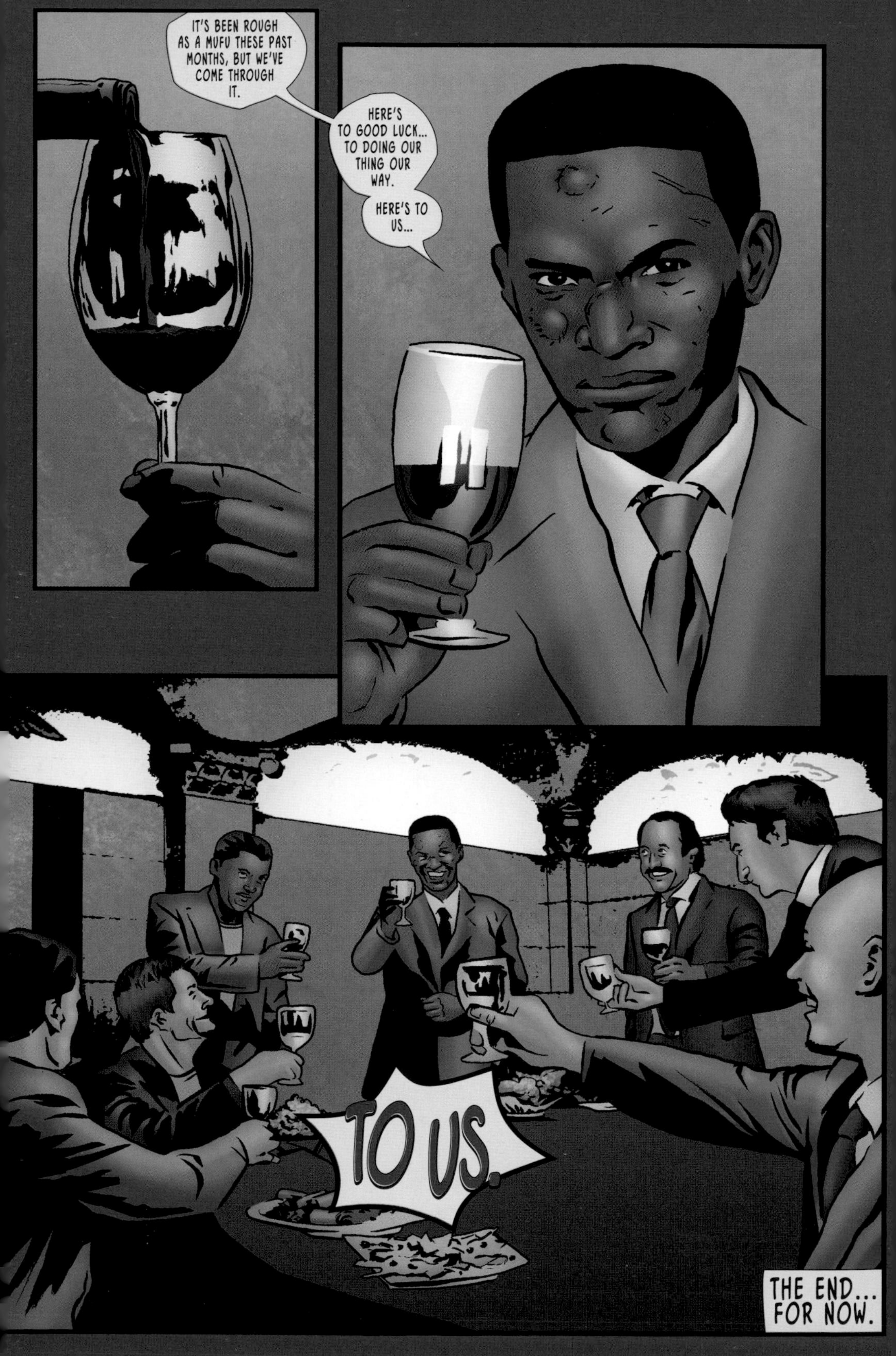
IT'S BEEN ROUGH AS A MUFU THESE PAST MONTHS, BUT WE'VE COME THROUGH IT.
HERE'S TO GOOD LUCK... TO DOING OUR THING OUR WAY.
HERE'S TO US...
TO US.
THE END... FOR NOW.

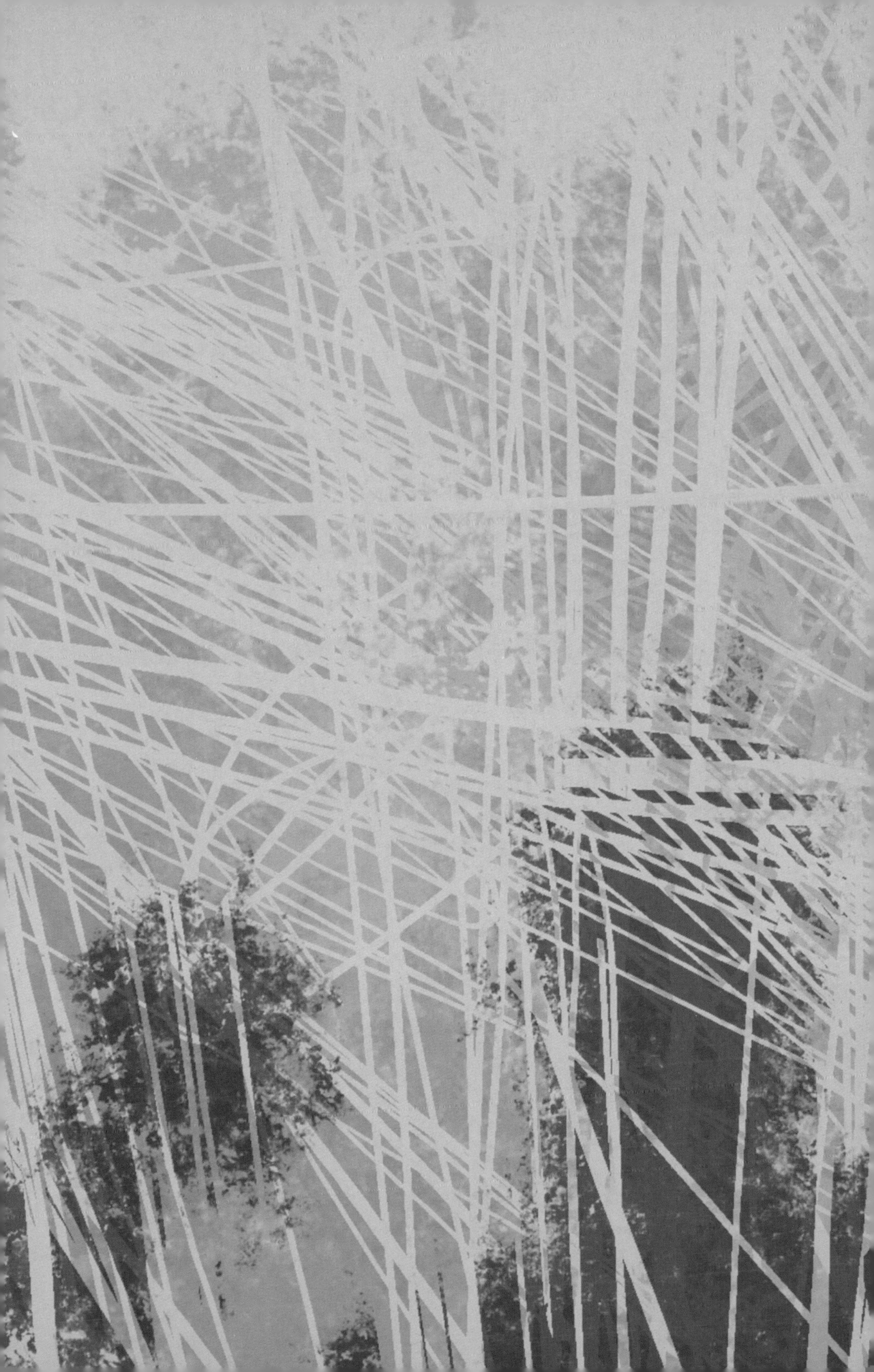

GREG RUCKA INTERVIEWS GARY PHILLIPS ABOUT HIGH ROLLERS

Gary Phillips has the distinction of being the only crime writer I've ever seen my dad get excited over. Considering that I'm a crime writer that'd be hard to take but considering it's Gary, it's forgivable.

The thing about Gary Phillips is that he's one of the biggest secrets going in two industries at once. In the world of crime novels he is known, loved, respected, and cherished for his noir style, prose so clean and sharp you can give yourself a bleeder just reading it. So hard-boiled, the yolk has turned green. In comics, he has delivered the same laser-focused fearlessness, taking his stories into uncharted terrain, effortlessly flipping over rocks that truly have been hiding the scum-of-the-earth beneath. And when you first meet Gary, you have no doubt that he can handle, personally, any-damn-thing that might come out from beneath said rock, looking for a fight.

Crime fiction isn't simply fiction about dropping bodies and stealing cash. At its heart, crime fiction is social activism, a way of focusing a lens on those elements of a flawed society that the rest of us would sleep much better ignoring. Crime fiction points to what is wrong and, while enticing you with its corruption, forces you to ask why it is the way it is and what can and should we do to repair the damage. At its best, crime fiction is societal redemption.

Gary Phillips is its best.

Which brings us to HIGH ROLLERS, and me, in Portland on a Sunday afternoon in April, sitting at my laptop and trying to think up questions to email to Gary. To be perfectly honest, I'd have much preferred to do this with a tape recorder and a couple of beers, but you take what you can get.

So, here you go. Greg Rucka interviewing Gary Phillips about HIGH ROLLERS:

Greg Rucka: I want to start off with a totally unrelated question. Think of this as me producing my bona fides, proof that I actually do know you and that this isn't all dog-and-pony

Why do you call me "Doc"?

Gary Phillips: Well of course you're the Doctor of the Word, but that's self-evident to anyone who'd read your comics or prose work. More to the point, Doc is one of those terms of, I won't say affection 'cause you know, we're both mas macho, but a term that arises from the 'hood. That is one guy might call another guy he knows and digs "Chief," "Doc," "Boss," "Homes"…in that vein.

GR: You realize you're the only person ever to give me 'hood cred. But that's a good segue into HIGH ROLLERS, actually. Let's talk about the series, here, first with an overview.

GP: HIGH ROLLERS is about the dark pursuit of the American Dream. It's the quintessential gangster story whose roots lie in works like W. R. Burnett's LITTLE CAESAR to THE SOPRANOS, though I hope with original flourishes. Our main character is Cameron Quinn, CQ, a rough and tumble chap who when we first meet him is an enforcer for a drug lord. But CQ is an ambitious lad, and is practicing his own brand of enlightenment; downloading audios of self-help business books to the WAY OF THE SAMURAI. He's going places and there's bound to be a few bodies strewn about on his road to success.

I should note too CQ is very much in that anti-hero mold. The balancing act is to give you a cat who is capable of bad, bad things, yet not so reprehensible that you as the reader aren't compelled to see what happens next with this complex, driven character.

GR: It's funny, because so often crime stories are short-handed as "morality tales." While you're certainly a moral writer, you've never been one to moralize. Given what you've said about CQ, how much a part do concepts like morality and ethics play in HIGH ROLLERS? And with that, I suppose, comes the question of companion concepts, like loyalty and honor.

GP: For me when you write the crime story, as distinct from a mystery story, morality is not left at the door so much as you present these characters, desperate in some form or another, wanting something, and leave it to the reader to make of them what you will. Often in a story about criminals, matters are relative, you compare and contrast one rough character against another. In a mystery story, generally speaking, our protagonist may be flawed but is more clearly delineated by his or her actions and their pursuit of justice against the criminals or the ones who have done a criminal act.

That's not to say within the crime story, innocents, civilians, aren't sometimes corrupted or unwillingly drawn into the criminals' orbit. This happens in HIGH ROLLERS in the nature of the complex relationship between CQ and his sister who has left the 'hood far behind – or so she hoped.

So in HIGH ROLLERS, while CQ is no choirboy, it becomes clear what he will and will not do. There is a code, albeit a bent and distorted one, that he adheres to in the course of events. And as you say, this then does get us to matters such as loyalty and honor. Groups embrace these ideals in the operation and functioning of that group. The police are often cited as being the Thin Blue Line, that line of defense that separates the civilized, law-abiding world from those who would invade and disrupt that order. We also know that sometimes loyalty and honor can be bent, as say when a cop looses control and there's a questionable shooting of a suspect. The cops might close ranks, take on a "us" versus "them" mentality as that incident is investigated.

CQ then embraces what he interprets as loyalty and honor, while he engages in building his criminal enterprise. This then brings him into contact with another pivotal character who is a criminal, but is guided by a higher ideal. I'm not looking to make excuses for these various players in the story, but hopefully present them in a dimensional way. How there is sometimes a collusion of interests and at other times, adversarial points of view. But characters who if you asked them, would tell you they believe in certain kinds of loyalty and honor.

GR: Whenever I read your stuff, I'm always struck by its verisimilitude. What kind of research went into the series?

GP: Like I'm sure you do, I read a lot of stuff, errant stuff, from articles in the NEW YORKER about the history of elevators to nanobots in WIRED, to political pieces in THE NATION. And TV, man, I'm a TV junkie. Just recently watched this great doc on PBS called KING CORN about how the homogenization of the one kind of corn we now grow in America winds up in us in inordinate amounts given this corn is mostly used for cattle feed and corn syrup. That these kernels are damn near all starch, little nutrients, as opposed to original corn, from Mexico, say, not even 60 years ago, was mostly protein. And this has health consequences. Family farms are being bought out, and so on.

Now shades of Obama's supposed elitist statements in San Francisco on the campaign trail, I'm not some brie eatin', designer water lovin' elitist. Ha. I'm hooked on LOST, and when they were younger, took my kids to their share of monster truck rallies.

I mean I might not ever do anything with that corn information, but that sort of thing gets you to thinking about something else, right?

Plus I know a few cops, a deputy (we call them that in L.A., not assistant) DA or two, play poker with a couple of criminal defense attorneys...I guess what I'm saying is as a writer, whether you're writing about crime and mystery, superhero stories, westerns, sci-fi, what have you, you want to absorb data and information from various sources.

The internet is a wonderful tool but nothing is better that reading it in a book, which at least has had some amount of vetting, and nothing beats anecdotal stories from people who are in that profession be it the uniformed cop, the steelworker, the social worker, etc.

GR: Explain the significance of SCARFACE on CQ.

GP: Both versions of SCARFACE are in my head as well as the other books and movies I referenced, as well as THE GODFATHER for that matter. What I'm really saying is the crime story is that funhouse warped mirror image of the American success story. "What Makes CQ Run" to paraphrase Budd Schulberg.

GR: Do you think the crime story is part of the American Dream, in that sense? All those examples we have in the pop culture, they're all in pursuit of the same things, it seems. What is it that CQ really wants? Does he even know?

GP: The crime story, particularly the modern crime story as it emerged in the late '20s as the Great Depression came on, is said to be the flip side of the pursuit of the American Dream. That is these are men and women who seek money, a certain station in life, power…influence even, but lack the tools, the sophistication and/or the wherewithal, to achieve it by say, being a captain of industry, pioneering doctor and so on.

But as Woody Guthrie sang in "Pretty Boy Floyd" of those times – and applicable now in the era of Bernard Madoff's grand thievery and post the white-collar rip offs of hard-working folks' monies and seniors of their life savings, that went on with such companies as Enron and WorldCom – "…some will rob you with a six-gun and some will rob you with a pen."

So yes, CQ's methods are not as refined shall we say as those corporate swindlers but he's after what he thinks is the ultimate, using his crude methods. But it so happens he's in an underground enterprise and a certain amount of violence is called for. But because he has a vision of being legit too, he's also keeping his mind on what's good for business. And like "Pretty Boy Floyd", there are conflicting tendencies in CQ. We see him as the ruthless enforcer, but also being thoughtful and not just thinking about himself.

So like a lot of guys blinded by the bling, initially CQ thinks what he wants is to run things. But even within this initial story arc, there'll be inklings that CQ will ask himself "is this all there is?"

GR: The pages I've seen look amazing. Where'd you find Sergio Carrera and what is it like working with him?

GP: That's the deft touch of my editor, Mark Waid. He found Sergio Carrera and brought him on board. Sergio is one hell of a draftsman. The way he handles body language, facial expressions…I just hope my script is up to his art!

GR: You guys seem to be working together very well, from what I've seen. You mentioned Mark there, and having worked with him on 52 and other things, I've gotten to know him pretty well. One of the things I discovered about him is that he is, I think, an excellent teacher, whether he knows it or not. What's the working relationship with him like?

GP: What I like in working with Mark is his notes and suggestions are clear to me. If we have points of disagreements we both can discuss those and arrive at a good compromise. Really, coming from the prose realm, I imagine people looking at comics from the outside don't have an appreciation of the amount of thinking, revision, and just sweat that goes into making these "funny books." Writing enough to get the point across, offer character shading, but not over-writing the material. Is the artist the right match for what this world is the writer is trying to get across? And for the crime story, set as it is in "our world," you have to have someone gearing their head differently. This is not drawing Jack Kirbyesque machines (and I love those types of stories too) with dudes who have competing muscle fitness mag physiques and women with butts you can balance a service tray on...so more than anything, I've come to appreciate how critical the "look" is to what I'm trying to convey.

GR: I've got to ask this, just because when it happens to me I'm always a little bewildered and delighted. Have you written anything in HIGH ROLLERS so far that's surprised you? Any of the characters taken off for you in a way you hadn't imagined or envisioned?

GP: As you know, you sketch out in text who your characters are, their relationship with each other, what they want and all that. But once you get to crafting the story, sometimes it's the nuances they reveal to you in what they say or what you have them not say. How do I get across a certain state of mind without being blatant about it? It could even be how the artist has rendered the character and this opens up other possibilities of who these people – 'cause you know they live in your head – are. For instance a plot point came to me that I hadn't outlined, and it came about as I thought about, then wrote this scene with two minor, but pivotal characters, in HIGH ROLLERS. Now of course I won't tell you what that is, as you've got to buy the book and read it.

GR: I suppose I've strayed far from the course – I thought I'd try to get answers for my questions as much as talk about HIGH ROLLERS. But that said, is there anything you'd like to add about the series?

GP: Just that I hope comics fans will give HIGH ROLLERS a read…it's not just about the bling. Maybe some of the readers who've followed my prose work will also take a chance and pick up a copy when it hits the stands. I think all concerned will be pleasantly surprised.

-END-

Greg Rucka is the author of nearly a dozen novels, six featuring bodyguard Atticus Kodiak. In comics, he has written the adventures of Superman, Batman, Wonder Woman, the weekly series 52, and his own creations WHITEOUT and QUEEN & COUNTRY for Oni Press. You can read more about Greg Rucka at his website here: www.gregrucka.com

Gary Phillips has written various crime and mystery novels, numerous short stories, and edited the anthologies POLITICS NOIR: DARK TALES FROM THE CORRIDORS OF POWER, and with Chris Chambers, THE DARKER MASK: HEROES FROM THE SHADOWS. He has also written a WWII novel, FREEDOM'S FIGHT, out now. In addition to BOOM! Studios Phillips has written comics for Oni Press, Dark Horse, Moonstone and DC/Vertigo: www.gdphillips.com

(This interview originally appea